# ADIRONDACK BOOKS 1966-1992: An Annotated Bibliography

With a partial listing of book-length materials for the year 1993

Compiled by

Douglas B. Welch

North Country Books
Utica, New York

1994

ADIRONDACK BOOKS 1966-1992:
An Annotated Bibliography



ISBN 0-925168-27-0

Library of Congress Cataloging-in Publication Data

Welch, Douglas B. 1951–
Adirondack Books 1966–1992: an annotated bibliography with a partial listing of book-length materials for the year 1993 / by Douglas B. Welch.
p. cm.
Includes index.
ISBN 0-925168-27 0
1. Adirondack Mountains N.Y.) – Biliography. I. Title.
Z1318.A2W45 1994
[F127.A2]
016.9747'5--dc20 94-7689
CIP

Published by
NORTH COUNTRY BOOKS, INC.
18 Irving Place
Utica, New York 13501

# *Contents*

# Acknowledgements

Any project the size and scope of *Adirondack Books 1966-1992* involves the cooperation, assistance and goodwill of numerous people. I would like to take this opportunity to thank those individuals and institutions who have contributed to the completion of this book.

Chuck Brumley of Saranac Lake assisted in delineating an initial strategy for this project. He also did some of the leg work, verifying a number of incomplete citations. His encouragement and "go for it" attitude was just what was needed when embarking on such a large project. Chuck also provided feedback on the essay on the history of Adirondack bibliography.

Janet Decker, of the Saranac Lake Public Library, provided an acquisitions list for the library that proved to be very useful in tracking down a number of titles. She was also of great assistance when I visited the Adirondack Room at Saranac Free Library.

Interlibrary loan services played a vital role that facilitated the completion of this project. Kathy LaClair of Crumb Library, SUNY at Potsdam, Mary Bucher, SUNY of Canton, and Julia Courtney and Laurie Davis of Owen D. Young Library, St. Lawrence University, Canton, N.Y. handled literally hundreds of interlibrary loan requests and did so with style, grace and good humor. I am deeply indebted to all of them.

Thanks also to Lynn Ekfelt and Nancy Alessi. Nancy kept me apprised of recent Adirondack acquisitions. Lynn, friend, colleague, and one-time supervisor, was a source of support, ideas, and practical suggestions in the first part of this project. Four years later she provided valuable editorial assistance when it came time to produce a final draft.

Other individuals who I would like to thank are: Jerry Pepper of the Adirondack Museum, Breck and Julie Turner of Lake Placid, Carol Levin and Melissa Jadlos of St. Lawrence University, John Hammond and Tom Blauvelt of North Country Reference and Research Resources Council, Kay Brown, Librarian at SUNY at Potsdam, Neal Burdick of Canton, Dick Irving of the Graduate Library at SUNY, Jon Montan of the St. Lawrence County Planning Office, Roger Hutchinson and John Kramer of the Canton Office of the Department of Environmental Conservation, Stephen Frisbee of Cubley Library at Paul Smiths College, Phil Eppard and Bill Katz of SUNY Albany School of Information Science and Policy, Nancy Heath of the Adirondack Park Agency, and Joe Swinyer and Laura Ingalls of Feinberg Library. Tony Cafarella, student assistant in Special Collections at Feinberg Library, provided excellent service when I visited that facility.

The Adirondack collection of Owen D. Young Library at St. Lawrence University, located only 10 miles from my home, greatly facilitated my efforts. Library Director Richard Kuhta and the Friends of Owen D. Young Library are to be commended for their continuing efforts to build the library's Adirondack Collection.

A number of individuals provided information and access to their works which made writing annotations possible. I would like to thank the following people for helping out in this way: Morris F. Glenn, David Starbuck, Wesley Winn, Steve Erman, James McLelland, William deLorraine, Don Mellor, Addie Shields and Alberta West.

The cover is a photo of "Evergreens," a piece of silhouette art, created in the late 1920s by the late Phoebe W. Hazelwood who lived in Sacketts Harbor, N.Y. A special thanks to Jean Golden for permission to use "Evergreens."

Dale Hobson of Potsdam, N.Y. was responsible for the design and layout of the book.

Breck Turner and Warder Cadbury reviewed a final draft of the manuscript.

I would also like to express my appreciation to Sheila Orlin of North Country Books. Her excellent communication skills and commitment to publishing regional books about New York State have made it a pleasure to work with her on the publication of this book.

No list of acknowledgements for this project would be complete without mentioning the late Dorothy Plum, editor of the *Adirondack Bibliography*. Thousands of people who have sought to learn more about the Adirondack region owe her a tremendous debt of gratitude. Her efforts marked an important watershed in the history of Adirondack bibliography.

Finally, a special thanks to my wife, Ginger Storey-Welch, and our three children Stephen, Kimberly, and Brian, whose support over the past five years made completion of this project possible.

# Introduction

### *HISTORY OF ADIRONDACK BIBLIOGRAPHY*

The tradition of Adirondack bibliography goes back to just before the turn of the 20th century. The current effort at an Adirondack bibliography can be better understood by a brief look at the important developments in the field over the past one hundred years.

Some early works on the Adirondack Region and Northern New York are listed in a catalog of the Press of Joel Munsell of Albany, New York, entitled *Bibliotheca Munselliana*. The book lists hundreds of works published by Munsell between 1828 and 1872, many on subjects other than the Adirondacks. (Those who would like to learn more about the printing career of Joel Munsell and Munsell's relationship to Adirondack literature are directed to *Joel Munsell: Printer and Antiquarian*, by David Edelstein, New York: Columbia University Press, 1950.)

Cecilia A. Sherill, a student at the New York Library School in Albany, wrote an enumerative bibliography on the Adirondack Region which appeared in the Fourth Annual Report of the New York State of Fisheries, Game and Forest Commission, 1898. Sherill's "Bibliography of the Adirondacks" was 18 pages long and contained 275 items. The bibliography was organized alphabetically by author or title. When available, the price of the publication listed was included. Book citations sometimes contained information about a book as a physical object: its format (8vo, for example), the number of pages, whether it had portraits, illustrations, or maps. Locations or annotations were not provided. Sherill's work marked the first bibliography dedicated exclusively to the Adirondacks.

Over two decades after Sherill's work a two-part bibliography was included at the end of the second volume of Alfred L. Donaldson's important work, *A History of the Adirondacks* (1921). The first part of this bibliography was a list of the contents of Donaldson's personal collection, which was donated to the Saranac Lake Public Library after Donaldson's death in 1923. The second part was a general bibliography on the region compiled by another library school student, James McMillen.

Donaldson's list aimed to be selective in what he included in his bibliography. Incidental materials on the Adirondacks were left out of his work. He attempted to meet the needs of both the collector and the average reader. Donaldson omitted the following materials from his bibliography: annual reports/yearbooks of clubs and associations, folders or booklets for advertising purposes, state government documents, state guide books, geographies, fiction, newspaper articles, and collections of scenic views.

The second part of the Donaldson bibliography was compiled by James McMillen, who, like Sherill, was a student at New York Library School and graduated in 1915. McMillen traveled to major city libraries to gather citations for his bibliography. Where McMillen's list duplicated the holdings of the Donaldson Collection, the item was deleted from McMillen's list. His actual effort was longer than it appears in Donaldson's book.

Dorothy Plum, a professional librarian and chair of the Adirondack Mountain Club's Bibliography Committee, writing in 1950, made comparisons between the Sherill and Donaldson bibliographies and offered the following analysis:

> An examination of the Sherill list shows that it contains a good deal of important material not noted in Donaldson—for example, early reports by Emmons, Colvin, Kemp, Sargent and others, as well as several of Governor Cleveland's messages, *The Natural History of the State of New York* and the Adirondack state land survey. In all there are 275 titles listed by Sherrill: of these a few are incomplete or duplicate entries; 43 are types of material omitted by Donaldson and 40 are found in the Donaldson Collection. The remaining 58 percent are titles that help to complete the bibliography in Donaldson's History. (from "Starting an Adirondack Collection," by Dorothy Plum in *Adirondac* (May-June 1950, p. 57.)

Sherill's work is less well-known today than Donaldson's bibliography, but Sherill's effort provided an important link to early materials on the Adirondack Region.

The effort that eventually produced what became known as *The Adirondack Bibliography* began as an update of Donaldson's bibliography. The story of *The Adirondack Bibliography* has two focal points, the

Adirondack Mountain Club and Dorothy Plum. The idea for the bibliography was the brainchild of Ed Nixon who was then president of the Adirondack Mountain Club. At the club's annual meeting in November 1948 Nixon presented his suggestion to the Board of Governors, which accepted the project as worthy of Club support.

In January 1949 the Bibliography Committee was formed, with Dorothy Plum as chair. As a preliminary step the Committee produced a pamphlet entitled, "An Alphabetical Index to the Bibliography in Donaldson's History of the Adirondacks," which was printed in late 1949. It became apparent to the Bibliography Committee that so much had been printed during the 30 years since Donaldson's book that their task amounted to a new work and not just an update.

Over the course of the next eight or nine years the Adirondack Bibliography Committee and numerous volunteers donated their time, energy and resources to collecting and verifying citations. But much of the burden fell to one individual. Dorothy Plum's efforts and energy have become so legendary, that *The Adirondack Bibliography* is known to many who use it regularly quite simply as "Plum."

The bibliography was also the story of an organization, the Adirondack Mountain Club. People volunteered their time to collect the information and their money to see the first volume printed 1958. Several times a year Dorothy Plum's column about the bibliography's progress appeared in the club's magazine *Adirondac*.

Individual collectors and institutions with Adirondack collections showed a spirit of cooperation through donations of time and access to materials. Without the combined contribution of Dorothy Plum, the Adirondack Mountain Club and other collaborators, *The Adirondack Bibliography* would have never happened.

*The Adirondack Bibliography*, published by the Adirondack Mountain Club, appeared in 1958, almost a decade after the update of Donaldson was begun. Dorothy Plum wrote the preface. The introduction by Russell M.L. Carson, a former Adirondack Mountain Club president, outlined a list of approximately 80 books that he believed should comprise a basic collection of Adirondackiana. In addition to an enumerative bibliography of 7,539 items with annotations, there was an index of terms, an appendix of unlocated titles and a listing of serials and sources cited.

The arrangement was by subject with 16 major subject areas and dozens of subheadings; most categories were organized alphabetically by author. Others were in chronological order. Books, pamphlets, periodicals, dissertations, mimeographed local histories, maps and atlases published through 1955 were included. Newspaper articles were not included.

*The Adirondack Bibliography* was a monumental achievement and was recognized as such at the time. Reviews in various New York publications such as the *The Conservationist*, *North Country Life*, and *New York History* were extremely positive. It was also mentioned in such professional journals as *Library Journal*, *College and Research Library News*, and *Wilson Library Bulletin*.

*The Adirondack Bibliography Supplement 1956-1965*, published in 1973 by the Adirondack Museum, continued the earlier work. It was a culmination of annual updates that followed the publication of the first volume. Older materials that did not appear in the first volume were included along with materials actually published between 1956 and 1965. There were 4,100 new items listed in the Supplement, and the numbering of entries continued from the first volume. The index found in the second volume was cumulative so that one need only consult one index.

Several new subject headings were added for the second volume. Dorothy Plum, who still chaired the Bibliography Committee, also edited the supplement. The lengthy Introduction by the late William K. Verner is still the definitive statement on Adirondack literature. His analysis is a chronological one that divides Adirondack history into eight eras, each with a descriptive name. These are: I. The Colonial Period: 1535-1785; II. After the Revolution: 1786:-1835; III. The Adirondack Wilderness: The Golden Years, 1836-1865; IV. The Wilderness Breached: The Gilded Age, 1866-1895; V. Conservation and Preservation: 1896-1915; VI. The Rise of Public Recreation: 1916-1945; VII. After Another War: 1946-1965; VIII. Since 1965. This last category might well be called "Wilderness in an Urban Society." For each era, developments in the Adirondacks and relevant books are linked, with the title in italics accompanied by the "Plum" number. Verner's chronological analysis is valuable in that it gives us an intellectual framework for understanding the history and development of the Adirondack Region. Like the original *Adirondack Bibliography*, the "Supplement" also contained an appendix of unlocated titles and a list of serials and sources cited.

There was also a much shorter paper supplement for the years 1966-68, which is usually overlooked by researchers. The work does not have an introduction or index, "Plum" numbers are not used, and a list of "Periodicals Cited" is not included. It appears to use the same system of subject headings. It was published in 1970, and edited by Dorothy Plum of the Bibliography Committee of the Adirondack Mountain Club.

That *The Adirondack Bibliography* was a significant achievement goes without saying. Like much of the literature about the Adirondacks, it was the labor of people who cared deeply about their subject. In addition to Dorothy Plum's central role, organizations and institutions donated their time, energy and financial resources to the laborious process of collecting and verifying citations. The fact that 24 years elapsed between the establishment of the Bibliography Committee and the printing of the bound supplement in 1973 is testimony to the arduous work of compiling a large bibliography. The late William K. Verner noted as much in his introduction to *Adirondack Bibliography Supplement 1956-65*: "... as with the making of many books themselves, with the making of bibliographies there is no end." (*Adirondack Bibliography Supplement 1956-1965*, p. xl). This is as true today as it was in 1972.

### *SINCE THE ADIRONDACK BIBLIOGRAPHY*

The production of Plum's bibliography marked a watershed in the development of Adirondack bibliography and indexing. While no single work matches the Adirondack Bibliography in its comprehensiveness, there have been a number of efforts to improve and increase access to the various materials and resources about the Adirondack region.

*Northern New York Historical Materials: A Union Catalog*, edited by G. Glyndon Cole with the assistance of Dorothy Plum was compiled by a committee of the North Country Reference and Research Resources Council and published cooperativley by the Council and The Adirondack Museum in 1968. The other members of the Committee headed by Mr. Cole were Edmund Arnold, Marion Brickey, Howard Miller, Dorothy Plum and Rose Waddell. Dorothy Plum was a contributor to this work, as was a colleague of Mr. Cole's, Donald Woodward. With some very important differences from its predecessor *The Adirondack Bibliography*, this volume continued the process of providing access to materials about the Adirondacks and Northern New York. As a union catalog, it differed from a bibliography in that it provided the locations of the items listed.

*Northern New York Historical Materials* was a union list of holdings of over 90 libraries and special institutions in Clinton, Essex, Franklin, Jefferson, Lewis and St. Lawrence Counties. The holdings of The Adirondack Museum, because of their size and significance to the region, were also included. The first edition of *Northern New York Historical Materials* contained over 2,700 entries that were published before 1961.

The geographical scope encompasses virtually all of Northern New York north of the Mohawk River, including the following counties: Clinton, Essex, Franklin, Fulton, Hamilton, Herkimer, Jefferson, Lewis, Oneida, St. Lawrence, Saratoga, Warren and Washington. It contains a number of different formats: books, pamphlets, leaflets, maps, newspapers, and magazines. The category of manuscripts, which the committee had hoped to include at one time, is *not* listed. Author and title indexes at the end of the work provide access by entry number. Headings include both subject headings and types of materials (such as atlases, maps, and directories).

The second edition of *Northern New York Historical Materials: A Union List* appeared in 1976 and was compiled and edited again by G. Glyndon Cole with the aid of a committee of the North Country Reference and Research Resources Council. Like the first edition, it included locations. The committee included H.C. Garretson, Donald Barden, Dorothy Plum, Richard Ward, Rose Waddell and Charles M. Snyder. It was once again published by the North Country Reference and Research Resources Council and The Adirondack Museum. This enlarged edition contained over 4,400 entries.

The geographic scope was expanded to include Oswego County, which had become part of the North Country Reference and Research Resources Council. The participating libraries numbered over one hundred and came from eight counties because the holdings of libraries and institutions in Hamilton and Oswego Counties had been added. Dissertations were added to the list of formats, but manuscripts were not included. A major change in organization was the creation of a County and Local History section, where all titles for a particular village or town are listed together rather than being scattered through the list by subject.

Two editions of *Northern New York Historical Materials* were valuable additions to the field, but it has already been over fifteen years since the second edition appeared. The overall trend, in the face of increased interest in the region and increased publication about the region, has been an inability to keep pace in terms of currency and comprehensiveness.

In the years that have elapsed since the appearance of the revised edition of *Northern New York Historical Materials: A Union List* no other comparable projects have been published to provide access to recent publications on the Adirondacks. This is not to say, however, that nothing at all has happened.

Neil Surprenant, a librarian at Paul Smiths College, has produced an index to *Adirondack Life* magazine. The most recent version was published by *Adirondack Life* and covers Volumes I-XV, 1970-1984. It lists 859 articles that have appeared in the magazine. The basic subject headings for this index come from *The Adirondack Bibliography*, with others added as needed from the Sears List of Subject Headings. Sears is a formalized list of subject headings used mostly by public libraries. In addition to articles listed by volume and issue, author and subject indexes are included as well.

The catalogs of Adirondack bookstores serve as de facto bibliographies for collectors and others interested in the Adirondacks. Published since the early 1980s, these catalogs provide information about recent books published about the region. The catalog of With Pipe and Book bookstore of Lake Placid listed author, title, year, a brief annotation, "Plum" number (if applicable), and price. No information on publisher or place of publication is provided. The catalog was divided into two sections. The first listed titles still in print. The second section listed books that are now out of print. The catalog also served as an informal source of information on the price of out-of-print Adirondack books. It was published twice a year. The main catalog appeared in late November or early December, with a shorter catalog of recently acquired materials published in July. Regular publication of catalogs was discontinued in 1993. During the early-mid-1980s Wildwood Books of Old Forge published a book list that was discontinued by 1990.

One major effort that originated outside of Northern New York also deserves mention—The *Guide to Historical Resources* publications for each county in New York State. Produced by the New York Historical Resources Center at Olin Library at Cornell University, these publications list the manuscript and archival holdings of historical agencies and college and public libraries. Since manuscript collections were not listed in either *The Adirondack Bibliography* or either edition of *Northern New York Historical Materials*, the *Guide to Historical Resources* publications have made a real contribution to access of manuscript materials about the Adirondacks and the rest of Northern New York.

In 1989 Chuck Brumley of Saranac Lake, N.Y. made an important contribution to the field of Adirondack bibliography. With a grant from the Essex County Council of the Arts, and working under time constraints, Brumley produced a list of items not listed in *The Adirondack Bibliography* through the year 1965. Brumley's list of nearly 1800 books, pamphlets, and periodical articles is important because it makes the Adirondack Bibliography more comprehensive. Brumley used the broad subject categories found in *The Adirondack Bibliography*. He also expanded the geographical scope to include selected areas outside the "Blue Line," the boundary of the Adirondack Park. Brief annotations are provided. It was printed in typeset form and in limited numbers.

For scholars, collectors, and researchers, Brumley's work is another source that can be consulted. If and when a new Adirondack bibliographic source is created, Brumley's project will be a valuable checklist for those involved.

The past fifteen years have seen a piecemeal approach to trying to maintain bibliographic control of the growing number of works about the Adirondacks. While each of the above tools has intrinsic value, they are all a part of a larger whole. The challenge that remains is to put all the pieces together in a comprehensive resource, and provide for its continuation in the future. Such a source would follow in the tradition of the original *Adirondack Bibliography* and would be an enduring and indispensable resource for anyone interested in the Adirondacks.

# Scope and Contents

*Adirondack Books 1966-1992* is an annotated bibliography of Adirondack books published since 1965. The two volumes that comprised *The Adirondack Bibliography* are a comprehensive listing of book, pamphlets, periodicals, and ephemera about the Adirondack region published through the year 1965. Charles Brumley's *Additions to the Adirondack Bibliography Through 1965* listed materials not previously included in *The Adirondack Bibliography*. It is an important step towards making coverage of pre-1965 Adirondack materials exhaustive.

The present bibliography has a different focus from these earlier works in that it concentrates on one format of materials, books, and provides annotations. Readers will note that some books published in 1993 have been included.

For the purpose of this work a "book" is defined as having 24 or more pages. The goal was to differentiate between book-length material and the shorter works such as leaflets, booklets, pamphlets, brochures, and papers. Adirondack Park Agency materials, theses, and technical papers are included as well.

Establishing this work's geographic scope has been a challenging and difficult issue. *The Adirondack Bibliography* used the Blue Line, or boundary of the Adirondack Park, in determining what was included in that work. It is important to keep in mind that the Blue Line is a political boundary (established in 1892) and not a geographical boundary. In reality, the Adirondack region has much in common socially, economically and culturally with adjacent areas of Northern New York. Depending on where one lives or on his or her interests, adjacent areas outside of the Blue Line may be considered "Adirondack." As Dorothy Plum, editor of *The Adirondack Bibliography*, so rightly noted in her preface to the first volume, "The literature of the Adirondacks knows no exact geographical boundary." (*Adirondack Bibliography*, q. v.)

As this discussion suggests, the geographic scope of this book is not strictly limited to materials relating to the region inside the Blue Line. All of Franklin and Clinton Counties are included; so are St. Lawrence County towns that lie within the Blue Line. Some works on towns adjacent to the southern and western boundaries of the Blue Line are listed here as well.

To the east, Lake Champlain and the eastern border of New York State south to the Blue Line form another boundary for the scope of this work. Lake Champlain is now part of the Adirondack Park. The inclusion of northeastern New York also recognizes the importance of historical events of the Colonial and Revolutionary War eras in the Lake Champlain/Hudson River corridor. The vast majority of works listed in the following pages, however, are about the region that lies within the boundary of the Adirondack Park.

*Adirondack Books 1966-1992* is aimed at a broad audience with a variety of interests in the Adirondack Region. Historians, book collectors, conservationists, young readers, scientists, naturalists, outdoor recreationists, conservationists, folklorists, artists, local history buffs, genealogists, and scholars will all find this work worthwhile for meeting their information needs about the region. As might be expected, the intellectual level of the materials listed varies widely from juvenile literature to photographic works to scholarly and scientific books.

The citations contain author's name, title, place of publication, publisher, year of publication and number of pages. The subtitle has been included as well, as has name of the author of the preface or introduction when different from the author of the work. Information on other printings and editions has been provided where known, but is not intended to be comprehensive. In the case of reprints, the name of publisher and the place and year of publication for both the original and first reprint edition since 1965 have been listed. Locations of the books listed have not been provided. While many of the books listed are now out of print, or have been in and out of print, many other titles are readily available through regional libraries or interlibrary loan service.

Brief, descriptive annotations ranging from one to five sentences in length are used. Besides offering additional information about the subject of the book, particularly when the title is obscure, the annotations aim to establish the connection of the book and/or its author to the Adirondack Region. The presence of photographs is noted, as is the name of an illustrator. Annotations have not been provided for cookbooks and some items published in 1993. The notation NAR (Not Available for Review) indicates the work exists as verified on RLIN or OCLC (national databases), but could not be readily located for inspection and review and may also be hard for readers to obtain. A small number of citations which could not be verified by sight or on a database have been listed separately as "Unlocated Titles" at the end of the bibliography section.

The arrangement of the material is by subject, organized alphabetically within each subject category by author. The one major exception to this format is in the "Adirondacks in Art and Literature" section where some of the categories denote literary formats instead of subjects. Consequently, some works in this section could also have been located under other subject categories. Elsewhere, the need to use a single subject heading per entry may not fully reflect the scope of a particular work. Additional subject terms have been added in the index to more completely represent a work's subject matter.

Subject headings for this work have been adapted from the broad subject headings found in *The Adirondack Bibliography.* This was done partly as a matter of convenience, but also for the sake of continuity with past efforts. Changes, additions, and deletions have been made to make the headings current. Environmental concerns, land use planning issues and the creation of the Adirondack Park Agency are some examples of the need for updating the subject headings. A separate section for reference materials has also been added. The cities and villages section has been subdivided by county.

Reprints of works with "Plum" numbers are listed for the convenience of contemporary readers. The name and year of original publication are listed, followed by the citation for the reprint. Reprints constitute approximately one out of ten Adirondack titles listed in *Adirondack Books 1966-1992*, testimony to the quality and continued popularity of these titles, and Adirondack books in general. Reprints of items without Plum numbers have been listed in the main bibliography section. As for reprints with Plum numbers, both the original citation and the reprint citation have been listed. The index is based on author and title, with other entries added from the annotations, titles and subject headings.

Citations will continue to be collected and annotations written for new books on the Adirondack Region, and for those older works that have inevitably been missed. A revised edition of this work will be considered if a larger, more comprehensive project to update the Adirondack Bibliography is not undertaken in the next few years.

# *Abbreviations*

**The following abbreviations are used in the bibliography:**

| | |
|---|---|
| advts. | advertisements |
| bib. | bibliography |
| comp. | compiled, compiler |
| ed. | editor, edited, edition |
| facs. | facsimile |
| illus. | illustration, illustrated |
| intro. | introduction |
| lvs. | leaves |
| mimeo. | mimeographed |
| n.d. | no date |
| n.p. | no place, publisher, printer |
| p. | pages |
| pls. | plates |
| pseud. | pseudonym |
| refs. | references |
| rep. | reprint |
| rev. | revised |
| s.l. | sine loco, no place of publication |
| s.n. | sine nomine, without name of printer or publisher |
| unpub. | unpublished |
| v., vol. | volume |
| var. | variant (edition) |
| var. pag. | various pagings |

# Adirondack Reference

## General

1. Adirondack Genealogical-Historical Society. *Index of Names and Places in the 1876 Franklin County, N.Y.Atlas*. Saranac Lake, N.Y., The Society, 1993. 1 v.

Name index for well-known Franklin County resource. Indexing provides name, village, township number, miscellaneous information, and page location. Very limited ed.

2. Chambers, Captain William. *Atlas of Lake Champlain: 1779-1780*. Bennington, VT., Montpelier, VT., Vermont Heritage Press; Vermont Historical Society, 1984. xxxi, 69.

Introductory essay by J. Kevin Graffagnino. Reprint of one of two known manuscripts. Many New York State sites. Folio.

3. Cole, George Glyndon. *Manuscripts for Research: Report of the Director of the North Country Historical Research Center 1961-1974*.Plattsburgh, N.Y., Feinberg Library, State University College, 1975. vii, 47.

List of manuscript material in North Country Historical Research Center, a department of Feinberg Library in 1975. Listing does not include photos, post cards or vertical file materials that also made up the Center's holdings.

4. Federation of Historical Services. *Historic Resources of the Upper Hudson, Champlain and Mohawk Valleys*. Troy, N.Y., The Federation, 1987. 135p.

Reference tool. County-by-county listing of museums, historical associations, libraries, and town historians. Of related interest to the Adirondacks: Clinton, Essex, Saratoga, Warren and Washington counties. Information included: name, address, phone, hours, collections and research facilities, activities.

5. Folwell, Betsy & Peggy A. Ingalls. *Cultural Resources in New York's North Country*. Blue Mountain Lake, N.Y., Adirondack Museum, 1980. 188p.

County-by-county listings of cultural resources in the North Country; museums, historical associations, institutes, historians, art collections.

6. Kirschenbaum, Howard. *The Adirondack Guide: An Almanac of Essential Information and Assorted Trivia*. Raquette Lake, N.Y., Sagamore Institute, 1983. 202p.

Excellent reference and statistical source. Topics covered are: geography and government, history, literature, economics, education, organizations, environment, arts and crafts, entertainment, recreation, transportation. Illus., charts, maps, index.

7. New York Historical Resources Center. *Guide to Historical Resources in Clinton County, New York Repositories*. Ithaca, N.Y., New York Historical Resources Center. Olin Library, Cornell University, 1987. 78, 181p.

Collection level listing of manuscripts and archive materials for Clinton County.

8. New York Historical Resources Center. *Guide to Historical Resources in Essex County, New York Repositories*. Ithaca, N.Y., New York Historical Resources Center. Olin Library, Cornell University, 1987. 51, 134p.

Collection level listing of manuscripts and archives materials for Essex County.

9. New York Historical Resources Center. *Guide to Historical Resources in Franklin County, New York Repositories*. Ithaca, N.Y., New York Historical Resources Center. Olin Library, Cornell University, 1987. 19, 44p.

Collection level listing of manuscripts and archives materials for Franklin County.

10. New York Historical Resources Center. *Guide to Historical Resources in Fulton County, New York Repositories*. Ithaca, N.Y., New York Historical Resources Center. Olin Library, Cornell University, 1984. 6, 20p.

Collection level listing of manuscripts and archive collections for Fulton County.

11. New York Historical Resources Center. *Guide to Historical Resources in Hamilton County, New York Repositories.* Ithaca, N.Y., New York Historical Resources Center. Olin Library, Cornell University, 1984. 37, 69p.
    Collection level listing of manuscripts and archive materials for Hamilton County.

12. New York Historical Resources Center. *Guide to Historical Resources in Herkimer County, New York Repositories.* Ithaca, N.Y., New York Historical Resources Center. Olin Library, Cornell University, 1984. 14, 31p.
    Collection level listing of manuscripts and archive materials for Herkimer County.

13. New York Historical Resources Center. *Guide to Historical Resources in Lewis County, New York Repositories.* Ithaca, N.Y., New York Historical Resources Center. Olin Library, Cornell University, 1987. 11, 29p.
    Collection level listing of manuscripts and archives materials for Lewis County.

14. New York Historical Resources Center. *Guide to Historical Resources in St. Lawrence County, New York Repositories.* Ithaca, N.Y., New York Historical Resources Center. Olin Library, Cornell University, 1987. 122, 296p.
    Collection level listing of manuscripts and archive materials for St. Lawrence County.

15. New York Historical Resources Center. *Guide to Historical Resources in Saratoga County, New York Repositories.* Ithaca, N.Y., New York Historical Resources Center. Olin Library, Cornell University, 1987. 36, 82p.
    Collection level listing of manuscript and archive materials for Saratoga County.

16. New York Historical Resources Center. *Guide to Historical Resources in Warren County, New York Repositories.* Ithaca, N.Y., New York Historical Resources Center. Olin Library, Cornell University, 1982. 27, 61p.
    Collection level listing of manuscripts and archive materials for Warren County.

17. New York Historical Resources Center. *Guide to Historical Resources in Washington County, New York Repositories.* Ithaca, N.Y., New York Historical Resources Center. Olin Library, Cornell University, 1983. 28, 74p.
    Collection level listing of manuscripts and archive materials for Washington County.

18. Rosevear, Francis. *A Chronology and Index to Verplanck Colvin in the Adirondacks.* Utica, N.Y., North Country Books, 1992. 142p.
    Reference work on Colvin's life and work. Includes index of illustrations in Colvin's writings. Prepared with the assistance of Barbara McMartin.

19. Surprenant, Neil. *Adirondack Life: An Index; Volume I-X, 1970-1979.* Jay, N.Y., North Country Reference and Research Resources Council, 1980. 45p.; rev. ed., *Adirondack Life Index: Volumes I-XV, 1970-1984.* Jay, N.Y., *Adirondack Life,* 1985. 29p.
    Valuable index to major Adirondack region periodical. Organized by author, subject as well as listed by issue. Based on an in-house index developed for Cubley Library at Paul Smiths College. Updated in 1985 with subject, author and photo index. Illus.

20. Wilson, Lorraine L. *A Directory of Art and Cultural Resources in the Adirondack North Country.* Lake Placid, N.Y., Adirondack North Country Association Arts Committee, 1989. 82p.
    Comprehensive list of organizations that contribute in some way to the arts; libraries, theaters, music, dance museums and historical associations. Covers 14 counties: Clinton, Essex, Franklin, Fulton, Hamilton, Herkimer, Jefferson, Lewis, Oneida, Oswego, St. Lawrence, Saratoga, Warren and Washington.

# Bibliography

21. Brumley, Charles K. *Additions to the Adirondack Bibliography: Titles Published Through 1965.* Saranac Lake, N.Y., Charles K. Brumley, 1989. 201p.
    Typescript. Listing of items found in regional libraries that did not appear in the *Adirondack Bibliography.* Organized by subject. Contains approximately 1,800 items.

22. Cole, G. Glyndon (ed.). *Historical Materials Relating to Northern New York: A Union Catalog.* Can-

ton, N.Y., North Country Reference And Research Resources Council, 1968. 307p.; rev. ed., 1976. 452p.

Updated 1976 edition of *Historical Materials Relating to Northern New York*, had over 4,400 entries. Includes books, pamphlets, broadsides, newspapers and magazines, maps, and theses and dissertations. Contains information for the following counties: Clinton, Essex, Franklin, Fulton, Hamilton, Herkimer, Jefferson, Lewis, Oneida, Oswego, St. Lawrence, Saratoga, Warren and Washington. Title and author indexes.

23. Nestler, Harold. *A Bibliography of New York State Communities, Counties, Towns, Villages.* Port Washington, N.Y., I. J. Friedman, 1968; reprints, *A Bibliography of New York State Communities.* Bowie, MD., Heritage Books, 1988. 118p.; rev. & enlarged ed., Bowie, MD., Heritage Books, 1990. 301p.

Rev. ed. of work first published in 1968. Contains 1,855 citations for histories of New York's smaller communities. Organized by county and town names. The 1990 edition has 2,500 entries including selections derived from author's own book catalogs. Arranged alphabetically by county then by town or community.

24. Plum, Dorothy. *Adirondack Bibliography Supplement 1956-65.* Blue Mountain Lake, N.Y., Adirondack Museum, 1973. 198p.

First book of the *Adirondack Bibliography* covered materials published through 1955. The Supplement includes listings through 1965. Lists new books, pamphlets, periodicals, and articles as well as missed titles through 1955. Introductory essay by William K. Verner still the definitive work on Adirondack literature.

25. Plum, Dorothy. *Adirondack Bibliography Supplement 1966-1968.* Glens Falls, N.Y., Adirondack Mountain Club, 1970. 46p.

Paper supplement to original *Adirondack Bibliography* brings materials up to date through 1968. Lists periodicals, books and pamphlets. Entries are not numbered. No indexing.

26. Versteg, Jennie G. *Lake Champlain: Reflections on Our Past; A Bibliography.* Burlington, VT., Center for Research on Vermont, University of Vermont, 1989. 90p.

Sources for each of eight eras that make up *Lake Champlain: Reflections on Our Past.* See # 76 for related work. Author index, illus.

# *History of the Adirondack Region*

## General History

27. Barnett, Lincoln. *The Ancient Adirondacks.* New York, N.Y., Time-Life Books, 1974.; rev. eds., Alexandria, VA., Time-Life Books, 1977, 1982. 184p.

Well-done work on Lake Champlain, High Peaks, Hudson River, the woods. Some regional history. Illus.

28. Bowman, Fred Q. *Landholders of Northeastern New York 1739-1802.* Baltimore, MD., Genealogical Publishing Co., 1983. 228p.

List of 9,000 landowners in Franklin, Clinton, Essex and Washington Counties, plus a list of 600 original land grantees. Appendix A contains dates the towns in Northeastern New York were organized prior to 1803; also population of region in 1790 and 1800. Appendix B: 200 landholders who are not listed elsewhere. Work is of obvious interest to genealogists. Index.

29. Bowman, Fred Q. *10,000 Vital Records of Eastern New York 1777-1834.* Baltimore, MD., Genealogical Pub. Co., 1987. vii, 356p.

Part of three volume series. Other two volumes pertain to Western and Central New York. This volume covers several regional counties including Clinton, Essex, and Saratoga. Based mostly on marriage and death announcements in newspapers before 1835. Alphabetically listed and numbered. Town of residence not necessarily limited to these counties.

30. Cross, David and Potter, Joan. *The Book of Adirondack Firsts.* Elizabethtown, N.Y., Pinto Press, 1992. 194p.

A potpourri of Adirondack regional history organized around first occurences of significant, interesting and unusual events. Entertaining reading. Illustrated by Alison Munoz.

31. Crowell, Marnie Reed. *North to the St. Lawrence.* Canton, N.Y., Raquette Press, 1975. 101p.

Short, general history of northern New York. A good introductory work on the region. Illus. by Lucretia Romey. Crowell lives in Pierrepont, N.Y. in St. Lawrence County. Appendix by Joan Kepes.

32. Daly, Sally, (ed.) *100 Years of Adirondack Park Roots: Families, Homesteads, Organizations, Businesses, 1892-1992.* Paul Smiths, N.Y., Committee for the 1992 Adirondack Park Centennial, 1992. 35p.

Lists long-term businesses, villages and towns, associations and clubs, organizations throughout the Adirondack Park.

33. De Sormo, Maitland C. *The Heydays of the Adirondacks.* Saranac Lake, N.Y., Adirondack Yesteryears, Inc., 1974, 1975. 262p.

A panoramic view of Adirondack history since the 1850s: railroads, resorts, log driving. Particular emphasis on Franklin County. Accompanied by numerous interesting photos of people and places of the times.

34. De Sormo, Maitland C. *The "Murray Rush" in Retrospect; Or, With the Multitude in the Adirondacks.* Saranac Lake, N.Y., Adirondack Yesteryears, 1989. 150p.

De Sormo's most recent work on the Adirondacks assesses W.H.H. Murray's *Adventure in the Wilderness.* At the time Murray was praised, criticized and made the object of satire. Over 80 illus. Front and back endpapers contain "Map of the Adirondack Wilderness" compiled by S.R. Stoddard. Special numbered ed. 1,500 copies.

35. Ludlum, Stuart D. (ed.). *Exploring the Adirondack Mountains 100 Years Ago.* Utica, N.Y., Brodock & Ludlum Publications, 1972. 65p.

Reproductions of woodcuts and engravings from the 19th century by Harry Finn, J. M. Hart, Winslow Homer and others. Reprints of several articles from nineteenth century publications.

36. McMartin, Barbara. *Hides, Hemlocks, and Adirondack History: How the Tanning Industry Influenced the Development of the Adirondacks.* Utica, N.Y., North Country Books, 1992. 332p.

Scholarly and comprehensive work. Tanning was an important early industry in the Adirondacks and created a demand for lumbering the region's vast softwood forests. General information on tanning as well as a county-by-county look at the industry's influence. Lengthy bibliography, notes, index, illus., maps.

37. Phelps, Orson Schofield. *The High Peaks of Essex: The Adirondack Mountains of Orson Schofield Phelps*. Fleischmanns, N.Y., Purple Mountain Press, 1992. 114p.

    Recently uncovered Phelps manuscript brought to light and edited by Bill Healy in 1990. Important primary material on Adirondacks. Phelps died in 1905. Bibliography.

38. Sherman, Gordon C. and Elsie L. Sherman. *An Illuminating History of the Champlain Valley and Adirondack Mountains, Volume I*. Elizabethtown, N.Y., Denton Publications, 1976. 213p.

    Most of Volume I covers Colonial and Revolutionary era history of Lake Champlain with emphasis on military personalities and their roles in events. First ed. limited to 500 copies.

39. Sherman, Gordon C. & Elsie L. Sherman. *An Illuminating History of the Champlain Valley and the Adirondack Mountains, Volume II*. Elizabethtown, N.Y., Denton Publications, Inc., 1977. 138p.

    Vol. II emphasizes non-military maritime history of Lake Champlain. Sailing vessels, passenger vessels, ferries and related topics discussed. First ed. limited to 500 copies.

## French Settlements and French and Indian Wars

40. Fitch, Jabez Jr. *The Diary of Jabez Fitch Jr. in the French and Indian War*. Glens Falls, N.Y., Rogers Island Historical Association, 1966. 40p.; rev, eds.,1968. 59p.; 1986. 60p.

    Rogers Island Historical Association Publication #1. Partial journal written by participant in French and Indian War in Eastern New York. Primarily the work of Richard Mason.

41. Krueger, John W. *A Most Memorable Day: The Battle of Lake George, September 8, 1755*. Saranac Lake, N.Y., Center for Adirondack Studies, North Country Community College, 1980. 61p.

    Account of Battle of Lake George during French and Indian War. Told from varying perspectives.

42. Pilcher, Edith. *Castorland: French Refugees in the Western Adirondacks, 1793-1814*. Harrison, N.Y., Harbor Hill Books, 1985. 256p.

    Recounts attempts by French aristocratic emigres to found a community named Castorland, along the Black River, during the French Revolution. Illus., maps, photos, bibliography and index.

43. Steele, Ian Kenneth. *Betrayals: Fort William Henry and the Massacre*. New York, N.Y., Oxford University Press, 1990. viii, 250p.

    Detailed analysis of massacre of English and American prisoners after their surrender at Fort William Henry on Lake George in August 1757. Footnotes and index.

## The Revolution

44. Bird, Harrison. *Attack on Quebec: The American Invasion of Canada, 1775*. New York, N.Y., Oxford University Press, 1968. 254p.

    Account of attempt by American colonies to capture Canada. Chapter on Lake Champlain's role in the attack. Map of northeastern states and Canada on inside covers. Index, chronological list of events.

45. Bowne, William L. *Ye Cohorn Caravan: The Knox Expedition in the Winter of 1775-76*. Schuylerville, N.Y., NaPaul Publisher, Inc., 1975. 81p.

    Story of the movement of heavy guns from Ticonderoga to Boston in 1775. The road between Ticonderoga and Boston was called the Knox Trail. The presence of the guns in Boston meant British ships could be effectively kept from occupying Boston Harbor-a major victory for the American colonists.

46. Cometti, Elizabeth (ed.). *The American Journals of Lt. John Enys*. Blue Mountain Lake, N.Y., Adirondack Museum, 1976. 377p.

    Preface by Harold K. Hochschild, Foreword by Julian P. Boyd. Journals of Englishman John Enys. As a 19-year old ensign, Enys participated in the Battle of Valcour Island on Lake Champlain. Later Enys returned to Lake Champlain and the Saranac River region on a fishing trip. At the end of his duty in North America he travelled south from Montreal, recording what he saw. 44 illus., 15 maps.

47. Everest, Allan S. *Moses Hazen and the Canadian Refugees in the American Revolution.* Syracuse, N.Y., Syracuse University Press, 1976. 217p.
    Interesting study about little known facet of American Revolution: Canadians who joined in the American cause to fight the British. Moses Hazen lead such a Canadian group and was commissioned as an officer in the Continental Army. After the Revolution some Canadian soldiers settled in Clinton County, New York.

48. Fowler, William M. Jr. *Rebels Under Sail: The American Navy during the Revolution.* New York, N.Y., Scribner, 1976. xi, 356p.
    Scholarly work on the naval history of the American Revolution. Chapter 9 entitled "The Freshwater Fleet," and Chapter 10 "Valcour Island" are relevant to Adirondack region. Notes, bibliography.

49. Hatch, Robert McConnell. *Thrust for Canada: The American Attempt on Quebec in 1775-1776.* Boston, MA., Houghton, Mifflin, 1979. xiv, 295p.
    Scholarly, well-written and readable account of American efforts to conquer Canada during 1775 and 1776. Since much of the focus is on the Montreal-Albany strategic corridor of Eastern New York this work will appeal to those interested in the Colonial and Revolutionary Era History of the Adirondacks.

50. Jones, Charles Henry. *History of the Campaign for the Conquest of Canada in 1776, from the Death of Montgomery to the Retreat of the British Army under Sir Guy Carleton.* Philadelphia, PA., Porter & Coates, 1882; reprint, New York, N.Y., Research Reprints, 1970. xiv, 234.
    Thorough historical study of the events in Eastern New York during 1776 covering Ticonderoga, Crown Point, Lake Champlain.

51. Klein, Milton M. (comp.). *New York in the American Revolution: A Bibliography.* Albany, N.Y., New York State American Revolution Bicentennial Commission, 1974. xxvi, 197p.
    Valuable reference tool with almost 1100 entries. Those interested in the Adirondack region during the American Revolution will find this work useful. Divided into chapters by subject. Index.

52. Reid, Arthur. *Reminiscences of the Revolution.* Utica, N.Y., Robert Books and Job Printer, 1859. 31p.; reprint, South Glens Falls, N.Y., Rt. 9 Book and Antique Shop, 1974. 32p.
    Facsimilie reprint about Fort Edward during the American Revolution.

53. Riedesel, Maj. Gen. *Memoirs, and Letters and Journals of Major General Riedesel.* Albany, N.Y., J. Munsell, 1868; reprint, New York: New York Times and Arno Press, 1969. 2v.
    Translated by W.L. Stone. Account of Burgoyne's campaign in Eastern New York during the American Revolution derived from the primary materials of a German military officer who was there. Biographical sketch of Riedesel.

54. Salsig, Doyen. *Parole: Quebec; Countersign: Ticonderoga; Second New Jersey Regimental Orderly Book 1776.* Rutherford, N.J., Farleigh, Dickinson Press, London, Cranbury, N.J., Associated University Presses, 1980. 310p.
    Edited and annotated primary source material about the Canadian Campaign between late 1775 and late 1776. Covers events in Eastern New York and the Champlain Valley. Brief notes about people involved. Approximately 40 illus.

55. Thurheimer, David C. *Landmarks of the Revolution in New York State.* Albany, N.Y., New York State American Bicentennial Commission, 1972, 1973, 1976. 57p.
    Six out of 40 entries have an Adirondack connection. They are: Saratoga National Historical Park, Stillwater, Saratoga Battle Monument, Bennington Battlefield, Fort Ticonderoga, Mount Hope, Crown Point. Each entry accompanied by short written entry and a photograph.

## The War of 1812

56. Bilow, John A. *Chateaugay, N.Y. and the War of 1812.* St. Lambert, Quebec, Paquette & Simms, 1984. 151p.
    Based on letters and diaries. Bilow was Town Historian when he wrote the book. Illus., bibliography, index.

57. Crisman, Kevin J. *The Eagle: An American Brig on Lake Champlain During the War of 1812.* Shelburne, VT., New England Press; Annapolis, MD., Naval Institute Press, 1987. xii, 276 lvs.

Thesis. Part I is a history of the Eagle. Part II is entitled "The Archaeological Reconstruction of the Eagle." 76 illus, several appendices, bibliography. Drawings of the Eagle on front and back endpapers.

58. Everest, Allan S. *The War of 1812 in the Champlain Valley*. Syracuse, N.Y., Syracuse University Press, 1981. viii, 239p.
Discusses the impact of the War of 1812 upon New York, Vermont and Canada. First chapter summarizes earlier history of the region. Bibliography.

59. Glenn, Morris F. *Glenn's History of Lake Champlain: Appendix A; Brigadier General Daniel Wright*. Arlington, VA., Glenn, 1980. Unpaged.
About the War of 1812 and Essex County, N.Y.

60. Glenn, Morris F. *Glenn's History of the Adirondacks: Volume 6; The 37th Regiment of Essex in the War of 1812*. Arlington, VA., Glenn, 1980. Unpaged.
Information of Essex Militia in Franklin County, Murray's Raid, and events surrounding the Battle of Plattsburgh. Contains excerpts of a manuscript entitled "Brigadier General Daniel Wright and the War of 1812 in Clinton, Franklin and Essex Counties."

61. Glenn, Morris F. *Glenn's History of the Adirondacks: Volume 7; The 37th Regiment of Essex Militia at the Battle of Plattsburgh*. Arlington, VA., Glenn, 1980. 43p.
Additional excerpts from "Brigadier General Daniel Wright and the War of 1812 in Clinton, Franklin and Essex Counties."

62. Glenn, Morris F. *History of the Adirondacks (Essex County, N.Y.): Volume 8; Documents Relating to the War of 1812*. Arlington, VA., Glenn, 1985. Unpaged.
Information on Gov. Daniel Tompkins, local payroll records from the Battle of Plattsburgh, and the Lost Prince, Eleazer Williams.

### Native Americans

63. Clinton County Historical Museum. *The Original People: Native Americans in the Champlain Valley*. Plattsburgh, N.Y., Clinton County Historical Museum, 1988. 32p.
Exhibit Catalog. Photos, drawings and text. Sections include geological history, the Ice Age, the Paleo-Indian, the Abenaki, the fur trade, settlement and European wars, surviving in the nineteenth century, as well as Native Americans today.

64. Graymont, Barbara. *The Iroquois in the American Revolution*. Syracuse, N.Y., Syracuse University Press, 1972. x, 359p.
Scholarly study of Iroquois and entanglements with Europeans in the American Revolution. Concerned with Iroquois culture as well as the military and political aspects of their lives. Notes, bibliographic essay. Also in paper.

65. Heller, Murray, (ed.) *Names, Northeast, Amerindian Names*. Saranac Lake, N.Y., North Country Community College Press, 1980. xxx, 111p.
Papers were presented as part of Second Annual Northeast Regional Names Institute which took place on September 12 & 13, 1980. North Country Community College is located in Saranac Lake, N.Y. References.

66. Jennings, Francis. *The Ambiguous Iroquois Empire*. New York, N.Y., Norton, 1984. xxv, 438p.
History of formal cooperation between Five Nations, their Amerindian allies and European powers. Bibliography, index.

67. Matthiessen, Peter. *Indian Country*. New York, N.Y., Viking Press, 1984. xii, 338p.
Accounts of Native American communities struggling to survive in the 20th century. Chapter 5 is an account of turmoil at Akwesasne Reservation in the 1970s. Index.

# Local History

### The Champlain-Hudson Valleys

68. Bellico, Russell P. *Sails and Steam in the Mountains: A Maritime and Military History of Lake George and Lake Champlain*. Fleischmanns, N.Y., Purple Mountain Press, 1992. 393p.
Story of these two historically important lakes from discovery through the nineteenth century. Maps, illus., bibliography, index.

69. Boyle, Robert. *The Hudson River: A Natural and Unnatural History.* New York, N.Y., Norton, 1969. 304p.

First 87 pages particularly relevant to those interested in the Adirondacks. Boyle's account offers both the postive and negative about the Hudson. Photos graphically contrast the beauty of the Upper Hudson and the degradation and the abuse in its lower sections. Bibliography.

70. Buckell, Betty Ahearn. *Stuff: The Absolute True Adventures of Men, Women, and Critters Who Happened to Have Lived, Loved, Breathed, Roamed and Died by the Beautiful Shores of Lake George and Lake Champlain.* Lake George, N.Y., Buckell Press, 1992. 174p.

Local history of Lake George and vicinity with humorous edge. Photos, drawings. Compilation of materials not incorporated into author's earlier works.

71. Glenn, Morris F. *The Capture and Burning of the Sloop Essex.* Arlington, VA., Glenn, 1981. 54p.

Published version of file from U.S. archives. Story of vessel commandeered by the U.S. Navy during the War of 1812 to ferry troops from Whitehall to Burlington, VT. Very limited ed.

72. Hill, Ralph Nading. *Lake Champlain: Key to Liberty.* Woodstock, VT., Countryman Press, 1976, 1977. vii, 296p. Vermont Bicentennial Edition. Other editions in 1987, 1991.

History of Lake Champlain beginning with geology and early native peoples of the region. Strategic importance of lake from colonial era to the War of 1812 is covered as well as its later commercial importance. Photos, maps, paintings and drawings help vividly capture the history of Lake Champlain.

73. Lake Champlain Committee. *Essays on Lake Champlain.* Burlington, VT., Lake Champlain Committee, 1988. 60p.

Seven essays on Lake Champlain and its surrounding bioregion. Topics: geology, natural history, Native American cultures, the commercial development of the Champlain Basin and a brief history of Burlington, Vt. Photos. Short biographies on each of the contributors.

74. New York State. Hudson River Valley Commission. *The Hudson: Report of the Hudson River Valley Commission.* Albany, N.Y., The Commission, 1966. 100p.

Report of Commission to study the Hudson, mostly Albany southward. Maps, photos. Discusses population, recreation, historic resources, farming, residential uses, etc. Outlines establishment of permanent commission and its structure and operations.

75. Stark, Bruce P. (ed.) *Proceedings of the Champlain Valley Symposium.* s.l., s.n., 1981. 50p.

Five historical articles on the Champlain Valley through the War of 1812.

76. Versteg, Jennie G. *Lake Champlain: Reflections on Our Past.* Burlington, VT., Center for Research for Vermont, University of Vermont, 1987. 299p.

Historical review of Lake Champlain divided into eight eras. A chapter is dedicated to each era and lists selected readings. Based on a project of public programs sponsored by the Center for Research on Vermont and Fletcher Free Library. See # 26 for related entry.

## Lakes, Streams and Mountains

77. De Sormo, Maitland C. *Summers on the Saranacs.* Saranac Lake, N.Y., Adirondack Yesteryears, Inc., 1980. 317p.

Book on the beautiful Saranac Chain of Lakes. Text and photos tell story of the clubs, boat builders, resorts and guides of the region. Front endpapers are a map of Upper Saranac Lake. Back endpapers contain a map of Lower Saranac Lake. References, index.

78. Fowler, Albert. *Cranberry Lake from Wilderness to Adirondack Park.* Syracuse, N.Y., Adirondack Museum/Syracuse University Press, 1968. 207p.

Collected materials about Cranberry Lake, third largest lake in Adirondacks. Region was developed later than others due to its remoteness. Three dozen illus. Chapters by Atwood Manley, Fay Welch, and others.

79. Lord, Thomas Reeves. *Stories of Lake George: Fact and Fancy.* Pemberton, N.J., Pinelands Press, 1987. 196p.

Contains descriptions of many prominent local geographical features; mountains, islands, bays, points. Local folklore and anecdotes. Illus., maps, photos, bibliography, index.

80. Ludlum, Stuart D. *(comp.) Exploring Lake George and Lake Champlain 100 Years Ago.* Utica, N.Y.: Brodick & Ludlum, 1972. 48p.

Illus. and essays on history of Lake George and Lake Champlain originally printed in the 1870s. Beautiful engravings. Essays: "The Violent Valley" (military history). "Lake George in the 1870s," and "Lake Champlain."

81. Sinnott, Trip. *Tea Island: A Perfect Little Gem; The Story of a Lake George Island.* Topsham, ME., Thirty-Three Press, 1983. 60p.; rev. ed., Clinton Corners, N.Y., Attic Studio Press, 1993. 64p.

Collection of lore-fictional and non-fictional accounts of Tea Island, which is the southernmost island in Lake George. Photos and drawings from various eras.

## Counties

82. 200th Anniversary Task Force. *Washington County, New York: 200th Anniversary, 1784-1984.* Fort Edward, N.Y., The Task Force, 1984. 51p.

Brief overview and map of county and one page descriptions of each Washington County town. Advts.

83. Allan, Helen, et. al. *Clinton County: A Pictorial History.* Norfolk, VA., Donning Co., 1988. 223p.

Photographic essay about Clinton County from its discovery to present. A fitting tribute to the bicentennial of Clinton County.

84. Bernstein, Burton. *The Sticks: A Profile of Essex County, N.Y.* New York, Dodd, Mead, 1972. 175p.

A well-written overview of Essex County in northeastern New York State. Sketches stress early strategic importance, early economic development in contrast to current poverty and economic problems.

85. Biondi, Mary H. *The Supervisor Story: St. Lawrence County, New York 1802-1973.* Canton, N.Y., Board of Supervisors and St. Lawrence County Historical Association, 1974. 124p.

Lists, photos, and biographical sketches of town supervisors for all of St. Lawrence County. Towns of Hopkinton, Piercefield, Colton, Parishville, Clifton, Clare, Fine and part of Pitcairn are inside the Blue Line.

86. Bowen, G. Byron. *History of Lewis County, New York 1880-1965.* Lowville, N.Y., County Board of Legislators, Lewis County, 1970. 563p.

General history of Lewis County plus history of individual towns. Towns of Watson, Greig, Lyonsdale, and part of Diana lie within the Blue Line of Adirondack Park. Some copies provided with 1969 highway map of Lewis County in back pocket. Bibliography.

87. Clinton County Historical Association. *Fire!: The History of Firefighting in Clinton County.* Plattsburgh, N.Y., Clinton County Historical Association, 1991. 68p.

Short history of firefighting in Clinton County. Contains brief articles about City of Plattsburgh's fire department as well as Clinton County's 24 volunteer fire departments. Pictures as well as lists of equipment and members accompany many of the articles.

88. Dunn, Violet B. (ed.). *Saratoga County Heritage.* s.l., s.n., (Syracuse, N.Y., Salina Press,) 1974. 608p.

History of Saratoga County, edited by Dunn who was then County Historian. Towns of Day, Hadley, Edinburgh, Corinth, Providence and Greenfield are completely or partly inside the Blue Line. Chapters on geology, political organization, highways, transportation, sports, culture and professional life as well as on individual towns. Index.

89. Fitch, Asa. *Their Own Voices: Oral Accounts of Early Settlers in Washington County.* Interlaken, N.Y., Heart of the Lakes Publishing Co., 1983. 158p.

Edited by Winston Adler. Collected by Dr. Asa Fitch. Compilation of newspaper articles gleaned from Fitch's manuscript, "Notes for a History of Washington County." Numerous oral accounts collected by Fitch during the 19th century. A few accounts are reminiscences of the late 18th century. Illus.

90. Harris, Ruth G. *Index of History of Essex County, N.Y. 1885.* s.l., s.n., 1978. 99p.

Reference work. Good tool for genealogists. Lists names with page numbers in Smith's book.

91. Herkimer County Historical Society. *Herkimer County at 200.* Herkimer, N.Y., The Society, 1992. xii, 338p.

    Geography, people, social and cultural life, transportation, economy, government, health, education and notable individuals. Photos. Brief sections on individual towns. Bibliography, footnotes, index. Appendix lists various officials in county and state government.

92. [Hough, Franklin B.] Compiled at St. Lawrence University. *Index of Place Names and Personal References in History of St. Lawrence and Franklin Counties.* Canton, N.Y., St. Lawrence County Historical Association and Franklin County Historical and Museum Society, 1971. 58p.

    Personal name index to Hough's book on Franklin and St. Lawrence Counties. Good resource for genealogists whose ancestors lived in one of these two counties.

93. Kozma, Ethel. *Remembering When: The Nineteenth Century in Essex County.* Wadhams, N.Y., United Church of Christ, 1983. 54p.

    Brief vignettes on all aspects of life in 19th century; travel, industry, recreation and politics. Illustrated by Sister Mary Felicitas Wells.

94. Lake Champlain-Lake George Regional Planning Board. *Data Book 1970: Clinton County.* Lake George, N.Y., The Board, 1970. 141p.

    Statistics and data describing Clinton County in 1970. Divided into three broad categories; A. Human Resources, (labor, population, income and housing) B. Community Resources (transportation, public utilities, education, community services, and business and industry). C. Physical Resources (Natural resources, agriculture, real estate, recreation and climate). Numerous maps, charts, graphs, tables. Spiral bound.

95. Lake Champlain-Lake George Regional Planning Board. *Data Book 1970: Essex County.* Lake George, N.Y., The Board, 1971. 256p.

    Statistics and data describing Essex County in 1970. Divided into three broad categories; A. Human Resources ( population, labor, income and housing) B. Community Resources (transportation, public utilities, education, community services, and business and industry. C. Physical Resources ( natural resources, agriculture, real estate, recreation, and climate. Maps, charts, graphs, tables. Spiral bound.

96. Lake Champlain-Lake George Regional Planning Board. *Data Book 1970: Hamilton County.* Lake George, N.Y., The Board, 1971. 148p.

    Statistics and data describing Hamilton County in 1970. Now mostly of historical value. Spiral bound. Organized in three broad categories; A. Human Resources (labor, population, income, and housing) B. Community Resources (transportation, public utilities, education, community services, and business and industry. C. Physical Resources (natural resources, agriculture, real estate, recreation and climate. Maps, charts, graphs, and tables. Spiral bound.

97. Lake Champlain-Lake George Regional Planning Board. *Data Book 1970: Washington County.* Lake George, N.Y., The Board, 1971. 185p.

    Statistics and data describing Washington County in 1970. Now primarily of historical interest. Organized into three general categories; A. Human Resources (labor, population, income, and housing) B. Community Resources (transportation, public utilities, education, community services, and business and industry. C. Physical Resources (natural resources, agriculture, real estate, recreation and climate. Maps, charts, graphs, and tables. Spiral bound.

98. Larson, Olaf F. *The People of New York State Counties: Clinton County; Trends in Human Resources and Their Characteristics to 1970.* Ithaca, N.Y., State College of Agriculture and Life Sciences, Cornell University, 1974. 48p.

    Clinton County population figures based on 1970 census. Tables.

99. Larson, Olaf F. *The People of New York State Counties: Essex County; Trends in Human Resources and Their Characteristics to 1970.* Ithaca, N.Y., State College of Agriculture and Life Sciences, Cornell University, 1974. 48p.

    Essex County population figures based on 1970 census. Tables.

100. Larson, Olaf F. *The People of New York State Counties: Franklin County; Trends in Human Resources and Their Characteristics to 1970.* Ithaca, N.Y., State College of Agriculture and Life Sciences, Cornell University, 1974. 48p.

    Franklin County populaton figures based on 1970 census. Tables.

101. Larson, Olaf F. *The People of New York State Counties: Fulton County; Trends in Human Resources and Their Characteristics to 1970.* Ithaca, N.Y., State College of Agriculture and Life Sciences, Cornell University, 1974. 48p.

Fulton County population figures based on 1970 census. Tables.

102. Larson, Olaf F. *The People of New York State Counties: Herkimer County; Trends in Human Resources and Their Characteristics to 1970.* Ithaca, N.Y., State College of Agriculture and Life Sciences, Cornell University, 1974. 48p.

Herkimer County population figures based on 1970 census. Tables.

103. Larson, Olaf F. *The People of New York State Counties: Lewis County; Trends in Human Resources and Their Characteristics to 1970.* Ithaca, N.Y., State College of Agriculture and Life Sciences, Cornell University, 1974. 48p.

Lewis County population figures based on 1970 census. Tables.

104. Larson, Olaf F. *The People of New York State Counties: Oneida County; Trends in Human Resources and Their Characteristics to 1970.* Ithaca, N.Y., State College of Agriculture and Life Sciences, Cornell University, 1974. 48p.

Oneida County population figures based on 1970 Census. Tables.

105. Larson, Olaf F. *The People of New York State Counties: St. Lawrence; Trends in Human Resources and Their Characteristics to 1970.* Ithaca, N.Y., State College of Agriculture and Life Sciences, Cornell University, 1974. 48p.

St. Lawrence County population figures based on 1970 Census. Tables.

106. Larson, Olaf F. *The People of New York State Counties: Saratoga County; Trends in Human Resources and Their Characteristics to 1970.* Ithaca, N.Y., State College of Agriculture and Life Sciences, Cornell University, 1974. 48p.

Saratoga County population figures based on 1970 Census. Tables.

107. Larson, Olaf F. *The People of New York State Counties: Warren County; Trends in Human Resources and their Characteristics to 1970.* Ithaca, N.Y., State College of Agriculture and Life Sciences, Cornell University, 1974. 48p.

Warren County population figures based on 1970 Census. Tables.

108. Larson, Olaf F. *The People of New York State Counties: Washington County; Trends in Human Resources and Their Characteristics to 1970.* Ithaca, N.Y., State College of Agriculture and Life Sciences, Cornell University, 1974. 48p.

Washington County population figures based on 1970 Census. Tables.

109. Morrison, James F. *A History of Fulton County in the Revolution.* Gloversville, N.Y., Fulton County Bicentennial Committee, 1977. 59p.

Northern Fulton County lies within the Blue line.

110. New York State. Department of Labor. *Occupational Survey: Franklin County.* Albany, N.Y., Department of Labor, 1970. 43p.

Discusses methods of making a livelihood in Franklin County circa 1970. Maps, charts and graphs.

111. Orr, Lois et. al. *Historical Markers in Clinton County.* s.l., s.n., 1980. 63 lvs.

Catalog of 55 markers in Clinton County. Part II lists potential new markers based on British Military action during the War of 1812. Part III is a reprint of a lecture about historical markers given by Simon E. Fitzpatrick before the Clinton Rotary on February 4, 1934.

112. Parrott, Virginia, and Marjorie Sexton. *Name Index to Crisfield Johnson's History of Washington County, N.Y. 1878.* Fort Edward, N.Y., Washington County Historical Society, 1984. 79p.

Reference tool. Alphabetical listing of names with Johnson's page numbers. Good aid of for genealogists and local historians.

113. St. Lawrence County Office of Economic Development. *St. Lawrence County Profile.* Canton, N.Y., St. Lawrence County Office of Economic Development, 1989. 86p.; rev. ed., 1992. 83p.

Statistics and data describing St. Lawrence County for economic development purposes. Quality publications with charts, maps, tables, illus. Chapters on population, public/ private services, education, labor and employment, industrial base, government assistance to business, and cultural and recreational opportunities.

114. Smallman, C. Walter. *Genealogical Index to Historical Sketches of Franklin County by Frederick J. Seaver*. Fort Covington, N.Y., Smallman, 1976. 58p.
Personal Name Index to Franklin County history. Organized by town for easy use.

115. Stommes, Eileen Mary. *The Impact of External Contacts: Development of Dependence; the Case of Clinton County, N.Y. 1870-1970*. Ithaca, N.Y., Cornell, 1978. 333 lvs.
Doctoral thesis. Historical study of Clinton County 1870-1970. Discusses integration of the county into larger state and national society. Notes shift of local economy from production of goods to service economy in late 1960s.

116. Vogel, Pamela J. *Our Waters, Potable and Notable: Warren County, New York*. Glens Falls, N.Y., P.J. Vogel, 1977. 58p.
Survey of various water resources in Warren County, New York. Organized by town. Illus., index.

117. Walton, Nina & Harriet Colton. *Name Index to History of St. Lawrence County, New York*. Canton, N.Y., St. Lawrence County, New York, 1980. 119p.
Name index to Everts' *History of St. Lawrence County*. Useful for genealogists.

118. Washington County Planning Board. *An Introduction to the Historic Resources in Washington County*. s.l., s.n., 1976. 113p.
Photo essay of historic resources and buildings of Washington County. Photos and maps.

## Cities, Villages and Towns

### Clinton County

119. Baker, Sarah and Patricia Allison. *The Saranac Valley, Volume I: The Pioneers*. Plattsburgh, N.Y., Baker, 1970. 54p.
The early settlement of Saranac Valley to the 1850s. Describes the pioneer potash-lumber-maple economy plus early roads, churches, politics, and Redford Glass. Illus. Typescript.

120. Baker, Sarah and Patricia Allison. *The Saranac Valley, Volume II: The Boom Days*. Plattsburgh, N.Y., Baker, 1970. 58p.
Covers logging, iron production and other economic development during 1870s and 1880s. Illus. Typescript.

121. Baker, Sarah and Patricia Allison. *The Saranac Valley, Volume III: The Plank Road Gazette*. Plattsburgh, N.Y., Baker, 1970. 42p.
Newspaper excerpts from 1870s and 1880s about Saranac Valley region. Organized by seasons. Materials garnered from *Press Republican* and *Plattsburgh Sentinel*. Illus. Typescript.

122. Barcomb, Peg (comp.). *Rouses Point Centennial Year: 1877-1977*. s.l., s.n., 1977. 100p.
Local history. Highlights schools, businesses, war veterans, with short section on prohibition. Map of Clinton County inside front cover. Photos. Does not have index or table of contents.

123. Campbell, Richard Dean. *The People of the Land of Flint*. Lanham, MD., University Press of America, 1985. xviii, 111p.
Story of Ganienkeh, a contemporary traditionalist Mohawk community in Clinton County. Group of Mohawks relocated from the tense and controversial situation at Moss Lake in 1984. Campbell was a Methodist minister in Plattsburgh at the time. Bibliography.

124. Clifford, John Garry. *The Citizen Soldiers: The Plattsburgh Training Camp Movement, 1913-1920*. Thesis, Indiana University, 1969. 303 lvs.; reprint, Lexington, KY., University of Kentucky Press, 1972. ix, 326p.
Scholarly treatment of the Plattsburgh Training Camp Movement preceding World War I. Garry's thesis is that the movement and its activities at Plattsburgh influenced public awareness and policy about military preparedness and the passage of the 1917 Selective Service Act.

125. Everest, Allan S. *Briefly Told: Plattsburgh, New York, 1784-1984*. Plattsburgh, N.Y., Clinton County Historical Assocation, 1984. 64p.
Bicentennial history of Plattsburgh, New York. Illus., bibliography.

126. Everest, Allan S. *Point Au Fer*. Plattsburgh, N.Y., Clinton County Historical Association, 1992. 53p.

Point Au Fer is a 500 acre arm of land reaching out into Lake Champlain south of Rouses Point. Everest documents the history of this particular place through the Colonial, French and Indian Wars, and Revolutionary era as well as the War of 1812.

127. Harkness, J. Warren. *A Collection of Articles on the History of Peru, Vol. I.* Peru, N.Y., Peru Bicentennial Committee, 1976. 115p.

Harkness lived from 1848-1937 and worked as a teacher, surveyor and community leader. He also wrote extensively. Early history of Peru beginning with its settlement by Quakers. Harkness focused on old roads and industries as well as early settlers.

128. Harkness, J. Warren. *A Collection of Articles on the History of Peru, Vol. II.* Peru, N.Y., Peru Bicentennial Committee, 1976. 96p.

Peru, N.Y. is near the boundary of the Adirondack Park. Harkness (1848-1937) was a farmer and a surveyor who lived in Peru. He wrote extensively about his times and events in the town. Harkness' writings are interspersed with those of other individuals.

129. Martin, David K. *Chazy and the Revolution.* West Chazy, N.Y., Town of Chazy Bicentennial Committee, 1976. 24p.

Story of Chazy during the American Revolution. Located on Lake Champlain which played a vital role in pre-War of 1812 American History. Illus., maps.

130. New York State. Department of Labor. *Proposed Zoning Ordinance, City of Plattsburgh, N.Y.* Albany, N.Y., Office of Planning and Coordination, 1969. 96p.

NAR

131. Nolan, Margaret (ed. and comp.). *Black Brook and Ausable Forks: Yesterday, Today and Tomorrow.* Elizabethtown, N.Y., Denton Publications, 1977. ix, 166p.

Local history of Black Brook and Ausable Forks in southern Clinton County. Both are Adirondack communities.

132. Orr, Lois (comp.). *Historical Review of the Town of Mooers, 1975-76, Bicentennial Edition.* Elizabethtown, N.Y., Denton Publications, 1976; reprint, 1985. 100p.

Mooers is in northeastern New York just outside the Blue Line and on the Canadian border. Book is a potpourri of people, places, buildings, businesses and professions down through the years. Illus., ports. Inside of front cover: reprint of 1869 map of Mooers Village, inside of back cover: 1869 map of Mooers Forks.

133. Plattsburgh Air Force Base Liason Committee. *Plattsburgh Air Force Base: 25 Years; Souvenir Edition 10-12 July 1981.* Plattsburgh, N.Y., Plattsburgh Air Force Base Liason Committee, 1981. 112p.

Emphasis on history of base. Appendices list air divisions and personnel. Map of base.

134. Plattsburgh, Town of. *200th Anniversary Souvenir Program: Town of Plattsburgh Bicentennial.* Plattsburgh, N.Y., Town of Plattsburgh, 1985. 85p.

Commemorative booklet. Essays on history of town and its historical markers. Photos of town officials. Letters of congratulations from President Reagan, Mario M. Cuomo, David Martin, Ronald Stafford, Andrew Ryan. Advts.

135. Plattsburgh, Town of. *Historical Sketches of the Town of Plattsburgh 1785-1975.* Plattsburgh, N.Y., Town of Plattsburgh, 1975. 56p.

Brief essays covering the historical highlights of the Town of Plattsburgh. Articles on Battle of Valcour in 1776, military history, industrial and economic development, religion, education, cultural affairs, and transportation.

136. Shields, Addie L. *Beekmantown: A Landmark in a Passageway.* Beekmantown, N.Y., Beekmantown Bicentennial Committee, 1976. 166p.

History of Beekmantown, N.Y., located east of the Adirondack Park and west of Lake Champlain. Landmark refers to rock formation that juts out into Lake Champlain channel between mainland and the Lake Champlain Islands. Brief chronology of town history followed by text and photos. This is the only work on Beekmantown by Shields. Nestler mistakenly cites another longer work on Beekmantown.

137. Shields, Addie L. *The John Townsend Addoms Homestead, Comstock Road, Clinton County, New York.* Plattsburgh, N.Y., s.n., 1979, 1981. 1 v.

Collected materials about Addoms site and the Underground Railroad in Clinton County, New York gathered for the purpose of having the Addoms House put on the National Historic register. Includes a list of oral and written sources. 1981 edition covers a chronological history of slavery, index. Photocopies of maps, photos, and documents.

138. Smith, Jessica. *A Reconnaissance Level Survey of the Historic Resources in the Towns of Ausable, Black Brook, Chesterfield, Jay and Village of Keeseville.* Keeseville, N.Y., Friends of Keeseville, 1991. 324p.

Photos. Typescript. Maps. Co-authored by Steven Engelhart and Ann Crossing.

139. Sullivan, Nell & David Martin. *A History of the Town of Chazy, Clinton County, New York.* Burlington, VT., George Little Press, 1970. iv, 360p.

Well done local history. Many photos and illus., lengthy and detailed text. Hardbound.

140. Sunderland, Lincoln (ed.). *History of Peru, N.Y.* Keeseville, N.Y., Bicentennial Committee of Peru, N.Y., 1980. 181p.

Third volume of history of Peru, N.Y. Material by various authors and from other sources consisting of articles, maps, lists, and obituaries. Illus. *(See #127 and #128.)*

141. White, Philip L. *Beekmantown, New York: Forest Frontier to Farm Community.* Austin TX., University of Texas Press, 1979. xv, 398p.

Academic historian's study of Beekmantown, N.Y. focuses on the changes a frontier community undergoes in becoming a farm community. White argues first generation settlers were higher in socio-economic status than later arrivals. By mid-1820s diminished timber resources meant a shift in economic life towards a more modest farm-based economy. Engravings in book from *The Pictorial Field Book of the War of 1812* by Benson J. Lossing. Maps, illus., index, bibliography.

142. Winans, Maggie (ed.) *Clinton County: I Remember When.* Plattsburgh, N.Y., Senior Citizens Council of Clinton County, 1983. 130p.

Edited interviews with Clinton County senior citizens. Divided by topic: "Growing up," "Farm Life," "School," "Good Times," "Work," "Life Stories," "Verse," etc. Each interview autographed and accompanied by a portrait of the interviewee. Over 100 entries.

Essex County

143. Essex Free Library Board of Trustees. *Essex, N.Y.: Lake Champlain's Historic Harbor.* s.l., s.n., 1969. Unpaged.

Chapters on Essex-on-the-Lake, agriculture, natural history, churches, cultural features, commerce and industry and Essex Village in 1969. Numerous photos of historical interest.

144. Carroll, George. *Lake Placid: The Adirondack Village that Became Famous.* Glens Falls, N.Y., Thomas F. Barton, 1968. 116p.

Foreword by Lowell Thomas. History of Essex County resort community; includes mention of John Brown, and the Olympics. Photos.

145. Clark, Raymond C. *A View of Westport, N.Y. on Lake Champlain, Gateway to the Adirondacks 1902-1972.* Elizabethtown, N.Y., Denton Publications, 1972. 64p.

Local history intended to update an earlier history of Westport which covered the events up to 1902. The western portion of the township lies within the Blue Line.

146. DuBois, Gaylord. *A Walk Around Whallons Bay, New York with Gaylord DuBois.* Arlington, VA., Glenn, 1984. vi, 99p.

Personal account of Whallons Bay, Town of Essex, New York. Based on exchange of letters between Morris Glenn and Dubois. Reminiscences of Whallons Bay, Dubois Farm. Lists of Dubois photo album and publications.

147. Fennessey, Lana. *The History of Newcomb.* Newcomb, N.Y., Fennessey, 1977, 1988. viii, 105p.

Newcomb, N.Y. is in southwestern Essex County. Information on history and settlement, the development of the mines, the Roosevelt Memorials, and the Santonomi Preserve are presented in separate chapters. Bibliography.

148. Glenn, Morris F. *Glenn's History of the Adirondacks Vol. 2: The Keene Flats of Old Mountain Phelps.* Arlington, VA., Glenn, 1987. xxxix, 93p.

Collected articles by Phelps that appeared in the *Essex County Republican* in the early 1870s. Phelps was an Adirondack Guide. Maps, photos, illus. 40 copies.

149. Glenn, Morris F. *Glenn's History of the Adirondacks (Essex County, New York) Vol. 3 Coon Mountain, Westport, N.Y.* Arlington, VA., Glenn, 1986. v, 150p.

Collected material on Coon Mt. near Westport, N.Y. Maps, photos, fold-in drawings. Errata sheet at the end. Special 1st ed.

150. Glenn, Morris F. *The Story of Three Towns: Westport, Essex and Willsboro, N.Y.* Arlington, VA., Glenn, 1977. 354p.

Town histories. Essex, and Willsboro lie outside Blue Line while part of Westport is within the Adirondack Park. Photos and maps. Glenn has written several other books about Essex County and Lake Champlain.

151. Historical Society of the Town of Chester. *Civic Directory: Organizations, Business and Professional Services, Daily Date Book and Personal Telephone Index of Chester.* Chestertown, N.Y., The Society, 1968. 49p.

Maps of Chestertown, business directory, history of the Town of Chester by Caroline H. Fish. List of organizations. Maps on back cover, illus. Advts.

152. Holt, Charles N. *Adirondack Frontier: Stories of Keene Flats After 1776.* Elizabethtown, N.Y., Denton Publications, 1976. 123p.

Essex County town. Chapter on the "year without winter." Photos, timeline.

153. Jaques, Adeline. *Echoes from Whiteface Mountain: A Brief History of Wilmington, N.Y.* s.l., s.n., 1980. 33p.

Originally a part of Jay, Wilmington was established in 1822. Emphasizes schools, churches. Text only.

154. Jones, Clarence. *When Does A Twig Become a Limb?* Middletown, Conn., Frankfort Publishing Co., 1988. vi, 194p.

Collected articles written by Jones between 1958 and 1983 for the publication of the Minerva Historical Society. A potpourri of stories, prose, reminiscences and local history. Minerva is located in southern Essex County. Illus.

155. Masters, Raymond D. *Social History of the Huntington Wildlife Forest.* Utica, N.Y., North Country Books, 1993. 96p.

Huntington Wildlife Refuge is located near Newcomb in East-Central Adirondacks. Information on Pendleton, Newcomb, logging, great camps, and Archer and Anna Huntington Wildlife Station. References, illus., appendices, no index.

156. Minerva Historical Society. *Minerva: A History of a Town in Essex County, N.Y.* New York, N.Y., Multiprint, Inc., 1967. 211p.; updated, Minerva Historical Society. *Minerva 1817-1985, Essex County, N.Y.: Supplement to the 1967 Town History.* Minerva, N.Y., Minerva Historical Society, 1986, 245p.

Local history. Information on professions and occupations, resorts and clubs, summer camps, organizations, utilities, railroads, town boundaries, and geology of the region. Index. Table of contents.

157. Ortloff, George C. and Stephen C. Ortloff. *Lake Placid: The Olympic Years, 1932-1980; A Portrait of America's Premier Winter Resort.* Lake Placid, N.Y., Macromedia, Inc., 1977. 204p.

Retrospective look at 1932 Winter Olympics in Lake Placid. Many excellent older photos. Anticipates the 1980 games, discussing interim events and sports activities.

158. Rossiter, Eleanor M. *Personal Names: A Supplement to the Index in BESSBORO, A HISTORY OF WESTPORT.* Elizabethtown, N.Y., Brewster Library, 1984. 41p.

Personal name index to existing local history. Names followed by page numbers where they appear in book.

159. State University of New York College at Plattsburgh. Technical Assistance Center. *Municipal Management and Consolidation Alternatives for the Town of North Elba and the Village of Lake Placid.* Plattsburgh, N.Y., The Center, 1975. 254p.

Study to identify ways to make local government more efficient and offer better services. Study identifies need to plan for 1980 Olympics.

160. Ticonderoga Historical Society. *Ticonderoga: Patches and Patterns From Its Past: The First Volume.* Ticonderoga, N.Y., Ticonderoga Historical Society, 1969. 343p.

Edited by Jane M. Lape. A civil history of Ticonderoga—the town, not the fort. Information on background, early history, as well as economic, social and cultural institutions. Periodic updates entitled, "Patches and Patterns Extended" initiated in 1990.

161. Town of Keene. *Proposal by Town of Keene for Visitor Interpretive Center.* Keene, N.Y., Town of Keene, 1985. 38p.

Quality publication to promote Keene as a location for a Visitors Interpretive Center. Emphasis is on Keene's central location, proximity to the High Peaks, and future possibilities. Maps, color photos.

162. Trancik, Roger, et. al. *Essex: A Land Use Planning Process.* s.l., s.n., 1975. 47p.

Town of Essex Land Use Planning publication. Valuable for its presentation of problems and community issues of a township adjacent to and similiar to the Adirondack Park region.

163. Walker, Carlin. *Bessboro Beginnings.* Westport, N.Y, Westport Library, 1988. 70p.

Compiled newspaper columns on history of Westport, New York. Photos, index.

164. West Alberta C. *Reber: 1800-1930.* s.l., unpub., 1980.

History of Adirondack community from its pioneer origins to its integration into a national culture. Reber is located in Essex County.

165. Winch, Oliver W. *Wilmington in the Adirondacks: A Brief History.* s.l., s.n., 1970. 95p.; rev. ed., *Wilmington of the Adirondacks.* s.l., s.n., 1974. 130p.

Wilmington, N.Y. is located in the northeastern corner of Essex County. Chapters cover topics like political history, early schools, Wilmington in the War of 1812, important families, census figures and local folklore.

Franklin County

166. Collins, Geraldine. *The Brighton Story: Being the History of Paul Smiths, Gabriels and Rainbow Lake.* Lakemont, N.Y., North Country Books, 1977. x, 202p.; 2nd ed., Saranac Lake, N.Y., Chauncey Press, 1986. x, 204p.

Thorough discussion of political, social, economic and cultural history of Brighton, which is located in south-central Franklin County, New York. Author started the library at Paul Smiths College and edited the Franklin County Historical Review. Second ed. in 1986, with index. Bibliography.

167. Daily, Frances Willson. *Lake Titus Potpourri.* Malone, N.Y., Daily, 1977. 34p.

Reminiscences of Lake Titus, camps and residents. Some photos date back to the early 1900s. Illus.

168. Dora, Donna & Mildred Keough (eds.). *A Past To Remember: A Future to Mold, Saranac Lake, N.Y.* Saranac Lake, N.Y., Women's Civic Chamber, 1977, 1985. 96p.

Photographic essay. Chronology of Saranac Lake on inside of front cover. Photos. First printing was 2,000 copies. Second ed. 1985.

169. Dumont, Diane S., et. al. *Reflections: A Brief History of Burke from 1797-1976.* Burke, N.Y., s.n., 1976. 48p.

Burke is located in Franklin County, near Malone, New York. Chronological outline history on inside of front cover. Maps of Burke on both inside and outside of back cover. Charts, photos.

170. Franklin, Town of. *For the Future 1836-1991 Town of Franklin "They Told Me So..." Vol IV.* Vermontville, N.Y., Town of Franklin, 1991. 59p.

Information about post office, reminiscences of school days, quilting, medicare and medicaid assistance program, 55+ Club, Retired Seniors Volunteer Program, and Vermontville forest fire. Photos, advts, maps.

171. Franklin, Town of. *150th Anniversary Town of Franklin 1836-1986 "They Told Me So...."* Vermontville, N.Y., Town of Franklin, 1986. 46p.

Information on Franklin Falls, Onchiota, Loon Lake House, and railroads. Reprinted clippings, local photos.

172. Franklin, Town of. *Town of Franklin 1836-1990 "They Told Me So..." Vol. III.* Vermontville, N.Y., Town of Franklin, 1990. 65p.

Topics include Onchiota, Humane Society, Retired Senior Volunteer Program, Office of Town Justice, Carney family Bible, Roakdale, and Buck Pond Public Campsite. Photos, advts.

173. Hyde, Floy S. *Water Over the Dam at Mountain View in the Adirondacks.* Mountain View, NY, Hyde, 1970, 1971, 1984. xx, 371p.

Local history of Mountain View in Central Franklin County, just inside the Blue Line. Also a case study of the development and decline of resort communities.

174. Saranac Lake Mid-winter Carnival. *Anniversary Album*. Saranac Lake, N.Y., Saranac Lake Mid-winter Carnival, 1967.

Program for 70th annual winter carnival. Includes programs of events and photos of earlier carnivals. Advts.

175. Simmons, Louis J. *Mostly Spruce and Hemlock*. Tupper Lake, N.Y., s.n., 1976. ix, 461p.

History of Tupper Lake, N.Y. in southern Franklin County. Now out of print and hard to find.

176. Simmons, Louis J. *Town of Altamont 1690-1990 Centennial Observance: August 11-19 1990*. s.l., s.n., 1990. 84p.

Centennial publication organized by Town Historian Louis Simmons. Pictorial with brief vignettes on all aspects of history of Tupper Lake in Franklin County. 50% advts.

177. Smith, Raymond C. *Those Were the Days: A History of Bangor, N.Y.* Bangor, N.Y., Bangor Town Board, 1977. 98p.

Local history of Bangor, N.Y., in Franklin County, just outside of the Blue Line. Photos, population charts, occupation lists and sections on politics and government, churches and fraternal organizations. Bibliography.

178. Stockwell, Ola. *Mini-Sketches of Westville*. Constable, N.Y., Stockwell, 1977. 116p.

A potpourri of information on Westville in the Town of Constableville in extreme northern Franklin County. Lists, charts, town records, photos as well as information on town government, schools, businesses and churches.

179. Surprenant, Neil. *Brandon: Boomtown to Nature Preserve*. Paul Smiths, N.Y., St. Regis Press, 1982. 58p.

History of Franklin County Town. Well written. Photos and index.

180. Taylor, Robert. *Saranac: America's Magic Mountain*. Boston, MA., Houghton Mifflin Co., 1986. 308p.

Story of tuberculosis, Dr. Edward Trudeau, and the village of Saranac Lake, New York. The appeal of the area to artists and writers as well as wealthy or famous tuberculosis victims contributed to the development of a diverse and unique Adirondack community.

181. Trim, Paula LaVoy. *Looking Back Upstream: St. Regis Falls and Its Past*. Saranac Lake, N.Y., Trim, 1989. 470p.

Reprinted clippings and articles accumulated by author following publication of her first book on St. Regis Falls, which is located in West Central Franklin County. Photos, maps.

182. Trim, Paula LaVoy. *Water Over the Falls: St. Regis Falls History*. Saranac Lake, N.Y., Trim, 1984. x, 276p.

Story of St. Regis Falls in Franklin County. Heavy emphasis on family history, with some material on social and economic history of the town. Illus. Bibliography.

Fulton County

183. Gerber, Morris. *Sacandaga Pictorial*. Albany, N.Y., Gerber, 1973. 32p.

Over three dozen photos of Sacandaga park, lake and river region.

184. McMartin, Barbara. *Caroga, the Town Recalls its Past*. Caroga, N.Y., Town of Caroga, 1976. vi, 250p.

History of town in northern Fulton County which lies just inside the Blue Line. Covers the founding of the town and early history and development. Deals with various sections of the township such as Wheelerville, Pine Lake, Canada Lake and Caroga Lake.

Hamilton County

185. Arietta Sesqui-Centennial Committee. *Arietta, Hamilton County, New York: Historical Book of the Town of Arietta*. s.l., s.n., 1986. 160p.

Town history. Arietta is located in Hamilton County. Chapters cover a wide variety of social, political, civic, cultural, religious and genealogical topics. Illus.

186. Boos, John E. *The Sacandaga Valley*. Albany, N.Y., Boos, 1972. 157p.

Lore and poetry of the Sacandaga Valley in the southern Adirondacks.

187. Girard, Ouida. *Griffin: Ghost Town in the Adirondacks and Other Tales*. s.l., s.n., 1980. 195p.
Story of Griffin, N.Y., once a larger, more active community in southern Hamilton County. Part reminiscence, part local history.

188. Hart, Larry. *The Sacandaga Story: A Valley of Yesteryear*. Schenectady, N.Y., Hart, 1967. 73p.
Before its creation in the 1930s the Sacandaga Reservoir was the Sacandaga River Valley. This work captures the way of life along this river before the inundation—the life of traditional Adirondack people: farmers, loggers, lumberjacks and millworkers. Many older photos of the dam construction that created the reservoir. Other printings in 1968, 1969, 1970, and 1973.

189. Russell, Earle, F. *A Glimpse into the Past: Memories of an Adirondack Town*. s.l., s.n., n.d. 32p.
Brief vignettes about Long Lake, N.Y.

190. Stanyon, Gladys & Mildred S. Colvin. *Reflections: Wells on the Sacandaga*. s.l., Boonville, N.Y., s.n., Boonville Graphics, 1975. 121p.
Life in the village of Wells in southern Adirondacks in the first quarter of the twentieth century. Captures the flavor of life in a simpler, less developed era. Recounts the flooding of the Sacandaga Valley in 1930 and the construction of the dam that created Lake Algonquin. 500 copies.

191. Timm, Ruth. *Raquette Lake: A Time to Remember*. Utica, N.Y., North Country Books, 1989. 321p.
History of Raquette Lake from its settlement through 1986. Information on resorts, camps, Alvah Dunning, and William W. Durant. Raquette Lake is in northern Hamilton County. Index.

192. Verner, Abbie S. (comp.). *The Guide to Long Lake and Vicinity*. Long Lake, N.Y., Tarbell Hill Press, 1973. Unpaged.
Listing of where to find a wide variety of goods during the summer in Long Lake in early 1970s. Map of Long Lake and location of various offices and businesses.

Herkimer County

193. Marleau, William R. *Big Moose Station*. Eagle Bay, N.Y., Marleau Family Publishing Co., 1986. xv, 350p.
History of Big Moose Station in northeastern Herkimer County, its establishment and its residents. Author was a Big Moose native who lived there for all but three years and worked as a New York State ranger for many years. Plates. Introduction by Thomas J. Marleau.

194. O'Brien, Clara. *God's Country, Eagle Bay Area: Fourth Lake in the Heart of the Adirondacks*. Sylvan Beach, N.Y., North Country Books, 1982. 278p.
History of Eagle Bay in Fulton Chain of Lakes. Topics discussed include chapters on railroads, tourism, local business, private clubs and preserves, summer camps, local residents and various organizations. Photos span several decades.

Lewis County

195. LeFevre, Dewitt C. *Grand-Pere's Legacy*. Beaver Falls, N.Y., Appleknockers, 1979. xii, 215p.
Personal work on Beaver Falls in Lewis County. Author was a journalist, and community, church, and business leader. Numerous drawings and photos.

196. Van Arnam, Lewis S. *A Beaver Falls Album*. Beaver Falls, N.Y., Beaver River Books, 1982. 96p.
Photo essay on social and economic life and the people of Beaver Falls: logging, sawmills, tanneries, schools, etc. Short essay on origins of Beaver Falls. List of significant events in the town history.

197. Van Arnam, Lewis S. *Beaver Falls Cavalcade 1794-1979*. Beaver Falls, N.Y., Van Arnam, 1979. viii, 222p.
Local history of village whose fortunes have been tied to paper industry. Other information on social, cultural, religious and economic life. Plates, bibliography.

198. Wilcox, Altsie. *Port Leyden and Vicinity: A Collection of Memorabilia*. s.l., s.n., 1977. viii, 72p.
Port Leyden is located just outside the Blue Line between the Adirondacks and Tug Hill Plateau in Lewis County. Short pieces on various aspects of community life and reprints of newspaper articles. Illus.

199. Williams, Emily Beebe & Ethel Evans Markham. *A History of Turin, Lewis County, New York.*

Lakemont, N.Y., North Country Books, 1974. 67p.

Story of Turin, New York from its earliest years to the establishment of Snow Ridge Ski area. Turin lies just west of the Adirondack Park Blue Line. Illus.

Oneida County

200. Crosten, William L. *Boonville and Beyond*. Utica, N.Y., North Country Books, 1989. 72p.

Photographic essay about this Lewis County community, located just west of the Adirondacks. Most photos were taken in the past two decades.

201. Davis, Margaret P. *Honey Out of the Rafters*. Remsen, N.Y., s.n., 1976, 1977, 1981. 136p.

Local history of Remsen and vicinity located just outside the Blue Line. Numerous photographs. Bibliography.

202. Ryder, Ron. *181 Years in Boonville, N.Y.: Facts, Dates, and Trivia, 1795-1976*. Boonville, N.Y., Boonville Graphics, 1976. 49p.

Bicentennial publication on Boonville. Plenty of photos, some old time advts. accompany text. Photos cover a wide range of subjects and time periods. Boonville lies just outside the Blue Line in northern Oneida County.

St. Lawrence County

203. Clarke, Susan. *The Birth of Russell 1807-1976: History of Russell, South Russell, North Russell, Clare, Degrasse*. s.l., s.n., 1976. 40p.

Bicentennial local history of these Southern St. Lawrence County towns. Russell is located just outside the Blue Line. Information on smaller communities within the township. Illus.

204. Colton Bicentennial Committee. *Colton: Story of a Town*. Gouverneur, N.Y., Town of Colton, 1976. 132p.; rev. and updated ed., *Colton: Story of a Town II*. Baltimore, MD, Gateway, 1993. 167p.

Bicentennial history of Colton, N.Y. Large but sparsely populated part of this town lies within the Adirondack Park. Features older photos of life in Colton, also photos from 1970s.

205. Freeman, LaVerne H. et. al. *Edwards on the Oswegatchie 1812-1976: Memories of Township #8*. Edwards, N.Y., Bicentennial Committee, 1976. 56p.

Local history of this southern St. Lawrence County community, just outside the Blue Line. Illus.

206. Keith, Herbert F. *Man of the Woods*. Syracuse, N.Y., Syracuse University Press/The Adirondack Museum, 1972. xi, 164p.

Intro. and Notes by Paul F. Jamieson. History of Wanakena in the southern St. Lawrence County Town of Fine. Founded as a lumber camp for the Rich Lumber Company, Wanakena is now a village surrounded by Forest Preserve. Three or four chapters on the Oswegatchie River. Other topics reflect the life and concerns of an Adirondack community: logging, hunting, fishing, and colorful local personalities. Photos. Paper ed. in 1976.

207. Parishville Historical Association. *Sketches of Parishville in Word and Picture, 1809-1976*. Parishville Historical Association, The Association, 1976. 45 lvs.

History of Parishville, N.Y. in St. Lawrence County from 1807 to 1976. The southern portion of the town lies within the Blue Line. Town is named after David Parish who owned large tracts of land in St. Lawrence County at the beginning of the nineteenth century. Describes many sections and neighborhoods that no longer exist.

208. Plumley, L.P. *100 Dam Years of Cranberry Lake: 1867-1967*. Gouverneur, N.Y., Cranberry Lake Centennial Committee, 1967. 40p.

Anniversary publication for Town of Clifton. Information on lumbering, resorts, chronological list of events in town history, 1845-1949. Illus., advts.

209. Reynolds, Jeanne & Bessie Decosse. *Two Towns... Two Centuries*. Gouverneur, N.Y., Clifton-Fine Bicentennial Committee, 1976. 224p.

Bicentennial History of Clifton and Fine, two southern St. Lawrence County towns inside the Blue Line. Many photos of local people and buildings as well as traditional occupations: logging, sugaring, and ice cutting.

210. St. Lawrence County Historical Association. *St. Lawrence County History: A View From the People*. Canton, N.Y., The St. Lawrence County Historical Association, 1975. 64p.

Bicentennial photographic essay on St. Lawrence County. Some photos are quite contemporary, while others reflect earlier times and generations.

211. Star Lake Centennial Committee. *Star Lake, NY Centennial 1878-1978.* Star Lake, N.Y., The Centennial Committee, 1978. 29p.
Information on Backus family, early hotels, Benson Mines, chronology of town 1837-1978. Brief passages on various community and organizations. Advts, illus.

Warren County

212. Germain, June and Roseanne H. LaFarr, (eds.) *Looking Forward to the Future While Cherishing the Past: 200th Anniversary, Thurman, N.Y.* s.l., s.n., 1992. 80p.
Bicentennial history of Warren County community. Illus.

213. O'Brien, Kathryn. *The Great amd the Gracious on Millionaire's Row: Lake George in Its Glory.* Sylvan Beach, N.Y., North Country Books, 1978, 1986. xiv, 278p.
Describes the homes of the rich and famous built on a 10-mile stretch of road between Lake George Village and Bolton Landing before the turn of the twentieth century. Well-researched, numerous photos of homes and their owners. Illus. Bibliography. Paper in 1986.

214. Ross, Wilford. *The History of Graphite, N.Y.* Glens Falls, N.Y., Ridgecraft Books, 1976. 46p.
Bicentennial local history of northern Warren County town. Typescript. Photos, personal name index.

215. Steinback, Elsa. *Sweet Peas and A White Bridge: On Lake George When Steam Was King.* Sylvan Beach, N.Y., North Country Books, 1974. 169p.
Anecdotes and tall tales of Lake George, mainly from the 19th century. Numerous photos, illus. by author.

216. Thomas, Lester. *Timber, Tannery and Tourists.* Lake Luzerne, N.Y., Committee on Publication of Local History, 1979. x, 166p.
Lake Luzerne is in southern Warren County. Title highlights stages of economic development. Other chapters on roads, religion, schools, prominent individuals and natural history. Interesting older photos.

217. Whipple, Janice M. *Stony Creek: Then and Now.* Stony Creek, N.Y., Stony Creek Historical Association, 1980. 71p.
Local history of southwestern Warren County town. Numerous old photos. Index.

Washington County

218. Buckell, Betty Ahearn (ed.). *No Dull Days at Huletts: With Reminiscences of Henry W. Buckell.* Glens Falls, N.Y., Buckell., 1984. 48p.
Excerpts from Henry Buckell's articles for the *Lake George Mirror.* Mr. Buckell was a landlord at Hulett House, a Lake George Area resort. Some text by the editor. Many excellent photos from Buckell family collection. Contains chronology of Huletts Landing, a list of owners and managers of Hulett House. Brief sections on other hotels and families from the Lake George area. Second printing in 1991.

219. Hansen, Katherine. *Hamlet Summers.* Hulett's Landing, Lake George, N.Y., K. Hansen, 1953; reprint, Fort Edward, N.Y., Washington County Historical Society, 1979. 81p.
Hulett's Landing is on the east shore of Lake George. Reminiscences, families, and other assorted information.

220. Morton, Doris Begor. *Day before Yesterday.* Whitehall, N.Y., Town Board of Whitehall, 1977, 1981. 100p.
Whitehall is adjacent to the Adirondack Park boundary in Washington County. Illus.

221. Rogers Island Historical Association. *Exploring Rogers Island, Fort Edward, New York.* Fort Edward, N.Y., Roger Island Historical Assoc., 1969, 1986. 35p.
History of Rogers Island. Photos and ink drawings. Several pages of plates of artifacts from Ft. Edward. Primarily the work of Richard Mason.

222. Stiles, Fred Tracy. *Old Days, Old Ways: More History and Tales of the Adirondack Foothills.* Hudson Falls N.Y., Washington County Historical Society, 1984. vi, 137p.
Reminiscences by Stiles of Ft. Ann and vicinity in Washington County. Many older photos of people and places. Bibliography.

## Other Cities and Villages

223. Glens Falls Historical Association. *Bridging the Years 1763-1978*. Glens Falls N.Y., Glens Falls Historical Association, 1978. 236p. Various printings.

History of Glens Falls, N.Y. located just outside the Adirondack Park. A mix of old-time and current pictures. Folio. Bibliography. Illus.

224. Van Dusen, Richard C. *Glimpses of the Past*. Glens Falls, N.Y., Glens Falls Historical Association, 1970. 78p.

Collected newspaper columns written by Van Dusen under the banner "Historical Museum Notes." Articles cover a variety of local history topics and acquisitions of museum.

# *Geography*

225. Brinley, Francis. *The Life of William T. Porter*. New York, N.Y., D. Appleton Co., 1860; reprint, New York, N.Y., Arno, 1970. vii, 273p.
Chapter VIII on angling entitled "Trout Fishing in Hamilton County" took place in 1844, which makes it an early account of the Adirondack Region.

226. Colvin, Verplanck. *Report of the Superindendent of the State Land Survey of the State of New York for the Year 1898*. Schenectady, N.Y., Adirondack Research Center, 1989. lxxvii, 343p.
First publication of this survey. Introduction on Colvin, his life, and role in the surveys and annual reports by Norman J. VanValkenburgh. Maps. Each copy numbered. 500 copies. Errata slip tipped in.

227. Dunwell, Francis F. *The Hudson River Highlands*. New York, N.Y., Columbia University Press, 1991. 282p.
Foreword by Robert F. Kennedy, Jr. Bibliographic refs. Some references to Adirondacks and historic role of Upper Hudson River Valley.

228. Harder, Kelsie B. and Mary H. Smallman. *Claims to Name: Toponyms of St. Lawrence County*. Utica, N.Y., North Country Books, 1992. 288p.
Alphabetically-organized book on place names of St. Lawrence County; their origins and reasons behind the names. Several southern St. Lawrence County towns are located within the boundary of the Adirondack Park. Also in paper.

229. Haydon, Roger. ed. *Upstate Travels: British Views of Nineteenth Century New York*. Syracuse, N.Y., Syracuse University Press, 1982. iii, 273p.
Intro. by the editor. First 30+ pages on Saratoga and the Champlain Valley relevant to the Adirondacks. Bibliography.

230. Heller, Murray. *Call Me Adirondack: Names and Their Stories*. Saranac Lake, N.Y., The Chauncy Press, 1989. 163p.
Entertaining and instructive book about names of Adirondack places. Index, bibliography. Also in paper.

231. Heller, Murray. *Names, Northeast*. Saranac Lake, N.Y., North Country Community College Press, 1979. 77p.
Proceedings of 1st Annual Northeast Regional Names Institute held on Sept. 21 and 22, 1979. Eight articles by various individuals on names and naming.

232. Morgan, Percy Reese. *On the Adirondack Survey with Verplanck Colvin: The Diaries of Percy Reese Morgan*. Fleischmanns, N.Y., Purple Mountain Press, 1991. 96p.
Edited by Norman J. VanValkenburgh. First person account of important 1895 and 1896 New York State surveys by a college student. Refs.

233. New York State University. Division of Archives and History. *Supplementary Index to Places in the Gazetteer of the State of New York by J.H. French*. Albany, N.Y., Division of Archives and History, 1966. 37p.
Lists communities not indexed in original work.

234. Silliman, Augustus E. *A Gallop Among American Scenery, Or, Sketches of American Scene and Military Adventures*. New York, Appleton, 1843; reprint, Freeport, N.Y., Books for Library Press, 1970. 267p.
Several pages on Lake George and Ticonderoga are an early account of the region.

235. Thompson, John H. *Geography of New York State*. Syracuse, N.Y., Syracuse University Press, 1966. 543p.; Supplement, 1977. 31p.
Covers whole state, but includes much on Adirondack region. Information on geography, climate, topography, old rail lines and canal routes. Illus., charts. Map in back pocket.

236. Van Zandt, Roland. *Chronicles of the Hudson: Three Centuries of Travellers' Accounts*. New Brunswick, N.J., Rutgers University Press, 1971. 369p.
Contains early references to Upper Hudson River Valley; William C. Redfield in 1837 and 1880 account by Charles Farnham. Illus.

237. Vesty, John. *Adirontreks: Places and People in the Adirondacks*. Indian Lake, N.Y., Crossroads Publications, 1990. xi, 267p.

A "*Blue Highways*" look at the town and villages of the Adirondacks. Photos, sketch maps.

238. Whitson, Peggy Hanford. *Once upon A Rowboat: Adventures on Lake Champlain, Or Weather or Not*. Colchester, VT., Whithaven Enterprises, 1986. 95p.

Guide to various locales and points of interest on both sides of Lake Champlain. Bibliography. Illus.

# *Adirondack Park and Adirondack Preserve*

## General and Historical

239. Adirondack Council. *State of the Park: A Look at Growth Trends Affecting the Adirondack Park.* Elizabethtown, N.Y., The Council, 1990. 32p.

Looks at real estate development and how it impacts natural setting of the Adirondacks. Promotes "compatible development" or screening of homes and large building projects. Dovetails with another Council publication on scenic vistas. See DiNunzio below #251.

240. Aspland, Patricia E. *Open Space Protection: An Examination of the 1972 New York State Environmental Quality Bond Act and An Evaluation of the Subsequent Land Acquisition Program for the Adirondack Park Forest Preserve.* College Park, MD., University of Maryland, 1984. viii, 187 lvs.

NAR

241. Association for the Protection of the Adirondacks. *Twenty Years of Change: Selected Reports of the Association for the Protection of the Adirondacks 1967-1987.* Schenectady, N.Y., The Association, 1987. 1 v.

Annual and special reports of this active organization concerned with the protection and conservation of Adirondack wilderness. Intro. by Paul Schaefer. Limited ed. of 25 copies in loose leaf binders.

242. Association for the Protection of the Adirondacks. *Wilderness and People: The Future of the Adirondack Park.* Schenectady, N.Y., The Association, 1993. 116p.

Nine original essays on the Adirondacks in honor of the Park Centennial from presentation made at a conference entitled "Visions For the Adirondack Park's Second Century held August 25-27, 1992 at Sagamore Institute. Edited by Linda M. Champagne. Illus., maps, annotations.

243. Brown, Eleanor. *The Forest Preserve of New York: The Great Adirondack and Catskill Public Forests, and Their Protection Through a Century of Conflict; A Handbook for Conservationists.* Glens Falls, N.Y., Adirondack Mountain Club, 1985. xii, 269p.

Informative work on Forest Preserve Lands in the Adirondacks and Catskills. Discusses the importance of Forest Preserve, what it is, how it was established, and the development of protection and recreational uses over the past century. Part II identifies and discusses a half dozen issues facing Forest Preserve lands: timber harvesting, wildlife management, water resources, transportation, land use and acquisitions and resource and recreation uses. Index.

244. Burdick, Neal S. ed. *A Century Wild 1885-1985: Essays Commemorating the Centennial of the Adirondack Forest Preserve.* Saranac Lake, N.Y., Chauncy Press, 1985. 126p.

Articles commissioned by *Adirondack Life* by well known contemporary writers to commemorate the founding of the Forest Preserve in 1885. Preface by editor.

245. Citizen's Advisory Task Force on Adirondack Hamlet Restoration and Development. *Final Report.* Ray Brook, N.Y., Adirondack Park Agency, 1978. 39p.

Identifies community concerns and issues then makes recommendations on information needs, historic resources, planning and Adirondack Railway. Identifies several sources of assistance and funding.

246. Cobb, Thomas ed. *Historic Preservation Issues in the Adirondack Park: Colloqium Proceedings December 4, 1982 Union College, Schenectady, N.Y.* Saranac Lake, N.Y., North Country Community College Press, 1983. 136p.

Conference proceedings focusing on preservation of cultural and architectural resources in Adirondack Park. Sagamore, Santononi and Topridge mentioned specifically.

247. Cornell University. *Adirondack Landowner Survey.* Ithaca, N.Y., Cornell University, 1985. 39p.

Published results of survey of property owners in 1982 and 1983. Lists survey questions and answers on attitudes towards Adirondack Park, land use, and development.

248. D'Elia, Anthony N. *The Adirondack Rebellion.* Onchiota, N.Y., Onchiota Books, 1979. 230p.

This book describes the position and outlook of those Adirondackers who oppose the Adirondack Park Agency as violating residents' property rights and concerns. Illus. by William Calhoun. Bibliography, index.

249. Davis, George D. *2020 Vision: Biological Diversity: Saving All the Pieces.* Elizabethtown, N.Y., Adirondack Council, 1988. 64p.

Delineates a vision of the Adirondack Park in the future that includes the preservation and expanded protection of the region's biological diversity. Photos, maps and charts.

250. Davis, George D. *2020 Vision: Completing the Adirondack Wilderness System.* Elizabethtown, N.Y., The Adirondack Council, 1990. 48p.

Addresses the preservation of wilderness within the context of the Adirondack Park and the Adirondack Forest Preserve. Contains proposals for new wilderness areas: Bob Marshall, Boreal, and Wild Rivers. Recommends expanding 13 existing wilderness areas. Photos, maps, charts, and appendices. Vol. 2. For related items see items 249, 261, and 275.

251. DiNunzio, Michael G. *Windows on the Park: Scenic Vistas of the Adirondacks.* Elizabethtown, N.Y., Adirondack Council, 1991. 24p.

Discusses development issues that impact scenic vistas. Photos. For related item see # 239 above.

252. Dwyer, John F. *New York Forestry.* Syracuse, N.Y., College of Environmental Science and Forestry, 1974. xx, 445 lvs.

Thesis. Chapters I-IV thoroughly cover Adirondack Park, the Forever Wild concept, land use and development in the Adirondacks. Presentation of both sides of the historical arguments on Adirondack Park-related issues. Bibliography.

253. Forsyth, Alfred S. *The Forest and the Law.* New York, N.Y., Sierra Club, 1970. 40p.

Legal and political history of the Forest Preserve in the Adirondacks and Catskills. Information on the Constitutional Conventions of 1894, 1915, and 1967. Cites numerous legal cases.

254. Graham, Frank, Jr. *The Adirondack Park: A Political History.* New York, N.Y., Knopf, 1978; reprint, Syracuse, N.Y., Syracuse University Press, 1984. xiii, 314p.

A political history of the Adirondack Park focusing on laws, issues, problems and conflicts regarding land use in the Adirondacks. The Park did not evolve in a vacuum but rather was shaped by the same forces, and started for the same reasons, as national parks and forests.

255. Holmes, Timothy P. *The Future of the Adirondacks: A Survey of Attitudes, a Report on the Finding of the Research.* Saranac Lake, N.Y., Holmes and Associates, 1990. 71p.

Survey results based on a sample of 462 queried participants on quality of life, recreation, land use/ development, administration of the Park, the Commission on the Adirondacks in the 21st Century. Tables, bibliography.

256. Houseal, Brian L. *A Sense of Place in the Adirondacks: The Practical Application of an Environmental Design Concept.* Syracuse, N.Y., State University of New York. College of Environmental Science and Forestry, 1976. viii, 217 lvs.

Thesis. Defines "sense of place." Uses Tupper Lake and Keene Valley to illustrate and discuss the concept in concrete terms. Bibliography.

257. Keller, Jane E. *Adirondack Wilderness: A Story of Man and Nature.* Syracuse, N.Y., Syracuse University Press, 1980. 241p.

Overview of the Adirondacks. Book divided into 3 main parts: (1) The First Adirondack Wilderness (Creation-1830) (2) The Wilderness in Transition (1830-1885) (3) The Contemporary Wilderness (1885-Present). Underlying theme is how people and nature impact each other. Photos are not numerous, but well-chosen.

258. Krupsak, Mary Anne. *Cultural Heritage in the Wilds: Conference Report; Conference at Topridge, May 25-26, 1978.* Albany, N.Y., The Report Committee, 1978. vi, 87p.

Proceedings of conference to address preservation and protection of cultural heritage of the Adirondacks.

259. Lake Champlain Basin Research and Planning Workshop. *Proceedings of the Lake Champlain*

*Basin Research and Planning Workshop.* Plattsburgh, N.Y., State University of New York at Plattsburgh, 1975. iv, 32p.

Conference proceedings on research and planning needs of Lake Champlain region. Included people from New York, Vermont and Canada. Work groups discussed 5 areas of concern; 1. Water Quality and Supply 2. Wetlands, Vegetation, Fish and Wildlife 3. Land Use 4. Human Resources and 5. Legal and Institutional Issues.

260. McMartin, Barbara. *Citizen's Guide to the Adirondack Forest Preserve.* Ray Brook, N.Y., Adirondack Park Agency, 1985. 30p.

Discusses state-owned land in the Adirondack Park. Briefly outlines numerous primitive, wilderness and wild forest areas. Index on inside of back cover lists individual areas by name. Photos, maps.

261. McMartin, Barbara. *2020 Vision: Fulfilling the Promise of the Adirondack Park: Realizing the Recreational Potential of the Adirondack Wild Forests.* Elizabethtown, N.Y., The Adirondack Council, 1990. 52p.

Makes case for addition to existing wild forests areas throughout the whole Adirondack Region. Maps, photos and charts. For related items see numbers 249, 250, and 275.

262. Nelson, Holly and Alan J. Hahn. *State Policy and Local Influence in the Adirondacks.* Ithaca, N.Y., Cornell University, Center for Environmental Research, 1980. iv, 43p.

Shorter work on the historical background and creation of the Adirondack Park Agency. Discusses constituencies supporting and opposing Adirondack Park Agency, and the various forms that opposition to the APA has taken. Draws conclusions. Refs.

263. New York State. College of Forestry. School of Landscape Architecture. *Documents and Statements Pertaining to a Proposal to Establish an Adirondack Mountains National Park.* Syracuse, N.Y., State University College of Forestry, 1968. Var. pag.

Contents were discussed in a program entitled "Seminar on the Proposed Adirondack Mountains National Park," held on December 13, 1967. Fay Welch was speaker and there was a panel consisting of four faculty members from the College of Forestry. Henry G. Williams Jr. served as moderator. Proposal is outlined. Subsequent section contains statcmcnts opposing thc proposal. No index or table of contents.

264. New York State. Conservation Department. *New York's Forest Preserve and a Proposed National Park.* Albany, N.Y., Conservation Department, 1968. 64p.

Provides historical and legal background of private land ownership in Adirondacks. Identifies strong impacts of a National Park upon wood industry and tourism. Appendices list various water resources and towns within the Adirondack Park.

265. Richardson, Raymond J. *A Seasonal Residence Inventory by Towns and Minor Civil Divisions for the Twelve County Adirondack Park Region.* Plattsburgh, N.Y., Technical Assistance Center. State University College, Plattsburgh, 1972. ii, 27p.

Survey of seasonal residences, their number, value and density in Adirondack counties. According to this survey number of season dwellings were undercounted in 1970 Census. Charts. Fold out maps.

265A. St. Lawrence University. *Conference on the Adirondack Park, 1971: First Conference on the Adirondack Park, August 19-21, 1971.* Canton, N.Y., St. Lawrence University, 1972. iii, 115p.

Conference proceedings edited by Allen P. Splete, Paul F. Jamieson, and William K. Verner. Presentations on the work of the Temporary Study Commission and the Adirondack Park Agency, water quality, the forever provision of the New York State Constitution, land use and zoning, forest practices.

266. St. Lawrence University. *Conference on the Adirondack Park, 1972: Second Conference on the Adirondack Park, June 16-17, 1972.* Canton, N.Y., St. Lawrence University, 1973. 125p.

Conference proceedings on Adirondack Park Agency. State master plan for state-owned lands and private land use planning.

267. St. Lawrence University. *Conference on the Adirondack Park 1974; Fourth Conference on the Adirondack Park, June 14-15, 1974.* Canton, N.Y., St. Lawrence University, 1976. vii, 99p.

Conference proceedings. Edited by Allen P.

Splete, Robert A. Clark, and Bonnie E. McGuire. Sessions covered land use planning nationally and in Vermont, socio-economic issues associated with development in the Adirondack Park, APA activities, the Adirondack Park Association, and the role of local government and review boards in the Park.

268. St. Lawrence University. *Conference on the Adirondack Park 1975; Fifth Conference on the Adirondack Park.* Canton, N.Y., St. Lawrence University, 1980. iv, 77p.

Conference proceedings of ten sessions. Adirondack Park Agency activities, property values, hiking and campers, Adirondack rustic furniture, history of the Saranac Lakes, air pollution, wetlands, and lake eutriphication.

269. St. Lawrence University. *Conference on the Adirondack Park 1977; Seventh Conference on the Adirondack Park, June 16-18, 1977.* Canton, N.Y., St. Lawrence University, 1980. iii, 61p.

Conference proceedings. Topics of the conference were economic development in the Adirondacks, recent state land master plan issues, and Adirondack Park Agency activities. Other sessions concerned obtaining health care in the Adirondacks and preparation for the 1980 Olympics.

270. St. Lawrence University. *Conference on the Adirondack Park 1978; Eighth Conference on the Adirondack Park, June 8-11, 1978.* Canton, N.Y., St. Lawrence University, 1980. v, 137p.

Conference proceedings. Edited by Allen P. Splete and Paul F. Jamieson. Sessions covered wide-ranging subjects: Adirondack rivers, local planning, wood energy in New York State and Vermont, boats, skiffs, and bateaus in the 19th century, the 1980 Olympics and the environment, and a session on John Bird Burnham.

271. St. Lawrence University. *Conference on the Adirondack Park, 1979; Ninth Conference on the Adirondack Park, June 7-9, 1979.* Canton, N.Y., St. Lawrence University, 1980. iv, 77p.

Conference proceedings. Sessions on unit management planning, open space, discussion with APA staff. Other sessions on species endangerment, oral tradition and the 13th Winter Olympics, and humorous look at Adirondack guides. Edited by Paul Jamieson, Allen Splete and Neal S. Burdick.

272. St. Lawrence University. *Conference on the Adirondack Park 1980; Tenth Conference on the Adirondack Park, June 26-28, 1980.* Canton, N.Y., St. Lawrence University, 1981. iv, 89p.

Conference proceedings. Eight sessions covering the following topics: wood as an energy source, acid rain, agriculture and alchohol fuel production, Verplanck Colvin as scientist and his relationship to Forest Preserve. Other sessions discussed Citizen's Advisory Committee on Open Space, dialogue with APA staff, and comparative issues for Adirondacks and Appalachian Mountains.

273. St. Lawrence University. *Conference on the Adirondack Park, 1981; Eleventh Conference on the Adirondack Park, June 11-13, 1981.* Canton, N.Y., St. Lawrence University, 1982. 57p.

Transcripts of 6 sessions of 1981 conference with emphasis on historical perspective as seen through the eyes of Department of Environmental Conservation, past leaders of the Adirondack Park Agency, and Conservation groups. Other sessions were about taxes and forest management. Edited by Allen P. Splete, Paul F. Jamieson, and Neal S. Burdick.

274. Sand, David E. *The Preservationist Ethic and the Origin of the Adirondack Park.* Princeton, N.Y., Princeton, N.J., 1979. 180 lvs.

Senior independent study project. Discusses various social forces and groups that lead to creation of the Adirondack Park in the 19th century. Specifically mentions the role of sportsmen, tourists and railroads. Bibliographic notes.

275. Sheehan, John F. *2020 Vision: A Summary of the Three Volume Series.* Elizabethtown, N.Y., Adirondack Council, 1992. 36p.

Abridged ed. of three other works. Produced to commemorate the centennial of the Adirondack Park. For individual works see items 249, 250, and 261 for more information. Illus., maps.

276. Terrie, Philip G. *Forever Wild: Environmental Aesthetics and the Adirondack Forest Reserve.* Philadelphia, PA., Temple University Press, 1985. 209p.

Study uses Adirondacks to discuss people's changing view of wilderness over time. Terrie is former Assistant Curator of the Adirondack Museum.

277. Trancik, Roger. *Hamlets of the Adirondacks: History, Preservation and Investment.* Ithaca, N.Y., R. Trancik, 1983. 60p.

Planning publication for Adirondack Park's 135 hamlets. Goal is to balance economic progress and environmental concerns. Study discusses history, analysis, groupings of Adirondack communities, and deals with individual hamlets. Final chapter offers planning ideas for future implementation. Bibliography.

278. Trancik, Roger. *Hamlets of the Adirondacks: A Manual of Development Strategies.* Ithaca, N.Y., s.n., 1984, 1985. 132p.

Uses a dozen smaller communities: Ausable Forks, Bloomingdale, Indian Lake, Keeseville, Long Lake, Lyon Mountain, Port Henry, South Colton, Speculator, Star Lake, Willsboro, and Wilmington to discuss various redevelopment strategies. These include: waterfront revitalization, recreation/tourism, industrial, human resource, re-use of various structures, public spaces, water and sewer. Numerous photos and drawings. Offers action strategies for redevelopment activities. The 1984 version entitled *Hamlets of the Adirondacks II* had a spiral binding.

279. VanValkenburgh, Norman J. *The Adirondack Forest Preserve: A Chronology; A Narrative of the Evolution of the Adirondack Forest Preserve of New York State.* Typescript, 1968. 370 lvs.; 1st thus, Blue Mountain Lake, N.Y., Adirondack Museum, 1979. xiv, 396p.

History of the development of the Adirondack Forest Preserve to 1968. Numerous appendices with interesting topics. For example, how many forest preserve acres were taken for the Northway? It's there in Appendix XI. Bibliography. First ed. in 1968.

280. VanValkenburgh, Norman J. *The Forest Preserve of New York State in the Adirondack and Catskill Mountains: A Short History.* Schenectady, N.Y., Adirondack Research Center, 1983. 53p.

Discusses the establishment and growth of state-owned lands in Adirondack region. Discusses Colvin, Hough, various state laws, the Temporary Study Commission and the founding of the Adirondack Park Agency. Illus., maps.

281. VanValkenburgh, Norman J. *Land Acquisition for New York State: An Historical Perspective.* Arkville, N.Y., The Catskill Center for Conservation and Development, 1980, 1985. 309p.

Author is retired from Department of Environmental Conservation where he was involved in land acquisition since 1961. Thorough treatment of land acquisition on a statewide basis. Much about Adirondacks. Discusses fisheries, reforestation, wildlife resource, and water resources as well as Forest Preserve. Index, bibliography.

282. VanValkenburgh, Norman J. *New York State Forest Preserve: Centennial Fact Book.* Albany, N.Y., New York State Department of Environmental Conservation, 1985. 20p.

Reference. Brief excerpts about New York State Forest lands. Divided into six categories: General history, Adirondack Forest Preserve, Catskill Preserve, Adirondack Park, Catskill Park, and New York State Constitution. Printed in green ink.

283. Vrooman, David Henry. *Two Essays in Public Sector Economics.* Albany, N.Y., State University of New York at Albany, 1976. 65 lvs.; Photocopy, Ann Arbor, Mich., University Microfilms, 1987.

Doctoral thesis. One of the essays is an analysis of factors affecting Adirondack land values. These factors include: proximity to a road or state land, location, land use classification, acreage, site, topography, and nonlocal buyers. Based on sales records from early 1970s. Typescript and thesis in 1976, reprinted in 1987.

284. Zinser, Charles I. *The Impact of Leisure Homes on the Economy of the Area within the "Blue Line" of the Adirondack Park.* Urbana, Ill., University of Illinois at Urbana, 1974. vi, 263p.

Thesis. Describes economic impact of leisure homes as positive with little negative social and environmental impact. Charts, works cited.

## Temporary Study Commission

285. New York State. Temporary Study Commission on the Future of the Adirondacks. *Financial Implementation.* Albany, N.Y., The Commission, 1970. 10p.

Covers various strategies and sources of funds for financing Temporary Study Commission recommendations. Technical Report #7.

286. New York State. Temporary Study Commission on the Future of the Adirondacks. *Forest, Minerals, Water and Air*. Albany, N.Y., The Commission, 1970, 1979. 103p.

Statistical and written description of natural resources. Charts, maps. Brief descriptions of specific regional industries and companies. Technical Report #3.

287. New York State. Temporary Study Commission on the Future of the Adirondacks. *The Future of the Adirondack Park*. Albany, N.Y., The Commission, 1970. 96p.

Recommendations of the Temporary Study Commission on the Future of the Adirondacks. Appointed by Governor Rockefeller, the Commission was to address concerns about growing infringements on the Adirondack Park. Recommendations led to the creation of the Adirondack Park Agency.

288. New York State. Temporary Study Commission on the Future of the Adirondacks. *The Future of the Adirondacks: The Technical Reports Vol. I & II*. Blue Mountain Lake, N.Y., Adirondack Museum, 1971. 2 v.

Reissue of the technical reports that were part of the findings of the Temporary Study Commission on the Future of the Adirondacks. Technical reports bound together in this reissue. Their titles are: Private and Public Lands; Wildlife; Forests, Minerals, Water and Air; Transportation and the Economy; Recreation; Local Government; Financial Implementation.

289. New York State. Temporary Study Commission on the Future of the Adirondacks. *Local Government*. Albany, N.Y., The Commission, 1970. 39p.

Discusses implications of Commission recommendations for local governments, concentrating in four areas: state funds for easements, the Fisher Law, changes in assessments, and tax exempt properties. Technical Report 6.

290. New York State. Temporary Study Commission on the Future of the Adirondacks. *Private and Public Lands, Part A*. Albany, N.Y., The Commission, 1970. 61p.

Topics covered include Adirondack Park Agency statutes, easements and covenants, outdoor advertising, and private land inventory.

291. New York State. Temporary Study Commission on the Future of the Adirondacks. *Private and Public Lands, Part B*. Albany, N.Y., New York State. Temporary Study Commission. 1970. 69p.

Mostly concerned with public lands, forest preserve, wild river system and non-forest preserve state land. Addresses regulation of aircraft, motorboats and motor vehicles.

292. New York State. Temporary Study Commission on the Future of the Adirondacks. *Recreation*. Albany, N.Y., The Commission, 1970. 74p.

Reports on recreation facilities, demands, and uses as well as hiking, canoeing and existing private recreation industry. Charts and graphs. Technical Report 5.

293. New York State. Temporary Study Commission on the Future of the Adirondacks. *Transportation and the Economy*. Albany, N.Y., The Commission, 1970. 45p.

Report focuses on ground transportation in the Adirondacks. At the time highway capacity exceeded demand. Noted that limited demand existed for rail and air transport. Recommended that Adirondack Park be ringed by expressways. Technical Report 4.

294. New York State. Temporary Study Commission on the Future of the Adirondacks. *Wildlife*. Albany, N.Y., The Commission, 1970. 55p.

Technical report. Discusses wildlife management, rare and endangered species and fish. Written for the commission by George D. Davis.

# Adirondack Park Agency

## General

295. Adirondack Park Agency. *Adirondack Economic Profile*. Ray Brook, N.Y., The Agency, 1976. 2v,

Part 1 is concerned with population and economic statistics. Part 2 covers conditions influencing the Adirondack land and real estate market. Charts, refs.

296. Adirondack Park Agency. *Adirondack Goals Program: Final Report on Community Workshops*. Ray

Brook, N.Y., Adirondack Park Agency, 1985. 60p.

Report on series of 17 statewide workships intended to create grassroots involvement in establishing future goals for the Adirondack Park. Adirondack North Country Association, Adirondack Conservation Council, Adirondack Mountain Club and Adirondack Council were involved in developing and carrying out the program.

297. Adirondack Park Agency. *Adirondack Park Agency Rules and Regulations.* Ray Brook, N.Y.., Adirondack Park Agency, 1974, 1979, 1982. var. pag.

Covers implementation of the the Adirondack Park Agency Act, the Wild, Scenic and Recreational River System, the Freshwater Wetlands Act, and Subtitle Q of Title 9 of the official compilation of Codes, Rules and Regulations of the State of New York.

298. Adirondack Park Agency. *Comprehensive Report.* Ray Brook, N.Y., The Agency, 1976. 2 v.

Report on Adirondack Park Agency mandated by law. Volume I describes the Adirondack Park, the APA program, its implementation, and new initiatives. Vol. II is a statistical analysis of APA activities.

299. Adirondack Park Agency. *Development Patterns in the Adirondack Park 1967-1987.* Ray Brook, N.Y., The Agency, 1990.

Discusses level of development, where it took place and where owners reside. Maps, charts.

300. Adirondack Park Agency. *New York State Wild, Scenic and Recreational Rivers System: Field Investigation Summary.* Albany, N.Y., The Agency, 1975. 1 v.

NAR

301. Adirondack Park Agency. *Pesticide Use in the Adirondack Park.* Ray Brook, N.Y., Adirondack Park Agency, 1983. 1 v.

Public forum. Presentation to pesticide users and applicators on government agency programs concerning pesticides.

302. Adirondack Park Agency. *Report of the Adirondack Park Agency to the New York State Legislature Regarding the Inclusion of Additional Rivers in the Wild, Scenic, and Recreational Rivers System.* Ray Brook, N.Y., The Agency, 1979. 25p.

Recommends addition of 104 miles of river to preexisting wild, scenic and recreational river system. Ink drawings of wild life and outdoor activities.

303. Davis, G. Gordon. *Conflict in the North Country: A Study of Regional Land Use Controls in the Adirondack Park.* Washington, D.C., Environmental Law Institute, 1979. 600p.

Discusses problems and issues of strict land use planning in a large area with year-round residents. Comparisons made with Vermont's Act 250. Notes, appendices, and selected bibliography.

304. De Rege, Carlo A. *Planning for the Adirondack Park: Issues and Conflicts.* New York, N.Y., New York University, 1972. 101 lvs.

Masters thesis. Adirondack Park history, Temporary Study Commission, Adirondack Park Agency and the Adirondack Park's Future. Discusses demand for open space and wilderness.

305. Ryder, Sarah Louise. *The Adirondack Park Agency: Captive or Captor?.* Charlotteville, VA., University of Virginia, 1986. 85 lvs.

Thesis. Concludes Adirondack Park Agency model is a workable alternative to federal protection of wilderness areas. Bibliography.

306. State University of New York College of Technology. Division of Business. *A Report on the Visitor Contact System for the Adirondack Park.* Utica, N.Y., SUNY College of Technology at Utica/Rome, 1978. iii, 32p.

Study on possible location for visitor contact system in Southwestern Adirondack region. Briefly describes a wide range of pertinent background and related information. Recommends 5 potential sites.

307. Voiland, Michael Peter. *Towards an Improved Methodology in the Analysis of Recreational Response Patterns: Trend Surfaces of Campers to Adirondack Park Signs.* s.l., s.n., 1974. iv, 52p.

Masters thesis. Outdoor recreational research. Discusses relationship between camper visits to the Adirondacks and the distances they must travel. Bibliography.

## Laws and Legislation

308. Adirondack Park Agency. *APA Act as Amended through the Close of the 1977 Legislative Session.*

Ray Brook, N.Y., Adirondack Park Agency, 1977. 64p.

Text of Executive Law Article 27, Sections 800-819.

309. Adirondack Park Agency. *APA Act as Amended through the Close of the 1978 Legislative Session.* Ray Brook, N.Y., Adirondack Park Agency, 1978. 64p.

Executive Law Article 27 more commonly known Adirondack Park Agency Act as updated through 1978. Law contains 19 separate sections.

310. Adirondack Park Agency. *Adirondack Park Agency Act.* Ray Brook, N.Y., Adirondack Park Agency, 1991. 45p.

This version contains additions to the Adirondack Park Agency Act through the end of the 1990 Legislative session. Outlines powers, duties and responsibilities of the APA.

311. Adirondack Park Agency. *Adirondack Park Land Use and Development Plan.* Ray Brook, N.Y., The Agency, 1973. 46p.

Contains provisions of land use and development plan from the Adirondack Park Act (Article 27, Executive Law). These provisons were adopted in May 1973 and went into effect in August 1973. This particular document does not contain information on administration and enforcement of the Plan. Section 810 on Class A and Class B Regional Projects.

312. Adirondack Park Agency. *Adirondack Park Land Use and Development Plan and Recommendations for Implementation.* Ray Brook, N.Y., The Agency, 1973. 35p.

1973 version of the Adirondack Park Agency Act. Executive law of the State of New York: Article 27, Sections 801, 802, 805, 806, 810. Outlines plan as well as how to carry it out including administration and enforcement.

313. Adirondack Park Agency. *Local Planning and Land Use Controls in the Adirondack Park.* Ray Brook, N.Y., The Agency, 1975. 41p.

Reprinted version of Article 27 of Executive Law of the State of New York, more commonly known as the Adirondack Park Agency Act. Specifically includes Sections 801, 802, 805, 806, 810 and 811. Also a working draft version.

314. New York State. Department of Environmental Conservation. *Model On-Site Sewage Disposal Ordinance for the Adirondack Park.* Albany, N.Y., Department of Environmental Conservation, 1979. 31p.

Generic sample law with definitions, standards, hearing procedures, and information on enforcement of septic and privy installations.

315. New York State. Legislative Commission on Expenditure Review. *Adirondack Park Planning and Regulation: Program Audit.* Albany, N.Y., The Commission, 1978. 68p.

Study to evaluate how effectively the Adirondack Park Agency carried out its functions. Tables, charts.

316. New York State. Legislature. *Adirondack Legislation: Study Bill; October 1991 Amendments to Article 27 Adirondack Park Agency Act.* Albany, N.Y., Legislature, 1991. 239p.

Proposed changes for Adirondack Park Act.

317. New York State. Legislature. *Adirondack Park Agency Act.* Albany, N.Y., New York State Legislature, 1981. var. pag.

APA Act with changes as of 1981. Contains 20 sections including 803A which provided for Adirondack Park Local Government Review Board.

318. Silverman, Michael Robert. *The Impact of Competing Pressure Groups on the Passage of the New York State Land Use Bill of 1973.* New York, New York University, 1976; photocopy, Ann Arbor, MI., University Microfilms, 1979. vi, 466 lvs.

Doctoral thesis. Discusses the political context in country and state in which Adirondack Park Agency was created. Role of regional press investigated. Tables, bibliography.

## Land Use Planning and Regulation

319. Adirondack Park Agency. *Adirondack Park State Land Master Plan.* Ray Brook, N.Y., The Agency, 1972, 1979, 1985. var. pag.

Written strategy for the administration of state lands within the Adirondack Park. Introduction outlines Adirondack Park Agency's mandate. Classification system for land and guidelines for its uses are discussed. Third section provides descriptions and locations of different categories of land uses. Map in pocket. Forest Preserve Centennial Ed. in 1985. Brief essay entitled, "The Forest Preserve: A Centennial Perspective" is new material.

320. Adirondack Park Agency. *Adirondack Park State Land Master Plan, 1987 Hearing Notice.* Ray Brook, N.Y., Adirondack Park Agency, 1986.

Hearing notice on wilderness areas acquired by State of New York. Maps of Bog River Flow, Fulton Chain Wild Forest boundary, Moose Plains Wild Forest and other smaller areas.

321. Adirondack Park Agency. *Administration of Local Land Use Controls in the Adirondack Park.* Ray Brook, N.Y., The Agency, 1983. 134p.

Planning manual designed for use by local governments within the Adirondack Park. Chapters discuss planning, zoning, subdivision regulations, enforcement, administrative procedures, and legal issues. Cooperatively produced by various agencies within the Adirondack Park.

322. Adirondack Park Agency. *A Citizen's Guide to Adirondack Park Agency Land Use Regulations.* Ray Brook, N.Y., The Agency, 1979, 1980. 24p.

Overview of development and land use planning in the Adirondack Park. Explains briefly how to obtain an Adirondack Park Agency permit. Checklist of projects requiring permits. Plates, maps.

323. Adirondack Park Agency. *Development in the Adirondack Park Objectives and Guidelines For Planning and Review.* Ray Brook, N.Y., The Agency, 1977. 158p.

Reference tool to assist in assessing private development in the Adirondack Park. Aimed at providing assistance in subdivision. Audience is state agencies, local governments, and individuals. Thorough in its treatment. 1976 version is an earlier draft of this document. Bibliography.

324. Adirondack Park Agency. *Draft Adirondack Park Agency Rules and Regulations: For Public Hearing.* Ray Brook, N.Y., The Agency, 1973.

Draft of initial rules and regulations under the August 1973 Land Use and Development Plan. Procedural aspects of Adirondack Park Agency's project review and jurisdiction.

325. Adirondack Park Agency. *Preliminary Private Land Use & Development Plan: Draft For Public Hearing Purposes.* Ray Brook, N.Y., The Agency, 1972. iii, 75p.

Draft land use development plan. Recommendations for implementing the plan plus additional miscellaneous recommendations for fiscal matters and outdoor advertising. Appendix A outlines and describes nine criteria for land use classifications. Map in pocket on inside of back cover.

326. Adirondack Park Agency. *Report of the Citizens' Advisory Task Force on Open Space to the Adirondack Park Agency.* s.l., s.n., 1980. 140p.

Citizen's report for Adirondack Park Agency. Charge of the group was to describe and define the nature of open space in the Adirondacks. Task force also made policy recommendations. Typescript. Appendices, maps and notes.

327. Adirondack Park Agency. *Rules and Regulations Governing the Wild, Scenic, and Recreational River System within the Adirondack Park.* Ray Brook, N.Y., Adirondack Park Agency, 1975.

Governs new land use and development on private land within the scenic, wild river system. Appendix lists affected areas. Maps, charts, maps, and definitions.

328. Booth, Richard S. *Developing Institutions for Regional Land Use Planning and Control: The Adirondack Experience.* Ithaca, N.Y., Department of City and Regional Planning in Conjunction with the Program in Urban and Regional Studies, Cornell University, 1980. 108p.

Discusses institutional structure of Adirondack Park Agency, problems created by dual duties in areas of planning and land use controls. Heavily footnoted.

329. Buhmann, Erich. *Inventory of Resource Distribution in the Adirondack Park Using Remote Sensing.* Syracuse, N.Y., State University of New York. College of Environmental Science and Forestry, 1983. ix, 133 lvs.

Thesis. Study about use of Landsat data for nature conservation mapping purposes. Discusses strengths and weaknesses of such a system. Study used image of 2.2 millon acres in Southwestern Adirondack Park. Maps, charts, bibliography.

330. Cochran, Ronald Perry. *Socioeconomic Impact of Conservation Legislation: An Analysis of the*

*Adirondack Land Use and Development Plan.* Syracuse, N.Y., Syracuse University, 1979; photocopy, Ann Arbor, MI., University Microfilms International, 1986. ix, 385 lvs.

Thesis. Study that draws parallels between Adirondacks and a colonial economy. Adirondack resources have been exploited for the benefit of those outside the region. Argues that State's Master Land Use Plan reinforces the colonial economic relationship. Uses Tupper Lake as a case study. Concludes Adirondackers bear disproportionate cost of maintaining wilderness character of the region. Bibliography.

331. Emery, Daniel W. *The Adirondack Park Agency: A Study of State Land Use Planning.* Syracuse, N.Y., State University of New York. College of Environmental Science and Forestry, 1978. iv, 102 lvs.

Thesis. Comprehensive view of APA's Land Use Plan. Part I provides background in terms of the national historical course of land use and development. Part II concerns the Adirondacks, the APA and land use regulation. Author has concentrated on social, political and legal issues. Bibliography.

332. Kanter, Jonathan. *The Adirondack Park Agency: Aesthetic Considerations in Project Review.* Syracuse, N.Y., State University of New York. College of Environmental Science and Forestry, 1980. xi, 256 lvs.

Thesis. Defines aesthetics and discusses legal aspects. Uses 3 projects as case studies of project review concerned with aesthetic considerations. Provides analysis, conclusions and recommendations. Bibliography.

333. Kay, David L. *The Adirondack Land Market: The Land, Its Value, Its Buyers 1968-1983.* Ithaca, N.Y., Cornell University, Department of Agricultural Economics, 1985. 53p.

Study concludes Adirondack Park Agency zoning regulations have not seriously impaired property values inside the Blue Line.

334. Liroff, Richard A. & G. Gordon Davis. *Protecting Open Space: Land Use Control in the Adirondack Park.* Cambridge, MA., Ballinger Publishing Company, 1981. 302p.

Analysis and description of the role of the Adirondack Park Agency and its impact on land uses. Chapter on lessons learned from the process of implementation.

335. Morton, Nancy L. *Environmental Considerations for Development in the Adirondack Park.* s.l., s.n., 1975. 29p.

Highlights soil and water conservation issues, and vegetation and wildlife concerns related to development. Goal is to minimize negative impacts in these areas during future growth within the Adirondack Park.

336. New York State. Department of Environmental Conservation. *Cranberry Lake Wild Forest Unit Management Plan.* Albany, N.Y., Department of Environmental Conservation, 1985. vi, 77p.

Overview of natural resources, existing uses, outlines policies and management strategy. Cranberry Lake is in southern St. Lawrence County and is located within the Blue Line. Maps, bibliography, appendices.

337. New York State. Department of Environmental Conservation. *Five Ponds Wilderness Unit Management Plan.* Albany, N.Y., Department of Environmental Conservation, 1987. 170p.

History and description of Five Ponds, located in Southern St. Lawrence County, south of Rt. 3. Lists trails and river routes in the area. Maps.

338. New York State. Department of Environmental Conservation. *Pepperbox Wilderness Area Unit Management Plan.* Albany, N.Y., The Department, 1985. v, 63p.

Pepperbox Wilderness Area is located in Northwestern Herkimer County north of Stillwater and is comprised of approximately 5 square miles.

339. Rogers, Golden and Halpern. *Policies for the Lake George Basin: Data Base Report: Submitted to Lake George Municipalities, Warren County, Adirondack Park Agency.* s.l., Rogers, Golden and Halpern, 1988. 1 v.

NAR

340. Rogers, Golden & Halpern. *Policies for the Lake George Basin Policy Report and Appendices: Submitted to Lake George Municipalities, Warren County, Adirondack Park Agency.* s.l., Rogers, Golden, & Halpern, 1989, 1988. 1 v.

NAR

341. St. Lawrence University. *The Horizon Case: An Adirondack Land Use.* Canton, N.Y., St. Lawrence

University, 1973. 58 lvs.

In 1970s Horizon Corp. proposed a large second home development in Colton, N.Y. Report of St. Lawrence University class summarizes their findings on wildlife, water samples in area near Horizon site. Also investigates history of forestry industry in St. Lawrence and Franklin Counties. Discusses land use issues in Adirondacks during the early 1970s and makes comparisons to Vermont. Maps, charts.

342. Smith, Stuart E. *Supplemental Information to Environmental Impact Study in Response to Comments by Adirondack Park Agency and Department of Environmental Conservation: Loon Lake Estates, Franklin County, New York.* Schenectady, N.Y., Environment One Corp., 1974. 470p.

NAR

343. Wissel, Peter A. *Adirondack Park Zoning: Property Values and Tax Bases, 1963-1983.* Albany, N.Y., State Board of Equalization and Assessment, 1988. x, 90p.

Did APA zoning subdivisions increase development costs? Did local tax bases suffer as a result of these costs? This study concludes "no" on both counts.

344. Wissel, Peter A. *New York's Adirondack Park: A Study of Land Price Effects from Developmental Restrictions.* Albany, N.Y., s.l., s.n., 1986. 42p.

Tentatively concludes that APA regulations negatively affect land values while local zoning tends to enhance land values.

345. Zinser, Charles I. *The Economic Impact of the Adirondack Park Private Land Use and Development Plan.* Plattsburgh, N.Y., State University of New York, 1978. xii, 411p.; reprint, Albany, N.Y., State University of New York Press, 1980. xvii, 319p.

A thorough study of the impact of the Adirondack Park Agency upon the economy of the Adirondack region. List of interviews conducted. Tables, maps, illus, index, references.

## Commission on the Adirondacks in the Twenty-First Century

346. Flacke, Robert F. Commission on the Adirondacks in the Twenty-First Century. *The Adirondack Park in the Twenty-First Century: Minority Report.* Lake George, N.Y., R. Flacke, 1990. 35p.

Makes case that overdevelopment is not a problem in Adirondacks and that Adirondack Park Agency control is adequate.

347. New York State. Commission on the Adirondacks in the Twenty-First Century. *The Adirondack Park in the Twenty-First Century.* Albany, N.Y., The Commission, 1990. 96p.

Summary of commission findings, divided into three sections: People and Government, Land Use and Financial Implementation. Distillation of longer volumes for consumption by the general public. Color Plates and folded map. There is also an abridged version consisting of 24 pages entitled, *The Adirondack Park in the Twenty-First Century: Summary.* Lists all 245 recommendations of the Commission on the Adirondacks in the Twenty-First Century and contains shortened text.

348. New York State. Commission on the Adirondacks in the Twenty-First Century. *The Adirondack Park in the Twenty-First Century: Technical Reports.* Albany, N.Y., State of New York, 1990. 2 v.

Vol 1: Reports are divided into 4 areas (1) History of the Adirondack Park (2) Forest Preserve and Other State Land Classification and Management Issues (3) Adirondack Park Land Acquisition, Management and Park Planning Issues (4) The Natural Reserves of the Adirondack Park. Vol. 2 contains technical reports 25-45. Also divided into 4 sections: (1) Economy and Quality of Life Issues (2) Private Land Regulation in the Adirondack Park (3) Subdivision and Development Trends in the Adirondack Park (4) Forestry in the Adirondack Park.

349. New York State. Department of Environmental Conservation. *Water Resources and Water Quality: Draft.* Albany, N.Y., Department of Environmental Conservation, 1989. 118p.

Technical report on water resources in Adirondack Park. Based on similiar report done by Temporary Study Commission in 1971. Describes five major watersheds, regional weather, climate, water resource planning, water quality. Study done for Commission on the Adirondacks in the Twenty-First Century.

350. Smith, David. *Environmental Health: Forest Resources and Quality: Issue Paper 5f: Draft.* Albany, N.Y., Commission on the Adirondacks in the Twenty-First Century, 1989. 84p.

History of Adirondack forests, current forest condition, and health of forests discussed. Pests, climatic changes may affect forests in the future.

# Conservation

## General

351. Burdick, Neal S. *The Evolution of Environmental Consciousness in Nineteenth Century America.* Cleveland, O., Case Western Reserve University, 1981. vii, 262 lvs.

Doctoral thesis. Two chapters related to Adirondacks. Discussion of Thoreau and James Fennimore Cooper and Verplanck Colvin and George Perkins Marsh.

352. Davis, George D. *Developing a Land Conservation Strategy: A Handbook for Land Trusts.* Elizabethtown, N.Y., Adirondack Land Trust, 1987. 38p.

Readable guide to planning and implementing a land trust strategy. Photos, charts, bibliography. Davis has numerous ties and connections to the Adirondack region, including service on two state commissions concerned with the future of the Adirondack Park. Bibliography.

353. Davis, George D. *Man and the Adirondack Environment: A Primer.* Blue Mountain Lake, N.Y., Adirondack Museum, 1977. 40p.

An introduction to the ecology of the Adirondacks by noted wildlife ecologist. Illus.

354. Lake Champlain Basin Environmental Conference. *Proceedings of the Annual Lake Champlain Basin Environmental Conference.* Chazy, N.Y., Institute for Man and Environment. SUNY Plattsburgh Miner Institute, 1976. 234p.

Transcripts of proceedings of conference held on July 15, 1976. Six sessions discussed watersheds surrounding Lake Champlain.

355. New York State. Department of Environmental Conservation. *Environmental Plan for New York State: Preliminary Edition.* Albany, N.Y., The Department, 1972. 91p.

Written plan for addressing problems with New York State's land, water, air, fish, wildlife, and energy. Intended as a resource for public and private decision-making in protecting environmental quality. Illus., maps.

## Wilderness

356. DiNunzio, Michael G. *A Gift of Wilderness: The Bob Marshall Great Wilderness.* Elizabethtown, N.Y., Adirondack Council, 1992. 24p.

Bob Marshall Wilderness Area in West-Central Adirondack Park. Star Lake, Raquette Lake, Long Lake, and Cranberry Lake form corners of this wilderness area. Numerous photos, most by Gary Randorf. Note says "Produced in Celebration of the Centennial of the Adirondack Park."

357. High Peaks Wilderness Advisory Committee. *Summary Findings Report.* Albany, N.Y., Department of Environmental Conservation, 1977. 39p.

Committee convened to deal with extensive deterioration of the trails in the High Peaks. Committee worked for two years on trail erosion and concluded a combination of human and natural forces were at work. Recommendations centered on planning, education, maintenance, rehabilitation, distribution; controlled use in some cases, and funding. Maps, graphs and appendices. Typescript.

358. Terrie, Philip. *The Adirondacks, from Dismal Wilderness to Forever Wild: A Case Study of American Attitudes Toward Wilderness.* Washington, D.C., George Washington University, 1979. iii, 288 lvs.

Doctoral thesis. Uses Adirondacks as focal point of his discussion of wilderness. Builds upon many early classic works on the Adirondack region. Chapters on the influences of W.H.H. Murray and Verplanck Colvin.

359. Terrie, Philip. *Wildlife and Wilderness: A History of the Adirondack Mountains.* Fleischmanns, N.Y., Purple Mountain Press, 1993. 175p.

Adirondack history interpreted through the wildlife of the region using historical and scientific information. Discusses Native Americans, sportsmen, and wildlife conservaton efforts by state government. Illus., indexes, bibliography.

360. VanValkenburgh, Norman J. *Unit Planning for Wilderness Management.* Schenectady, N.Y., As-

sociation for the Protection of the Adirondacks, 1987. 26p.

Addresses the concept of intentional wilderness. Attempts to define wilderness, describe its ecology, and identify its users and how many can be properly handled. Planning is presented as a crucial part of wilderness management in an urban society.

# Forestry

361. Adirondack Park Agency. *Revision of the Adirondack Park Agency's Rules and Regulations in Regard to Timber Harvesting That Includes Clearcutting.* Ray Brook, N.Y., The Agency, 1982. 1 v.

Spells out requirements and enforcement procedures for APA Act, Wild Scenic and Recreational River Systems Act, and Freshwater Wetlands Act. Bibliography.

362. Beatty, Charles T. *A Study of Public Regulatory Controls As They Affect Private Forest Land.* Syracuse, N.Y., State University of New York. College of Environmental Science and Forestry, 1976. v, 174 lvs.

NAR

363. Briesch, Alvin Ray. *Multi-dimensional Ordination of Boreal and Hardwood Forests On Whiteface Mountain.* Albany, N.Y., State University of New York at Albany, 1969. 64 lvs.

Thesis. Study of distribution of various tree species according to moisture and altitude on Whiteface Mt. Use computer program for purposes of analysis. Bibliography, numerous charts and graphs.

364. Committee Policy Forum. *Intensive Timber Harvest Study Steering Committee, Policy Forum.* Ray Brook, N.Y., Adirondack Park Agency, 1980. 2 v.

Meeting of 13 experts discussing forest practice issues in the Adirondacks: clear cutting, chemical herbicides for forest management, and wood-for-energy plants.

365. Governor's Task Force on Northern Forest Lands. *Northern Forest Lands Study 1990 Final Report.* Washington, D.C., The Task Force, 1990. viii, 206p.

Draft in 1989. Study covering Maine, New Hampshire, Vermont, and New York. Describes biological, recreation uses of forest land, timber characteristics, ownership of forest land, ways in which forests are changing, significant areas, inhabitants, strategies to protect forests.

366. Joint Government-Industry Conference on Intensive Timber Harvest in Private Adirondack Forests. *Intensive Timber Harvest in Private Adirondack Forests.* Ray Brook, N.Y., Intensive Timber Harvest Study Steering Committee, 1982. 64p.

Conference proceedings. Topic is clear cutting on private forest land and other options for land owners. Transcript of remarks, photos and conference program.

367. Richards, Karyn B. *Strategic Plan for Forest Resources in New York State.* Albany, N.Y., Department of Environmental Conservation, 1985. 186p.

Five year plan containing recommendations for diverse uses of forest resources: wood energy, recreation, aesthetics, wildlife, future timber supplies. Emphasizes the development of goals and the planning process.

368. Roman, John Ross. *Vegetation-Environment Relationships in Virgin, Middle Elevation Forests.* Syracuse, N.Y., State University of New York. College of Environmental Science and Forestry, 1980. xxv, 477 lvs.

Doctoral thesis. Research on Five Ponds Wilderness Area in Southern St. Lawrence County. Correlates specific tree communities to certain environmental characteristics. Charts, graphs, photos, tables. Interesting study. Bibliography.

369. Uebler, Robert L. *The Effect of Timber Harvesting on Soil: Physical Properties For Tree Harvesting Methods in Two Areas of New York State.* Syracuse, N.Y., State University of New York. College of Environmental Science and Forestry, 1975. v, 78 lvs.

Thesis. Technical forestry study in Camden on Tug Hill and Northville near Sacandaga Reservoir. Bibliography.

# Fish and Game

370. Bailey, James A. *Crude Protein in Adirondack Deer Browses.* Syracuse, N.Y., State University College of Forestry, 1966. xi, 152p.

Doctoral thesis. Field work done at Huntington Forest Wildlife Station. Discusses protein content levels of witch hobble browse and how to increase it through applications of nitrogen or lime for the purposes of deer herd management. Includes tables, literature cited.

371. Behrend, Donald F. *Behavior of White-Tailed Deer in an Adirondack Forest.* Syracuse, N.Y., State University College of Forestry, 1966. xii, 206 lvs.

Doctoral thesis. Research done at Huntington Forest Wildlife Station. Study of distribution and activity of white-tailed deer. Field work concentrated on documenting daily and seasonal distribution and activity patterns in relation to environmental factors and the physical and psychological nature of deer. Bibliography.

372. Wiersma, George Bruce. *Seasonal Deer Browsing in an Adirondack Forest.* Syracuse, N.Y., State University College of Forestry at Syracuse, 1968. xiii, 194 lvs.

Doctoral thesis. Study carried out at Huntington Forest Wildlife Station in the Eastern Adirondacks found that deer browsed sugar maple and witch hobble at different times of the year. Study also looked at browsing based on whether the area in question had been clearcut or partial cut. Literature cited. Graphs, charts, maps and figures.

# Soil and Water Conservation

## General

373. Adirondack Lakes Survey Corporation. *Adirondack Lakes Study: An Evaluation of Fish Communities and Water Chemistry 1984-1987.* Ray Brook, N.Y., Adirondack Lakes Survey Corporation, 1989. 2 v.

Covers Lake Champlain, St. Lawrence, Raquette, Oswegatchie, Black River, and Mohawk-Hudson watersheds. Discusses methodology, watershed measurements, data collection, statistics, chemistry results. Executive summary, references, glossary. Second volume is appendix that contains numerous tables on water chemistry, fish species, etc.

374. Adirondack Lakes Survey Corporation. *Adirondack Lakes Survey: An Interpretive Analysis of Fish Communities and Water Chemistry 1984-1987.* Ray Brook, N.Y., Adirondack Lakes Survey Corporation, 1990. 1 v.

Comprehensive study of region's water quality and fish resources. Sixteen volume set covering 1,200 Adirondack Lakes. Technical information. Volume sixteen is index. Charts, maps, graphs accompany written findings.

375. Atmospheric Sciences Research Center. *Langmuir Circulations and Internal Waves in Lake George.* Albany, N.Y., Atmospheric Sciences Research Center, 1966. 42p.

Discussion of how heat and momentum are tranferred in lakes in comparison to trade winds in the Carribean. Field work was done at Lake George in 1964 and 1965. Maps, graphs, references.

376. Atmospheric Sciences Research Center. *A Preliminary Study of Water Motions in Lake George and Lake Champlain.* Albany, N.Y., Atmospheric Sciences Research Center, 1966. 49p.

NAR

377. Greeson, Phillip E. and F. Luman Robinson. *Characteristics of New York Lakes: Part 1; Gazetteer of Lakes, Ponds, Reservoirs.* Albany, N.Y., Department of Environmental Conservation, 1970; second ed., 1985. 124p.

Printouts and tables listing and statistically describing New York State's lakes and ponds. Information includes quadrant, county, size of basin, latitude and longitude, elevation, surface in square miles, and miles of shoreline.

378. Hunsaker, C.T. *Empirical Relationships Between Watershed Attributes and Headwater Lake Chemistry in the Adirondack Region.* Oak Ridge, Tenn., Environmental Sciences Division. Oakridge National Laboratory, 1986. xi, 123p.

NAR

379. McMartin, Barbara. *Citizen's Guide to Adirondack Lakes.* Ray Brook, N.Y., Adirondack Park Agency, 1986. 27p.

General document on lakes and ponds. Highlights social and natural value of these aquatic resources. Briefly discusses physical properties and ecology of lakes. Short article on acid rain. Maps, illus, photos.

380. McMartin, Barbara. *Citizen's Guide to Adirondack Rivers and Roads.* Ray Brook, N.Y., Adirondack Park Agency, 1986. 23p.
Provides guidelines for use of roads and rivers within the Adirondack Park. Emphasis on diversity of roads and rivers and their enjoyment. Maps, photos, illus.

381. New York State. Conservation Department. *Developing and Managing the Water Resources of New York State.* Albany, N.Y., Water Resources Commission, 1967. 52p.
Divides New York into several regions for purpose of analysis. Adirondacks covered by 2 basins; Hudson-Mohawk and St. Lawrence-Lake Champlain-Black River Basin. Identifies problems and strategies for solutions. llus.

382. New York State. Energy and Research Development Authority. *Acidic Deposition and Adirondack Forest Soil Fertility: An Appraisal.* Albany, N.Y., New York State Energy and Research Development Authority, 1991. 64p.
Scientific study of acidic deposition and forest growth in conifer forest near Warrensburg, New York. Study concluded that the influence of tree species on soil acidity levels was greater than the impact of acid rain. Charts, graphs, bibliography.

383. New York State. Legislature. Joint Legislative Committee to Study the Conservation, Development, and Equitable Use of Water Resources of the State. *How to Conserve, Develop, and Use the Water Resources of New York State.* Albany, N.Y., Joint Legislative Committee, 1968. 207p.
Discusses water resource problems and the role of state government in solving these problems.

384. New York State. Temporary Commission on Water Resources Planning. *Progress Report: 1967.* Albany, N.Y., The Commission, 1968. 278p.
NAR

385. Rosen, A.E. *An Adirondack Watershed Data Base: Attribute and Information Mapping Information for Regional Acidic Deposition Studies.* Oakridge, TN., Oakridge National Laboratory, 1988. xiv, 65p.
Technical work about various factors in acidification of Adirondack lakes and rivers. These factors include morphology, physiography, bedrock, vegetation, wetlands, human activities, presence of beaver, and precipitation. Bibliography.

## Wetlands

386. Bedor, Melissa C. *Wetland Regulation in the Adirondack Park.* Syracuse, N.Y., State University of New York. College of Environmental Science and Forestry, 1981. v, 294 lvs.
Thesis. Delineates various positive characteristics of wetlands and the Adirondack Park Agency's approach to wetlands management. Bibliography

387. Bogucki, D. J. *Wetlands Interpretation & Mapping Project for the Adirondack Park: Final Report.* Ray Brook, N.Y., Adirondack Park Agency, 1982. 32p.
Technical report on establishing systematic wetland management plan in Adirondacks. Work done by Research Foundation of SUNY for Adirondack Park Agency. Maps, tables, appendices, methods and recommendations.

388. McMartin, Barbara. *Citizen's Guide to Adirondack Wetlands.* Ray Brook, N.Y., Adirondack Park Agency, 1985. 27p.
Educational publication about Adirondack wetlands. Discusses value of wetlands, their characteristics and types. Illus.

389. Westfall, Gregory J. *A Water Quality Study at Two Adirondack Wetlands.* Syracuse, N.Y., State University of New York. College of Environmental Science and Forestry, 1975. ix, 165 lvs.
Environmental science thesis. Field work was done in southern St. Lawrence County within the Blue Line. Dovetails with other work around that time. See Karlin (#465) and Hardin (#476). Contains tables, summary, conclusions and bibliography.

## Water Quality

390. American Petroleum Institute. *Acid-Rain Related Reconnaissance of Water, Rock, Soil, and Sediment Chemistry in the Adirondacks During Fall 1981.* Washington, D.C., American Petroleum Institute, 1982. 33p.

Concludes acid rain alone can not account for low pH in Adirondack waters and soils.

391. Boyle, Robert H. and R. Alexander. *Acid Rain.* New York, Schocken Books, 1983. 146p.
Book of general interest on the subject of acid rain. Specific references to New York State and the Adirondack region. Index, bibliography.

392. Harr, Thomas E. and P.E. Coffey. *Acid Precipitation in New York State.* Albany, N.Y., New York State Department of Environmental Conservation, 1975. vi, 52p.
Early review of the literature on acid rain from mid-1970s. Contains information on acid precipitation in Adirondacks/Northern New York. Charts, maps, and references.

393. Hendry, George R. *Effects of Acidification on Aquatic Primary Producers and Decomposers.* Upton, N.Y., Brookhaven National Laboratory, 1981. i, 22 lvs.
Study uses Lake Colden in the Adirondacks as a case study for discussing effects of acidification.

394. Izard, Harold H. *Public Meeting on Acid Precipitation.* Albany, N.Y., Science and Technology Staff, New York State Assembly, 1979. vii, 161p.
Several of the studies deal specifically with acid precipitation and water quality in the Adirondack region. Maps, charts, graphs and references cited.

395. Johannes, A. H. *Characterization of Acidic Precipitation in the Adirondack Region.* Palo Alto, CA, Electric Power Research Institute, 1981. 215p.
Acid rain study conducted simultaneously at Sagamore Lake, Panther Lake, and Woods Lake. Concentrates on precipitation or wet deposition, but also dry deposition, snowmelt, moisture that penetrates the forest canopy. This latter area is specifically cited as an area in need of research. One surprising observation was the high level of nitrates in the snow cover.

396. Katzenstein, Alan W. *Understanding Acid Rain.* Washington, D.C., Edison Electric Institute, 1983. 50p.
Excellent short introduction to issue of acid rain. Uses Adirondacks as a case study. Photos, index, bibliography.

397. Mandelbaum, Paulette A. *Acid Rain, A New York State Agenda: Proceedings.* Glens Falls, N.Y., Adirondack Mountain Club, 1985. 59p.
Conference proceedings. Summarizes presentations on acid rain in New York State, the economic implications of controlling it, and how it can be reduced. Acid rain is considered a threat to many Adirondack lakes.

398. Martin, Scott C. *An Evaluation of Phosphorus Budgets and Trophic Status Models For Adirondack Lakes.* Potsdam, N.Y., Clarkson College of Technology, 1979. xii, 200 lvs.
Master thesis. Study of 6 Adirondack lakes to determine level of atrophy. Purpose is to explore potential for a management strategy for Adirondack Lakes. Tables, charts, and bibliography.

399. Mast, James Floyd. *Acidity Status Characterization of Freshwater Lakes in Adirondack Mountain Park, New York Using Landsat MSS Data.* Terre Haute, IN., Indiana State University, 1983. xi, 90 lvs.
Thesis. Study of acidity of lakes in Adirondacks based on computer-generated information. One purpose of the study is to build rationale for future monitoring of acidity in the lakes. Introduction has geographical/ geological description of the Adirondacks. Bibliography, tables and figures.

400. Metz, William C. *Adirondack Tourism: Perceived Consequences of Acid Rain.* Upton, N.Y., Brookhaven National Laboratory, 1984. vii, 45p.
Report prepared for the U.S. Department of Energy asserts short term effects of acid rain are minimal, but in the long term acid rain may damage certain Adirondack areas. Real or perceived environmental damage could eventually affect tourism.

401. Morey, Edward R. *The Impact of Acid Rain: A Characteristics Approach to Estimating the Demand for and Benefits from Recreational Fishing.* Williamstown, MA, Williams College, 1986. 26p.
NAR

402. Murdoch, Peter S. *Hydrologic Analysis of Two Headwater Lake Basins of Differing Lake pH in the West-Central Adirondack Mountains of New York.* Albany, N.Y., U.S. Geologic Survey, 1987. v, 49p.
Study compares neutral Panther Lake and acidic Woods Lake in 1980 and 1981. Concludes

watershed storage and groundwater contribution are greater in neutral lake basins.

403. Pfeiffer, Martin H. *Acidity Status of Lakes in the Adirondack Region of New York in Relation to Fish Resources.* Albany, N.Y., Bureau of Fisheries, Division of Fish and Wildlife, New York State Department of Conservation, 1980. 36p.

Technical study. Purpose of study is to establish acidity of Adirondack lakes and ponds as a basis for future comparison. Attempts to correlate changes in alkalinity to changes in fish species. Charts, maps.

404. Raynal, D. J. *Actual and Potential Effects of Acid Precipitation on a Forest Ecosystem in the Adirondack Mountains.* Albany, N.Y., New York State Energy Research and Development Authority, 1980. xix, 264p.

NAR

405. Raynal, D. J. *Characterization of Atmospheric Deposition and Ionic Input at Huntington Forest, Adirondack Mountains, N.Y.* Syracuse, N.Y., College of Environmental Science and Forestry, 1983. vi 85p.

Huntington Wildlife Forest is located near Newcomb, N.Y. Scientific study on acid rain. Charts, graphs, references.

406. Retzsch, Walter C. *Adirondack Land Use: A Commentary On Past and Present Impacts on Terrestrial and Aquatic Ecosystems.* Rockville, Md., Everett and Associates, 1983. xii, 96p.

Concludes decreases in fires and agricultural land, and increases in forest land are contributing factors in mounting acidity of Adirondack lakes and streams.

407. Retzsch, Walter C. *Influence of Natural Acidity and Fisheries Management Activities upon the Status of Adirondack Fish Populations.* Washington, D.C., American Petroleum Institute, 1981. vi, 76p.

NAR

408. Rinkoff, June. *Analysis of Individual On-Site Sewage Disposal System Sanitary Surveys.* Raybrook, N.Y., Adirondack Park Agency, 1976. 35p.

Report done by student intern for Adirondack Park Agency. Purpose was to determine effectiveness of septic systems for purposes of protecting water quality. Charts, tables, appendices.

409. Simonin, Howard A. *A Water Chemistry Comparison of Several Quebec and New York Lakes in Relation to Acidification.* Albany, N.Y., Department of Environmental Conservation, 1986. ix, 83p.

Acid deposition study that compares 4 lakes in Quebec to 4 lakes in the Adirondack region. Adirondacks had higher nitrate and sulfate levels. Study concluded that Adirondacks were more affected by acid emissions. Lakes were most acidic during spring snowmelt.

410. Springer, Mark Lincoln. *A Statistical Analysis of Wet Loading Models for the Adirondack Park.* Stillwater, OK., Oklahoma State University, 1987. x, 142 lvs.

Thesis. Acid rain research in Central Adirondacks. Analyzes quality of rain using scientific models. Bibliography.

411. Wood, Lindsay W. *Limnology of Remote Lakes in the Adirondack Region of New York State, with Emphasis on Acidification Problems.* Albany, N.Y., New York State Department of Health, 1978. 65p.

Acid deposition study of 57 lakes considered to be representative of all lakes. Most were in Hamilton, Essex and Herkimer Counties. Numerous charts, tables. Works cited.

# *Natural History*

## General

412. Department of Environmental Conservation. *A Natural History of the Adirondack Park, N.Y.* Ray Brook, N.Y., Adirondack Park Agency, 1980, 1983. 53p.
    Short introductory work giving overview of the natural history of the Adirondacks. Chapter on ancient geology and the ice age. Chapters on forests, wildlife, rivers and lakes round out the discussion. Illus.

413. DiNunzio, Michael G. *Adirondack Wildguide: A Natural History of the Adirondack Park.* Elizabethtown, N.Y., The Adirondack Conservancy Committee and The Adirondack Council, 1984. 160p.
    Numerous beautiful drawings, paintings and photos. Illus. by Anne E. Lacy. Appendices include checklists of fishes, birds, amphibians, reptiles, mammals and trees.

414. Fosburgh, Hugh. *A Clearing in the Wilderness.* Garden City, N.Y., Doubleday, 1969. xvii, 134p.
    An entertaining four-season look at the Adirondack woods and wildlife as seen in a particular place, Baker's Clearing, in the Central Adirondacks. Photos.

415. Frahn, M. Winnifred. *Wondering as I Wandered: Along an Adirondack Lake.* s.l., M.W. Frahn, 1987. 163p.
    Journal-like text with actual photos by the author—full of observations about plant and animal life.

416. Frahn, M. Winnifred. *Wondering as I Wandered: Along an Adirondack Lake, and Stream, by Foot, by Dinghy, by 'Scope.* s.l., M.W. Frahn, 1988. 162p.
    Similiar format to first book. Journal entries of observations, 55 photos by R. Kendall, author's brother.

417. Glenn, Morris F. *Lake Champlain Habitat.* Alexandria, VA., Glenn, 1980. 37 lvs.
    Nature observations of Whallons Bay on Lake Champlain.

418. Ketchledge, E. H. *A Guide to the Natural History of Mt. Jo.* Glens Falls, N.Y., Adirondack Mountain Club, 1979. 24p.
    Comp. by Natural History Committee of Adirondack Mt. Club. Specifically uses Mt. Jo as a case study, but much of the information applies to Adirondacks in general. Twenty-five stops are listed and described.

419. Klinger, Lee Francis. *Global Patterns in Community Succession.* Bronx, N.Y., New York Botanical Gardens, 1990. 50p.
    Scientific study that uses Alaska and northern New York to examine long standing hypothesis that forest decline is part of the natural succession process. Charts, maps, bibliography.

420. McCabe, Timothy. *Atlas of Adirondack Caterpillars: with a Host List, Rearing Notes and a Selected Bibliography of Works Depicting Caterpillars.* Albany, N.Y., New York State Museum, 1991. iv, 114p.
    Prolific photos and drawings of caterpillars. Indices, bibliography.

421. Mihalyi, Louis. *More of Nature, Nurture, and Nostalgia: Gleaned from the Black River Journal.* Utica, N.Y., North Country Books, 1990. 137p.
    Second volume of collected newspaper columns on natural history of the North Country. Illustrated with wildlife drawings.

422. Mihalyi, Louis. *Nature, Nurture and Nostalgia: Gleaned from the Black River Journal.* Sylvan Beach, N.Y., North Country Books, 1985. 125p.
    Collected newspaper columns published under the title, *Black River Journal.* Articles have nature-related and outdoor themes. Illustrated by John Norton.

423. New York State. Hudson River Valley Commission. *The Hudson: Biological Resources.* Bear Mt., N.Y., The Commission, 1966. 47p.
    Identifies 92 biologically significant sites in the Hudson River basin, nine of which are in Saratoga, Herkimer, Warren or Washington Coun-

ties. Establishes goals in protecting site and recommends legislative and administrative actions to accomplish goals.

424. Pringle, Laurence. *Wild River.* Philadelphia, PA. and New York, N.Y., Lippincott, 1972. 128p.
Photographic essay on the ecology of rivers. First photo of Mt. Marcy and Lake Tear of the Clouds which is the source of the Hudson River.

425. Slack, Nancy G. *85 Acres: A Field Guide to the Adirondack Alpine Summits.* Lake George, N.Y., Adirondack Mountain Club, 1993. 43p.
Identifies alpine tree, shrubs, flowers. Color plates. Discusses timber line, wilderness disturbance, and spruce-fir forests as they relate to alpine ecosystems.

# Geology

426. American Geophysical Union. *The Adirondack Mountains: A Section of Deep Proterozoic Crust.* Washington, D.C., American Geophysical Union, 1989. vii, 63p.
Part I is an overview of Adirondack geology. Second part is road log for an 8-day field trip, with a significant part of excursion in northern and central Adirondacks. Numerous maps and lengthy bibliography.

427. Baillieul, Thomas A. *The Cascade Slide: A Mineralogical Investigation of a Cacsilicate Body On Cascade Mountain, Town of Keene, Essex County, New York.* Amherst, MA., Department of Geology, University of Mass, 1976. vii, 128 lvs.
Technical geological treatment of Cascade Slide in High Peaks region. Bibliography.

428. Bates, Roy E. *Winter Thermal Structure, Ice Conditions and Climate of Lake Champlain.* Hanover, N.H., The Laboratory Cold Region Research and Engineering Lab, 1980. 26p.
Report of field measurements taken on Lake Champlain between 1974 and 1977. Plenty of charts, graphs and photos.

429. Beddoe, Theresa Anne. *Anorthositic Sills of the Southern Adirondack Mountains of New York State.* Blacksburg, VA., Virginia Polytechnic Institute, 1981. vii, 250 lvs.
Masters thesis. Geologic study of area roughly enclosed by Indian Lake, Gore Mt., Wells and Speculator in Southern Adirondacks. Includes chemical and mineral analyses. Bibliography, figures, tables.

430. Connerney, John E. P. *Deep Crustal Electrical Conductivity in the Adirondacks.* Ithaca, N.Y., Cornell University, 1979. xv, 217 lvs.
NAR

431. DeLorraine, William F. *Geology of the Fowler Orebody, Balmat #4 Mine, Northwest Adirondacks, Northwest Adirondacks, New York.* Amherst, MA., University of Massachusetts, 1979. viii, 159 lvs.
Geology thesis on Balmat Mine in southwest St. Lawrence County, outside of Blue Line. Outlines ideas for future works and exploration. Bibliography, maps.

432. Fallon, S. Page. *Stratigraphy and Structural Geology of the Long Lake Area, Adirondack Mountains, New York.* Amherst, MA., University of Massachusetts, 1990. xiv, 313 p.
Doctoral thesis. Technical geological study of Long Lake in Central Highlands of the Adirondacks. Directed by Dr. Jaffe, who has also written about the geology of the Adirondacks.

433. Foose, Michael Peter. *The Structure, Stratigraphy and Metamorphic History of the Bigelow Area, New York Adirondacks.* Princeton, N.J., Princeton University, 1974; reprint, Ann Arbor, MI., University Microfilms, 1984. xv, 224 lvs.
Thesis. Describes geologic development of the Adirondack Lowlands to the northwest of the Adirondacks proper. Bibliography.

434. Geddes, Eugene M. *Investigations into the Origin of an Anorthosite Body on the East Branch of the Sacandaga River, South Central Adirondacks, New York.* Canton, N.Y., St. Lawrence University, 1984. iv, 55p.
B.S. Honors Thesis in Geology. Based on research in southern Adirondacks in Sacandaga River Valley. Petrologic study. Makes observations but does not draw any conclusions. Color and black and white plates, references, figures, and maps.

435. Glennie, James Stanley. *Precambrian Geology of the Piseco Lake Area.* Syracuse, N.Y., Syracuse University, 1973; reprint, Ann Arbor, MI., University Microfilms, 1984. v, 45 lvs.

Doctoral thesis granted in 1973. Geologic description of Piseco Lake region with many technical drawings. Bibliography.

436. Goldblum, Deborah R. *The Role of Ductile Deformation in the Formation of Large Garnets at Gore Mountain, Southeastern Adirondacks.* Philadelphia, PA., Temple University, 1988. viii, 109 lvs.

Thesis. Geologic study. References, figures, maps, plates.

437. Gooley, Larry. *A History of Altona Flat Rock, Located in Clinton County, New York State.* Elizabethtown, N.Y., Denton Publications, 1980. 103p.

Flat Rock is the name given to a rugged geologic formation covering approximately 15 square miles in town of Altona, Clinton County, N.Y. Gooley describes wilderness features of Flat Rock, its geologic history and its place in town history. Informative study of unique natural formation. Illus., maps. Cover by Paula Gooley.

438. Isachsen, Yngvar W. *Ground Investigations of Projected Traces of Focal Mechanisms for Earthquakes at Blue Mountain Lake, Raquette Lake and Chazy Lake, Adirondack Uplift, New York.* Washington, D.C., Nuclear Regulatory Commission, 1979. vi, 33p.

Mapping project to establish presence of faulting in Central and Northern Adirondacks. Results were inconclusive.

439. Jaffe, Howard. *Bedrock Geology of the High Peaks Region, Marcy Massif, Adirondacks, New York.* Amherst, MA., Department of Geology and Geography, University of Massachusetts, 1983. 78 lvs.

Technical field guide to High Peaks; extensive charts, graphs, maps and photos. Part of remapping project using updated methods. 300 copies.

440. Kelley, William Morgan. *Chemistry and Genesis of Titaniferous Magnetite and Related Ferromagnesian Silicates, Sanford Lake Deposits, Tahawus, New York.* Amherst, MA., University of Massachusetts, 1979. x 181 lvs.

NAR

441. Kelly, Patrick V. *A Characterization of the Rock Types in and around a Portion of the Oregon Dome, Adirondacks, New York.* Canton, N.Y., St. Lawrence University, 1984. vii, 54 lvs.

B.S. Honors thesis. Study of anorthosite bodies in Oregon Dome in South-Central Adirondacks. Reviews past and current work as well. Color photos, refs., map in folder.

442. Lochhead, Alison A. *The Structural Fabric of the Eastern Piseco Anticline.* Amherst, MA., University of Massachusetts, 1992. xiv, 143 lvs.

NAR

443. McLelland, James and Richard W. Wiener. *Stratigraphy and Structural Geology of the Adirondack Mountains, New York.* Boulder, CO., Geological Society of America, 1984. 55p.

Offers alternative view of geologic development of the Adirondack region. Illus., notes, bibliography.

444. Morrison, Jean. *Petrology and Stable Isotope Geochemistry of the Marcy Anorthosite Massif, Adirondack Mountains, New York.* Madison, WI., University of Wisconsin, 1988. v, 200 lvs.

NAR

445. Nekut, Anthony G. *Crustal Electrical Conductivity Structure in the Adirondacks.* Ithaca, N.Y., Cornell University, 1979. ix, 116 lvs.

NAR

446. New York State Geological Association. *Adirondack Field Trips.* s .l., The Association, 1992. 75p.

Two field trips. First, by James McLelland of Colgate University, also includes discussion of geology of region. Two-day trip in Franklin and Essex Counties. Second entry is discussion of geology and field trip in the AuSable Forks, Elizabethtown, and Willsboro area in northeastern Adirondacks. Both include figures, tables and bibliography.

447. New York State. State Education Department. *Geology of New York: A Simplified Account.* Albany, N.Y., State Education Department, 1991. x, 284p.

Chapter 4 on the geology of the Adirondack region.

448. Olson, Karin Elizabeth. *Mafic Magnetism in the Adirondacks, New York.* Amherst, MA., University of Massachusetts, 1990. xvii, 230 lvs.

Thesis on Al-Fe magmas in the Adirondacks.

Lengthy bibliography.

449. Reed, Susan Elizabeth. *The Late-Glacial and Post-glacial Diatoms of Heart Lake and Upper Wallface Pond in the Adirondack Mountains, New York.* San Francisco, CA., San Francisco State University, 1982. viii, 192 lvs.

Thesis. Geological study of high diatoms in two lakes in the High Peaks region. Diatoms are microscopic one-cell algae that can serve as indicators of water chemistry. Diatom research has made it possible to develop biological histories of bodies of fresh water. One of the conclusions of this study is that Heart Lake and Wallface Pond will be susceptible to dramatic decreases in pH level due to acid rain. Bibliography.

450. Seal, Thomas Lee. *Pre-Grenville Dehydration Metamorphism in the Adirondack Mountains, New York: Evidence from Pelitic and Semi-Pelitic Metasediments.* Stony Brook, N.Y., University of New York at Stony Brook, 1986. ix, 84 lvs.

Master thesis. Discusses pressure, temperature and role of water in shaping geology of Colton, Russell, and Edwards. Bibliography, charts, figures.

451. Stoddard, Edward F. *Granulite Facies.* Los Angeles, CA., UCLA, 1976; reprint, Ann Arbor, Mich., University Microfilm International, 1976. xvii, 271 lvs.

Doctoral thesis. Technical study of Rainbow Falls region in southern part of the town of Colton, N.Y.

452. VanDiver, Bradford B. *Geological Studies of the Northwest Region: Field Trip Guidebook.* Brockport, N.Y., New York State Geological Association, 1971. 1 v.

Six field trips, mostly northern Adirondacks and St. Lawrence County. Each trip includes maps, written description, tables and bibliography.

453. VanDiver, Bradford B. *Roadside Geology of New York.* Mountain Press Publishing Co., Missoula, MT., 1985, 1989. x, 411p.

Part of Chapter IX and XI will be of the most useful to people interested in the Adirondacks. Very readable-makes geology understandable to the average person. Maps, photos, illus.

454. VanDiver, Bradford B. *Rocks and Routes of the North Country, N.Y.: Geological Guide for Tours, Minerals Rock Climbing and White Water.* Geneva, N.Y., W. F. Humphrey Press, Inc., 1976. xv, 204p.

Part I provides geologic background of the North Country, Part II describes field trips, Part III deals with mineral collecting and Part IV discusses rock climbing and white water. Index.

455. VanDiver, Bradford B. *Upstate New York: Field Guide.* Dubuque, Iowa, Kendall/Hunt Publishing Co., 1980. xv, 276p.

Covers four-fifths of New York State outside of New York City. Chapters 1-3 about Highland Adirondacks, Lowland Adirondacks, and St. Lawrence Lowlands. Other chapters on Lake Champlain, Lake George and Tug Hill and Adirondack eskers. Contains information on geologic sights, their locations. Index, references.

456. Wiener, R.W. *Detailed Studies of Selected, Well-Exposed Fracture Zones in the Adirondack Mountains Zone, N.Y.* Washington, D.C., U.S. Nuclear Regulatory Commission, 1987. x, 82p.

NAR

457. Wyckoff, Jerome. *The Adirondack Landscape: Its Geology and Landforms; a Hiker's Guide.* Gabriels, N.Y., Adirondack Mountain Club, 1967. 72p.

Geology for the general reader. Guide to educate hikers to what is around them while visiting the Adirondacks. Fifth printing in 1980. Out of print.

458. Yang, Yingping. *Igneous Petrogenesis and Tectonics of the Rocks in the Adirondack Mountains, New York.* Miami, OH., Miami University, 1992. xi, 161 lvs.

NAR

459. Ziegler, John F. *The Metamorphosis and Origin of the St. Regis Anorthosite.* New Orleans, LA., Tulane University, 1986.vi, 42 lvs.

Thesis. Geologic study of rare geologic formation, one of which is located in the St. Regis Triangle in Franklin County. Tables, charts and references.

# Mineralogy

460. Tervo, William A. *The Rock Hound's Guide to New York State Minerals, Fossils and Artifacts.* New York, N.Y., Exposition Press, 1967. 148p.

First several chapters on counties in and around Adirondack region. Each chapter highlights significant geological and mineralogical features. Later edition in 1976.

## Plant Science

461. Bessette, Alan E. *Mushrooms of the Adirondacks: A Field Guide.* Utica, N.Y., North Country Books, 1988. 145p.

In addition to plates and descriptions there is an introductory section on mushroom collecting. Information on eating, preserving, and cooking wild mushrooms. Indexes of common names, genera and species.

462. Bessette, Alan E. & Bill Chapman. *Trees and Shrubs of the Adirondacks.* Utica, N.Y., North Country Books, 1990. 150p.

Written descriptions and color plates. Other features such as index to common names, index to botanical names and a chapter on making a pressed leaf collection. Written description lists Latin name, family name, plate location, description, occurence and comments.

463. Cutler, Lewis Michael. *Studies of the Flora and Vegetation of the Cranberry Lake Watershed, New York.* Syracuse, N.Y., State University of New York. College of Environmental Science and Forestry, 1975. viii, 223 lvs.

Thesis. Extensive, multi-faceted study of natural history of Cranberry Lake area with information on virgin stands of white pine in Five Ponds area. Bibliography, illus., and charts.

464. DiNunzio, Michael G. *A Vegetational Survey of the Alpine Zone of the Adirondack Mountains, New York.* Syracuse, N.Y., State University of New York. College of Environmental Science and Forestry, 1972. vii, 109 lvs.

Thesis. About alpine (tundra) flora that exists in the Adirondacks. Mentions 18 peaks. Color photos, tables, bibliography.

465. Karlin, Eric F. *Wetland Plant Communities of the Adirondack Mountain Region.* Syracuse, N.Y., State University of New York, College of Environmental Science and Forestry, 1975. vii, 99 lvs.

Thesis. Wetland ecology. Concentrates on various wetland plant communities and their composition, structure and environmental factors that shape their development. Ties in with other works; see Westfall (#389) and Hardin (#476) Short section entitled "Successional Characteristics of Adirondack Wetlands." Bibliography.

466. Ketchledge, E. H. *Trees of the Adirondack High Peaks Region.* Gabriels, N.Y., Adirondack Mountain Club, 1967; 2nd ed., Glens Falls, N.Y., Adirondack Mountain Club, 1979. 103p.

Pocket-size guide book to each of 34 species found in High Peaks region of the Adirondacks. Pictures of leaves of each species. Short sections on Forest Preserve history, conservation ethic and checklist.

467. Kudish, Michael. *Adirondack Upland Flora: An Ecological Perspective.* Saranac, N.Y., Chauncy Press, 1992. 320p.

Definitive scientific work on alpine flora on Adirondack peaks.

468. Kudish, Michael. *Paul Smiths Flora: A Preliminary Vascular Flora of the Paul Smiths, Saranac Lake Area, the Adirondacks, New York, with Notes on the Climate, Geology and Soils.* Paul Smiths, N.Y., Paul Smiths College, 1975. 136p.

Scientific description of the plant life of the area surrounding Paul Smiths and Saranac Lake as well as climate, geology and soils. Interesting information about the region.

469. Kudish, Michael. *Paul Smiths Flora II: Additional Vascular Plants; Bryophytes (Mosses and Liverworts); Soils and Vegetation; Local Forest History.* Paul Smiths, N.Y., Paul Smiths College, 1981. ii, 162p.

Continues 1975 work. Additional vascular plants; mosses, liverworts plus information on soils, vegetation and local natural history.

470. MacKenzie, Katherine. *Wild Flowers of the North Country: Northern New York, Vermont, New Hampshire, Maine.* Plattsburgh, N.Y., Tundra Books, 1973. 96p.

Pocket-size field guide. Each short description of a flower is accompanied by a watercolor painting. Contents are divided into 4 categories: Spring Flowers, Early Summer Flowers, Late Summer

Flowers, and Wild Orchids. An elegant little book.

471. McGrath, Anne with Joanne Treffs. *Wildflowers of the Adirondacks.* Sylvan Beach, N.Y., North Country Books, 1981. xvi, 109p.

Regional field guide to most common wildflowers. Meant for the general reader. 120 color plates. Written description of flowers and indexes of common and botanical names. Index, Other printings in 1984, 1988, 1990.

472. Ogden, Eugene C. et. al. *Field Guide to Aquatic Plants of Lake George, N.Y.* Albany, N.Y., University of the State of New York, State Education Department, 1976. iv, 65 lvs.

Scientific field guide with both Latin names and common names. Excellent drawings of various plants. Location of plants in and around Lake George are listed.

473. Remillard, Marguerite Madden. *Use of Aerial Photography to Study Beaver Impact on Plant Community Succession in the Adirondacks of New York.* Plattsburgh, N.Y., State University of New York at Plattsburgh, 1984. ix, 143 lvs.

Biology thesis. Correlates plant community succession and beaver activity in Adirondacks using aerial photography. Numerous tables. Bibliography.

474. Whitehead, Donald R. *The Regional Vegetational History of the High Peaks (Adirondack Region) New York.* Albany, N.Y., State Education Department, New York, 1990. iv, 27p.

Recounts various stages of vegetation in High Peaks since deglaciation. Existing vegetational zones have developed over the past 2,000 years. Maps, charts, literature cited.

# Zoology

## General

475. Gretch, Mark. *The Wildlife Heritage of Clinton County.* Plattsburgh, N.Y., Clinton County Historical Museum, 1989. 47p.

Educational manual accompanying a 1989 temporary exhibit for Clinton County Historical Association. Background of each species, their relationship to people and unique or special characteristics are described.

476. Hardin, David L. *Animal Community Structure of Adirondack Wetlands.* Syracuse, N.Y., State University of New York. College of Environmental Science and Forestry, 1975. ix, 192 lvs.

Thesis. Wetland ecology. Purpose was to correlate a wide range of animal communities to plant communities and physical characteristics of the wetlands. Ties in with work of Karlan (#465) and Westfall (#389). Bibliography.

## Fish

477. Decker, Daniel J. *Guide to Freshwater Fishes of New York.* Ithaca, N.Y., Distribution Center, Cornell University, 1980, 1985. 140p.

Short descriptions of freshwater fishes of New York State. Shaded line drawings by Tom Parker. Not as useful as color plates or drawings.

478. George, Carl J. *The Fishes of the Adirondack Park.* Albany, N.Y., New York State Department of Environmental Conservation, 1980, 1981. iii, 93p.

Chapter on influence of natural setting and historical background on native species of fish in the Adirondacks. Mostly about 92 native species. Bibliography, and index of common and scientific names. Table 1 groups fish by zoological and geographical criteria. No plates or illus.

479. Smith, C. Lavett. *The Inland Fishes of New York State.* Albany, N.Y., New York State Department of Environmental Conservation, 1985. xi, 522p.

Comprehensive reference book of fishes. Listed by species. Standard description includes common and scientific names, identification, description, habitat and distribution, feeding habits, and maps of geographic locations. Illus., glossary, bibliography.

480. Werner, Robert G. *Freshwater Fishes of New York State: A Field Guide.* Syracuse, N.Y., Syracuse University Press, 1980. vi, 186p.

Field guide for the general reader, fishing enthusiast and naturalist as well as for the scientific minded. Bibliography.

## Birds

481. Beehler, Bruce M. *Birdlife in the Adirondack Park*. Glens Falls, N.Y., Adirondack Mountain Club, 1978. 210p.

Bird field guide for the Adirondack Park. In addition to information on particular species, there are sections on the Adirondack Park, regional history, and conservation. Another chapter focuses on the Adirondack environment and bird life. Now out of print.

482. Bessette, Alan E. *Birds of the Adirondacks: A Field Guide*. Utica, N.Y., North Country Books, 1992. 240p.

Co-authored by William K. Chapman, Doug Pens, and Warren Greene. 185 color plates. Describes over 200 species found in the Adirondacks, divided into several categories. Additional information on feeding, and bird watching. Checklist, illus., indexes.

483. Bull, John L. *Birds of New York State*. Garden City, N.Y., Doubleday, 1974. 655p.; additional material, *Supplement to Birds of New York State*. West Hempstead, N.Y., Federation of New York State Bird Clubs, 1976; reprint, *Birds of New York State: Including the 1976 Supplement*. Ithaca, N.Y., Comstock Publishing Associates, 1985. 703p.

Comprehensive work on bird life of New York. Written description includes information on each bird: its range, status, breeding, as well as more general information. Reprint of 1974 ed. with 1976 corrections compiled by Federation of New York State Bird Clubs. Bibliography. Supplement contains new bird distribution information. Plates, maps, illus, bibliography, index.

484. Carleton, Geoffrey. *Birds of Essex County, N.Y. Thru December 31, 1975*. Essex, N.Y., High Peaks Audubon Society, 1976. 29p.

Lists birds sighted in Essex County. Half dozen categories from abundant to rarity. Graphics, maps, bibliography plus supplement through December 31, 1976.

485. Drennan, Susan R. *Where to Find Birds in New York State: The Top 500 Sites*. Syracuse, N.Y., Syracuse University Press, 1981. 499p.

General information such as birding sites listed by region. Sections 6 and 7 deal with St. Lawrence and Adirondack-Champlain Region. Description of site, location, and map. Site's value rated for all four seasons. Bibliography. Also in paper.

486. Dunning, Joan. *The Loon: Voice of the Wilderness*. Dublin, N.H., Yankee Books, 1985; reprint, Boston, MA., Houghton Mifflin, 1991. 143p.

Excellent work on loons for general reader. Author introduced to loons in Cranberry Lake, New York. Discusses life patterns of loon during the course of the year. Fine illus. by author. Bibliography.

487. Fritz, Robert S. *The Distribution and Population Status of the Spruce Grouse in the Adirondacks*. Syracuse, N.Y., State University of New York. College of Environmental Science and Forestry, 1977. viii, 115 lvs.

Thesis. Scientific study of spruce grouse population, density, and habitat. Correlates amount of conifer forest and presence and size of spruce grouse populations. Uses models to establish probability that smaller population groups are more likely to disappear. Tables, maps, bibliography

488. Klein, Tom. *Loon Magic*. Ashland, WI., Paper Birch Press, 1985. xiii, 130p.

General work on loons. Many excellent, unusual color plates. Instructive book. Edited by Jeff Farr. Preface by Sigurd T. Olson. Photography by Woody Hagge. Also a children's version. Bibliography, index.

489. Liotta, P. H. *Learning to Fly: A Season with the Peregrine Falcon*. Chapel, N.C., Algonquin Books of Chapel Hill, 1989. 201p; New York, N.Y., Ballantine Books, 1990. 241p.

Deeply personal first-hand account of working with young peregrine falcons at a central Adirondack site. The purpose of the program is to re-establish falcons in their natural environment. Author makes some inner explorations of his own. Notes, bibliography.

490. McIntyre, Judith W. *The Common Loon: Spirit of Northern Lakes*. Minneapolis, MN., University of Minnesota Press, 1988. 228p.

Work of general interest about loons. Author is professor of biology at Utica College. Part of her research was done in the Adirondack region.

491. Parker, Karl E. *Foraging and Reproduction of the Common Loon.* Syracuse, N.Y., State University of New York. College of Environmental Science and Forestry, 1985. x, 144 lvs.

Masters thesis on the ability of loons to adapt to acid deposition in the waters which they inhabit. Maps, charts, suggestions for future research, bibliography.

492. Taylor, Kip. *Loon.* Saranac Lake, N.Y., Taylor, 1988. 175p.

Beautiful, unusual color plates. Text on loon life cycle, behaviors and activities. Illus.

493. Warren, Philip H. *Birds of Clinton County.* Plattsburgh, N.Y., National Audubon Society: Northern Adirondack Chapter, 1979. 68p.

A preliminary study of the diverse birdlife to be found in Clinton County, New York. Lists over 200 bird species. No illus. Best used in conjunction with traditional field guides. States its limitations and outlines areas where more study and research is needed.

## Mammals

494. Adirondack Life. *Adirondack Life Book of Animal Tracks: Signs of Animals Common to the Adirondack Woods.* Jay, N.Y., Adirondack Life, 1976, 1985. 40p.

Field guide. Signs of animals common to Adirondack woods. Illus. of animal tracks by Jim Arnosky.

495. Betters, Francis. *Meet the Animals of the Adirondacks.* Wilmington, N.Y., Adirondack Sports Publications, 1991. 68p.

Adirondack writer who frequently writes about fishing uses interview format to write about wildlife of Adirondack region. Informative. Art by Mary Monique.

496. Chapman, William K. with Dennis Aprill. *Mammals of the Adirondacks: A Field Guide.* Utica, N.Y., North Country Books, 1991. 160p.

Quality guide. Description, photos, footprints, index to common names, index to Latin names, and glossary. Written description focuses on physical description, habitat, food, and reproduction.

497. Elliott, Lang. *Social Behavior and Foraging Ecology of the Eastern Chipmunk (Tamias Striatus) in the Adirondack Mountains.* Washington, D.C., Smithsonian Institution Press, 1978. vi, 107 lvs.

Discusses mating and social behavior of chipmunks. Field work was done near Onchiota. Bibliography, illus., charts, graphs.

498. Linck, David B. *Summer Activity Patterns of the Eastern Chipmunk in an Adirondack Forest.* Syracuse, N.Y., State University of New York. College of Environmental Science and Forestry, 1971. vi, 54 lvs.

Thesis. Study done at Huntington Forest fills void in research on chipmunk. Discusses "summer disappearance" of chipmunks when activity is reduced or less conspicuous (late July-August). Suggests that second breeding season may account for "disappearance." Bibliography.

499. Richards, Dorothy with Hope Sawyer Buyukmihci. *Beaversprite: My Years Building an Animal Sanctuary.* San Francisco, CA., Chronicle Books, 1977. Interlaken, N.Y., Heart of the Lakes Publishing, 1983. 191p.

Story of Richards' long time interest in beavers. Richards lived in the southern Adirondacks.

500. Saunders, D. Andrew. *Adirondack Mammals.* Syracuse, N.Y., Adirondack Wildlife Program, State University of New York College of Environmental Science and Forestry, 1988. 224p.

Mammals of the Adirondack region. Drawings of each mammal and its range on a map of the Adirondack Park. Written description covers each animal's range, habitat, food and feeding behavior, activity, reproduction characteristics, predators, social habits and communication patterns.

# *Social and Economic Development*

## General

501. Bethlen, Francis Rhedly and David A. Singer. *A Study of the Agricultural Economy and Agricultural Water Use in the Five County Lake Champlain-Lake George Region: A Research Report.* s.l., s.n., 1967. 306p.

Analyzes agricultural land management programs on a regional basis. Part II discusses agricultural economy and water use. Inventory of agriculture covers soil, water, climate, land use, farms and land in farms, dairy, and other farming activities such as livestock and crops. Mimeo. Tables, works cited.

502. Birmingham, Stephen. *The Right People: A Portrait of the American Social Establishment.* Boston, MA., Little, Brown, 1968. 360p.

Short section on the Adirondacks, Lake Placid Club and Lake George as playground for the rich.

503. Black River-St. Lawrence Economic Development District. *Overall Economic Development Program.* Canton, N.Y., The Commission, 1968. 99p.

Contains by-laws and justification for designation as an economic development district which covers Franklin, St. Lawrence, Jefferson and Lewis Counties. Short discussions of economic history of region, commuting patterns, community patterns, and population characteristics. Charts, graphs.

504. Dempsey, William M. *Statistical Abstracts and Analysis of Clinton County, N.Y.* Plattsburgh, N.Y., State University College, Office of Analytical Studies and Long Range Planning, 1970. 111p.

Statistics on Clinton County compiled from other sources. Intended to clarify past socio-economic trends in county, serve as a resource for current economic development needs in the 1970s, and be useful for future economic development planning. Mimeo. Tables, charts, maps.

505. DeVries, Gordon. *Tac Stats: A North Country Statistical Digest.* Plattsburgh, N.Y., Economic Development and Technical Assistance Center, State University of New York at Plattsburgh, 1979. iv, 136p.; rev. ed., *Tac Stats: A Statistical Digest of 16 Northern New York Counties.* Plattsburgh, N.Y., Technical Assistance Center, State University of New York at Plattsburgh, 1990. 109p.

Statistical description of 16 Northern New York counties during the 1970s. Areas covered are: population, income, employment, retail sales, housing, land use and miscellaneous categories. Graphs, charts, maps, references. Revised ed. based on 1988 population estimates.

506. Eastern Adirondack Economic Development Commission. *Overall Economic Development Program.* Albany, N.Y., New York State Office of Planning Coordinator, 1967. 102p.

Document provides rationale and statistical justification for the creation of an economic development zone in the eastern Adirondacks.

507. Environmental Consulting Group. *Regional Development Concepts for the Lake Champlain-Lake George Region.* Hanover, N.H., Environmental Consulting Group, 1971. Var. pag.

Preliminary regional planning tool focusing on shared regional strategic planning of recreation and transportation issues. Supplemented by economic, housing and law enforcement statistics. Maps.

508. Erman, Steven. *Economic Development Needs of the Adirondack Park.* Ray Brook, N.Y., Adirondack Park Agency, 1983. Unpaged.

Identifies Adirondacks' lack of economic diversity as their chief problem, and their natural character as their most important economic asset. Points out the important role of lumbering and tourism in the regional economy. Contains appendix of social/economic data. Delineates economic development goals and specific strategies for achieving those goals. Graphs, charts.

509. Essex County. Division of County Planning and Development. *Directions For Development: Planning for Essex County in the 1980s.* Elizabethtown, N.Y., Essex County, N.Y., 1980. 137p.

Descriptive work and inventory on Essex County. Discusses priorities, needs of residents, and the nature of the county's business and commercial sectors.

510. Hardy, Philip J. *Iron Age Community of J. and J. Rogers Iron Company: Au Sable Valley, N.Y. 1825-1900*. Bowling Green, OH., Bowling Green State University, 1985. v, 315 lvs.
Thesis. Discusses the role of major employer in Essex County community. By first quarter of twentieth century wood products had replaced iron mining. Bibliography.

511. Ives, Jane K. *Survey of Social Welfare Needs and Resources, Lake Champlain-Lake George Region*. Albany, N.Y., New York State Department of Social Welfare, 1966. 83p.
Outlines welfare programs for families and children as well as Economic Opportunity Programs in the region. Tables, charts, graphs, maps, and list of interviewees.

512. Jancar, Barbara W. *Warren and Hamilton Counties Opportunity Report for Submission to the Warren-Hamilton Counties Action Committee on Economic Opportunity*. Lake George, N.Y., Action Committee on Economic Opportunity, 1966. 287p.
Report based on survey instrument is fact finding document for the War on Poverty Program in Warren and Hamilton Counties. Summary and recommendations for better use of people and economic resources. Survey covered education, jobs, welfare, health, housing, economic development, transportation and law enforcement services. Charts, tables, illus.

513. Kalish, Richard J. *An Economic Study of the Adirondack-Mohawk Region, 1940-1960*. Albany, N.Y., Office of Planning Coordination, 1966. xi, 536p.
Discussion of economic welfare of Fulton, Hamilton, Herkimer, Lewis, Montgomery and Oneida counties. Economic conditions declined in several key areas in the early post-World War II era. Charts and graphs.

514. Kalish, Richard J. *Mohawk Regional Economic Study: Part I Basic Inventory*. Albany, N.Y., Office of Planning Coordination, 1968. 172p.
Income, history, population, economic development, migratory patterns for southern Adirondack counties of Herkimer, Hamilton, Fulton, and Lewis counties. Index, numerous tables, maps.

515. Kelley, Jeffrey A. *Recent Farm Life as Examined from the Archaelogical Remains of the Rickert Allen Site in Peru, N.Y.* Plattsburgh, N.Y., State University College at Plattsburgh, 1983. x, 252 lvs.
Senior honors thesis. Analysis of archaelogical dig. Drawings and refs.

516. Lake Champlain-Lake George Regional Planning Board. *Economic Report on Lake Champlain-Lake George Region: Reappraisal of Regional Potential and Problems*. Syracuse, N.Y., Economic Consultants Organization, 1971. 112p.
Update of similiar report from late 1960s. Discusses need for economic growth and agricultural and industrial development. Tables chronicle income, population, retail and wholesale figures. Summary and recommendations.

517. Lake Champlain-Lake George Regional Planning Board. *Proposed Rural Area Land Development Plan for Lake Champlain-Lake George*. Lake George, N.Y., The Board, 1974. 40 lvs.
Draft. Lists goals and analyzes current resources. Discusses physical features, sewer and water, growth trends, population, present land uses, economic activity and transportation. Based on data from Adirondack Park Agency. Three large maps in pockets. Makes recommendations. Bibliography.

518. Lake Champlain-Lake George Regional Planning Board. *Regional Housing Study*. Lake George, N.Y., The Board, 1972. 53p.
Overview of housing in Clinton, Essex, Hamilton, Warren and Washington Counties. Describes existing housing in terms of structures, population and the regional economy. Identifies substandard housing, mobile homes, seasonal dwellings and supply problems. Discusses lack of support services and lack of land use controls as issues. Charts.

519. Lewis County Planning Board. *Overall Economic Development Plan*. s.l., s.n., 1968. 65 lvs.
Mimeo. Describes Lewis County and the basis for economic growth: its cultural, forest, agricultural and industrial resources. Charts, graphs, maps.

520. Maxwell, John F. *The Economic Impact on the Lake Placid Area of Hosting the 1980 Olympic Winter*

*Games*. Plattsburgh, N.Y., State University College, Technical Assistance Center, 1974. 36p.

Estimates that Lake Placid area should see a $30,000,000 benefit in the 1980s after the Winter Olympics. Concludes that development for Olympics will be compatible with land use plan of the Adirondack Park Agency.

521. Miller, Wayne L. *Franklin County Facts and Figures: A Comprehensive Survey of People and Places, and Their Development Outlook*. Malone, N.Y., Franklin County Employment and Training Administration, 1978. 87p.

Exhaustive statistical description of Franklin County, New York. Heavily draws upon State and Federal sources. Chapter I: Population; II: Economic and Social Characteristics; Chapter III: Social and Economic Atlas of Franklin County; Chapter IV: Health; Chapter V: Government; Chapter VI: Labor and Industry.

522. Miller, Wayne L. *Franklin County: Poverty or Prosperity*. Malone, N.Y., Franklin County Employment and Training Administration, 1978. Unpaged.

Tables and text provides thorough statistical description of Franklin County, its people, the social and economic characteristics of the county, business, political and governmental and educational trends. Directory of various levels of government, large employers, and educational institutions.

523. Moore, Dan E. *One Approach to Rural Outreach: Community Development Centers, Clinton County, New York*. Plattsburgh, N.Y., Clinton County Rural Development Program, 1974. 69p.

Promotes role of existing community development centers in complying with federal Rural Development Act of 1972.

524. New York State. Department of Commerce. *Business Fact Book, Part 2: Profile of People, Jobs and Housing, Northern Area*. Albany, N.Y., Department of Commerce, 1974. 28p.

Statistical description by county of population, employment and housing. Covers Jefferson, Lewis, St. Lawrence, Franklin, Clinton and Essex counties. Charts. Part 1 of this publication contains numerical information on manufacturing, business and agriculture.

525. New York State. Department of Commerce, Bureau of Business Research. *Economic Profile of Northern New York*. Albany, N.Y., Department of Commerce, 1985. 57p.

Basic economic information on northern New York, specifically Clinton, Essex, Franklin, Jefferson, Lewis and St. Lawrence Counties. Low wages, high unemployment, seasonal work, and high structural unemployment characterize the northern New York economy. Farm-related work, and businesses that exploit natural resources dominate the regional economy. Over 1,700 manufacturing jobs have been lost in recent years. Book has two parts; general statistics and county-by-county economic profiles.

526. New York State. Hudson River Valley Commission. *The Hudson: Population*. Bear Mountain Park, N.Y., The Commission, 1966. 43p.

Population trends in Hudson Valley on a county-by-county basis. Includes Adirondack region counties. Charts, ref.

527. Office of Planning Coordination. *Adirondack Skier Market*. Albany, N.Y., Office of Planning Coordination, 1970. 40p.

Technical study. Discusses potential for skiing in eastern New York, specifically, Lake Champlain/Lake George area. Charts, graphs.

528. Richardson, Raymond J. *Lake Placid Center for Music, Drama and Art; Its Economic Development; A Study For the New York State Council on the Arts*. Plattsburgh, N.Y., State University College, Technical Assistance Center, 1973. 30p.

In 1973 the Center accounted for a $1,000,000 impact on Lake Placid. In a survey 45% of visitors to the Center were tourists, 21% were Lake Placid residents and 34% were vacation home owners or northern New York residents. Charts, graphs, and estimated expenditures by tourists at the Lake Placid Center.

529. Sargent, Donald E. *The Uses of Wollastonite*. Schenectady, N.Y., Chemical and Allied Industries, 1972. 111p.

Wollastonite is a mineral found in large quantities in Essex County, useful in plastics, electrical equipment, paints and abrasives. Discusses physical, ceramic and chemical properties of wollastonite. References.

# Commerce and Industry

## General

530. Brown, Tommy L. and Nancy A. Connelly. *Tourism in the Adirondack Region of New York.* Ithaca, N.Y., Cornell University, 1984. ix, 68 lvs.

Initial study of tourism in northern New York. Summer tourism declined in late 1970s, while winter tourism increased. Work points out need for additional efforts in planning tourism and need to interview potential tourists for their impressions of the region.

531. Chugh, Ram L. *Adirondack North Country Tourism.* Lake Placid, N.Y., Adirondack/North Country Association, 1986. i, 191p.

Transcript of September 1985 conference held at SUNY College at Potsdam. Main topics concern financing and planning tourism projects.

532. Chugh, Ram L. & Prem P. Gandhi. *North Country Successes: Case Studies of Successful Entrepeneurs in ANCA.* Lake Placid, N.Y., Adirondack North Country Association, 1987. vi, 142p.

Case studies and attributes of selected regional entrepeneurs. Outlines objectives, overview, design and statistical characteristics of the study. Chapter 6 delineates a plan of action and a marketing strategy for the region.

533. Feldman, Robert Larry. *Effectiveness of Audio-Visual Media For Environmental Interpretation to Recreating Motorists.* Ithaca, N.Y., Feldman, 1975. x, 213 lvs.

Lengthy doctoral thesis that compares use of audio-cassettes and brochures in informing tourists. Field work done in 1974. Brochure was more effective overall. Audiocassette was more effective with first time visitors.

534. Hyde, Floy S. *Adirondack Forests, Fields and Mines: Brief Accounts and Stories Concerning Lumbering, Forest-Related Products, Farming Specialties, and Mining, Yesterday and Today.* Lakemont, N.Y., North Country Books, 1974; Saranac Lake, N.Y., Chauncy Press, 1986. xvi, 223p.

Excellent book on traditional ways of making a living in the Adirondacks. Provides contemporary glimpses as well as historical perspective. Focuses on wood-related industries, farming and mining. A realistic and respectful treatment of the subject. Numerous plates. Bibliography.

535. Ratner, Shanna E. *Strategies for Community Economic Development through Natural Resource Use in Northern New York.* Ithaca, N.Y., Cornell University, Agricultural Experiment Station, 1985. 38p.

Local self-reliance approach to economic development in northern New York emphasizing available natural resources and small business. Ratner has hit upon an important, but often overlooked, concept.

## Arts and Crafts

536. Adirondack Museum. *The Rustic Artistry of Clarence O. Nichols: Furniture in the Collection of the New York State Museum.* Blue Mountain Lake, N.Y., Adirondack Museum, 1987. 35p.

Exhibit catalog. Two short essays on Nichols by John L. Scherer and Craig Gilborn. Photos of 20 pieces of Adirondack rustic furniture.

537. Gilborn, Craig A. *Adirondack Furniture and the Rustic Tradition.* New York, N.Y., Abrams, Inc., 1987. 352p.

Book on Adirondack furniture placing it in the rustic tradition. Manufacturers listed. Over 350 photos, approximately 50 in color.

538. Harrell, Dr. Loy S. *Decoys of Lake Champlain.* West Chester, PA., Schiffer Publications, 1986. 128p.

Decoys and people who carve them. Maps of Lake Champlain on inside covers and fly leaves, both front and back-three-fourths are from Vermont side. Real contribution to regional folklife and folk art. Illus.

539. Ketchum, William C. *Early Potters and Potteries of New York State.* New York, N.Y., Funk and Wagnells, 1970. x, 278p.; rev. ed., *Potters and Potteries of New York State 1650-1900*, Syracuse, N.Y., Syracuse University Press, 1987. x, 626p.

Contains chapter on Washington and Saratoga Counties and the Adirondack region.

540. Lumsden, Linda. *Adirondack Artists & Craftspeople.* Saranac Lake, N.Y., Adirondack Publishing Co., 1986. 118p.
Profiles of 15 Adirondack artisans and craftspeople. While most are not natives of the region, Lumsden holds up these artists as reflecting the region's own aesthetic sensibility and values of independence and quality workmanship. Photos by John Santoro. Edited and designed by Sara Henry.

541. Osborn, Susan. *American Rustic Furniture.* New York, Harmony Books, 1984. 149p.
Book on various styles of rustic furniture including Adirondack. Sections on furniture construction and a list of sources for rustic furniture. Illus.

542. Stapleton, Constance. *Crafts of America: A Guide to the Finest Traditional Crafts Made in the United States.* New York, N.Y., Harper and Row, 1988. 341p.
Listings of various crafts people. Photo and text on each individual. A few Adirondack artisans listed: Carl Heilman, Bill Smith, Gene Valk, and Ken Heitz.

543. Tatham, David ed. *Prints and Printmakers of New York State, 1825-1940.* Syracuse, N.Y., Syracuse University Press, 1986. 277p.
Chapter 3 about St. Lawrence County. Chapter 8 is about humorous wood engravings of the Adirondacks. Numerous prints. Index, bibliography, notes.

## Forestry and Lumbering

544. Amigo, Eleanor & Mark Neuffer. *Beyond the Adirondacks: The Story of St. Regis Paper Co.* Westport, Conn., Greenwood Press, 1980. xi, 219p.
History of St. Regis Paper Company from its beginnings in Watertown, N.Y. in 1899 to its status as one of the nation's 110 largest corporations in 1979 with over 31,000 employees. St. Regis has owned mills and woodland throughout northern New York State. Bibliography.

545. Black River/St. Lawrence Resource Conservation & Development Council. *Directory of Adirondack Wood Products and Firms.* Watertown, N.Y., The Forestry Committee, 1990. 32p.
Lists questionnaire respondents and members of American Wood Workers Association; alphabetical listing of firms and products, and forests product index covering baskets to windows. Advts.

546. Irland, Lloyd C. *Forest Products Industry Development Programs in the ANCA Area, New York State: Report to ANCA.* Augusta, ME,. Irland Group, 1988. 56 lvs.
Discusses wood-based development efforts in Adirondacks, and the role of wood in regional development. Makes comparisons to similiar programs in Michigan, Maine and Pennsylvania.

547. Joint Government-Industry Steering Committee on Intensive Timber Harvesting. *Clearcutting in the Adirondacks.* Albany, N.Y., The Committee, 1981. 37p.
Committee report. Outlines 5 goals for Adirondack forests. Divided into 3 chapters: (1) The Future of the Adirondack Forest (2) Today's Adirondack Forest (3) Adirondack Forest Management. Photos, tables, figures, notes.

548. Northeastern Forest Experiment Station. *Preliminary Forest Survey Statistics by Counties and Units: New York.* Upper Darby, PA., Northeastern Forest Experiment Station, 1968. iii, 33p.
NAR

549. Reinckens, Thomas E. *Wood for Fuel: Generating Electricity in Tupper Lake, N.Y.* Plattsburgh, N.Y., State University of New York, Technical Assistance Center, 1978. 52 lvs.
Investigates wood and its cost and availability for 8 megawatt electricity-producing plant in Tupper Lake. Charts, graphs and appendices.

550. Temporary State Commission on Tug Hill. *Wood Energy Development and the Future of the Forests: Opportunities and Concerns.* Watertown, N.Y., Temporary State Commission, 1985. 95p.
Transcripts of 2 public forums sponsored by the Commission. Forums took place on May 8 and 9 in 1985 in Camden, New York and Lowville, New York respectively. Comments on the impact of large scale industrial/commercial wood energy development upon forests and employment.

### Resorts and Hotels

551. Bensen, Arthur L. *The Story of a New York City Tenderfoot and His Adirondack Mountain Adventure.* North Hudson, N.Y., Frontier Town Productions Inc., 1970. 130p.

Human interest story of Frontier Town, a tourist attraction in North Hudson, New York. A potpourri of information about Frontier Town, and the history, social and economic life of the eastern Adirondacks.

552. Buckell, Betty Ahearn. *Old Lake George Hotels: A Pictorial Review.* Lake George, N.Y., Buckell, 1986. 99p.

Each photo or illus. accompanied by short written description. Illus.

553. Higby, Roy C. *A Man From the Past.* Big Moose, N.Y., Big Moose Press, 1974. 157p.

Edited by Ray Hanlon, illustrated by Donald Lux. The story of the Higby family resort at Big Moose Lake from its beginning in 1875. Social history of the region, especially the rural life skills that were common until the past generation or two. Two printings in 1974.

554. New York State Ski Area Operators Association. *Statement of Review and Recommendations.* s.l., The Association, 1973. 27p.

NAR

555. Richardson, Raymond J. *Big Tupper Ski Area Expansion: An Economic Impact Study.* Plattsburgh, N.Y., State University of New York, Technical Assistance Center, 1972. 33 lvs.

Positive statement of impact of expansion of Big Tupper Ski Area on Big Tupper region. Discusses primary and secondary job impact, and expected increase in the number of skiers and their spending. Tables, charts and map.

556. Wessels, William L. *An Old Time Inn: Blue Mountain Lake House; Adirondack Museum.* Lake George, N.Y., Adirondack Resorts Press, 1972. 32p.

Story of Blue Mountain House property over 100 years from post-Civil War era through early 1970s. Property became site of Adirondack Museum.

## Communications, Transportation and Public Works

### General

557. Adirondack Economic Development Corporation. *Airport Master Plan: Phase II Report: Adirondack Airport, Saranac Lake, New York.* Liverpool, N.Y., Calocerinos & Spina, 1990. 1 v.

Presents and evaluates various alternatives for Airport project. Focuses on environmental considerations. Maps, tables, charts.

558. Maxwell, John F. *Air Travel in the North Country of New York and Vermont.* Plattsburgh, N.Y., State University of New York, Technical Assistance Center, 1974. 88 lvs.

Technical study of air travel in northern New York and northern Vermont in mid-1970s. Study concluded that gathered data could be used to support arguments for upgraded service to air carriers. Tables, graphs.

### Railroads

559. Allen, Richard S., et al. *Rails in the North Woods.* Lakemont, N.Y., North Country Books, 1973. xiii, 194p.; Sylvan Beach, N.Y., North Country Books, 1978. xiii, 202p.

Story of shortline railroads in northern New York. Rev. ed. includes 2 or 3 rail lines not covered in the first ed. Illus. by John Mahaffy.

560. Borrup, Roger. *Plattsburgh Traction Company, Plattsbrugh, N.Y. 1895-1929 Transportation Bulletin No. 78.* Warehouse Point, CT., Connecticut Valley Chapter, National Railway Historical Society, 1971, 1992. 48p.

Brief history of 6.5 mile trolley line that served Plattsburgh between 1895 and 1929. Reprints and photos from Plattsburgh newspapers tell the story of this rail line.

561. Dempsey, William M. *A Study of the Economic Feasibility and Economic Impact of Restoring Selected Services on the Remsen-Lake Placid Railroad.* Plattsburgh, N.Y., State University of New York,

Technical Assistance Center, 1975. iv, 84 lvs.

Detailed, statistical analysis of economic issues in reopening Remsen-Lake Placid railroad. Maps, charts, bibliography.

562. Gardner, Edward. *Adirondack Vistas.* Harrison, N.Y., Harbor Hill Books, 1974. 49 lvs.

Railroads in the Adirondack region. Maps, timetables, illus.

563. Harter, Henry A. *Fairy Tale Railroad: The Mohawk and Malone: from the Mohawk through the Adirondacks to the St. Lawrence.* Sylvan Beach, N.Y., North Country Books, 1979; Utica, New York, 1992. 310p.

History of Mohawk and Malone R.R. with information on branch and connecting lines. Appendices contain additional information: companies, stations, chronology, derailments and accidents. Photos, bibliography. Paper in 1992.

564. Kudish, Michael. *Where Did the Tracks Go: Following Railroad Grades in the Adirondacks.* Saranac Lake, N.Y., Chauncy Press, 1985. 246p.

Valuable work on railroad lines in Adirondack region. Provides location, date of establishment/abandonment, details of daily operations. Substantive introductory essay.

565. Lahey, Carol. *Marketing Analysis for Proposed Adirondack Railroad.* Plattsburgh, N.Y., Economic Development and Technical Assistance Center, 1982. 90p.

Study of 118-mile-long Adirondack railroad from Utica to Remsen to Lake Placid. Discusses history, anticipated benefits, historical passenger use of railroad line and a financial analysis. Maps, appendices.

566. Nestle, David F. *A History of the Hudson Valley Railway: Saratoga through Car.* Greenwich, N.Y., Nestle, 1967. 104p.

Railroad served Glens Falls and Lake George at its northern end. Photos, charts, schedules.

567. Nimke, R.W. *The Rutland: 60 Years of Trying: Vol. VI, Part 1 & 2, The O & LC Division.* Walpole, N.H., R.W. Nimke, 1989. 2 v.

The Ogdensburg and Lake Champlain Line served northern Clinton, Franklin and St. Lawrence Counties. Charts, maps, elevation drawings and reprints of assorted company documents. Part II is about passenger and freight operations. Both volumes have folded maps. No table of contents or index. Illus.

568. Shaughnessy, Jim. *Delaware & Hudson.* Berkeley, CA., Howell-North, 1967, 1982. xii, 476p.

History of Delaware & Hudson railroad with 3 chapters about northern New York and the Adirondacks.

## Roads and Bridges

569. Allen, Richard S., (comp.) *Old North Country Bridges.* Utica, N.Y., North Country Books, 1983. 110p.

Pictorial on covered bridges in Adirondack/North Country region. Not all bridges are located within the Adirondack Park. Nicely done tribute to a once practical and aesthetically pleasing type of bridge.

570. Engelhart, Steven. *Crossing the River: Historic Bridges of the AuSable River.* Keeseville, N.Y., Friends of Keeseville, Inc., 1991. 42p.

Chronicles bridges of AuSable River Valley. Community-by-community description of bridges. Plates, maps.

571. Gurney, Gary F. *Evaluation of Adirondack Park Highway Signs.* Albany, N.Y., Engineering Research and Development Bureau, New York State Dept. of Transportation, 1977. 40p.

Research report assessing aesthetics and visibility of Adirondack Park yellow and brown signs. Charts, illus.

## Steamboats and Other Carriers

572. Buckell, Betty Ahearn. *Lake George Boats.* s.l., Buckle Press, 1990. 181p.

Discusses steam and gasoline boats and launches. Work also covers water regattas and various steamboat and commercial operations. Many individual boats are mentioned by name and/or pictured. Index, photos, bibliography, glossary. Map of Lake George on inside covers.

573. Crisman, Kevin J. *The History and Construction of the United States Schooner Ticonderoga.* Alexan-

dria, VA., Eyrie Publications, 1983. 82p.

The Ticonderoga was a commercial vessel, then a warship on Lake Champlain during the War of 1812. Part I is a history of the schooner, and Part II is an in-depth recapitulation of the vessel's construction. Appendices, bibliography. Limited ed.

574. Crowley, William. *Rushton's Rowboats and Canoes: The 1903 Catalog in Perspective.* Blue Mountain Lake, N.Y., Adirondack Museum; Camden, ME., International Marine Pub. Co., 1983. xiii, 80p.; 2nd printing, 1992.

Reprint of Rushton's 1903 catalog with introductory essay by Crowley on Rushton and his canoe business. Photos from Adirondack Museum's canoe collection. Index.

575. Durant, Kenneth. *The Naptha Launch.* Blue Mountain Lake, N.Y., Adirondack Museum, 1976. 31p.

Short work on naptha power boats in the Adirondacks. Naptha is a volatile, petroleum-based fuel. Illus., 1500 copies.

576. Durant, Kenneth & Helen Durant. *The Adirondack Guide-Boat.* Blue Mountain Lake, N.Y., Adirondack Museum; Camden, ME., International Marine Pub. Co., 1980, 1986. xviii, 250p.

Popular Adirondack book. Based on Ken Durant's lifelong interest in guide-boats; completed by his wife Helen Durant. Guide-boat plans and commentary by John Gardner. Part I provides historical background and context of the guide-boat's development. Description, construction and use of guide boats covered in Part II.

577. Glenn, Morris F. *Glenn's History of Lake Champlain (New York and Vermont): Volume 1; The Naptha Launch on Lake Champlain.* Alexandria, VA., Glenn, 1980. 27 lvs.

Naptha-fueled boats were familiar in the 1880s on Lake Champlain, and were the first individually-owned power craft. Naptha launches were popular with the wealthy of the day. Author was surprised by the dearth of information on the subject. Discusses operating a naptha launch, and the naptha engine. References, plates, illus.

578. Glenn, Morris F. *Glenn's History of Lake Champlain (New York and Vermont) Volume 2: Occasional Lists of Shipping on Lake Champlain.* Alexandria, VA., Glenn, 1980. 62 lvs.

Only 10 copies. Selected commercial shipping records for Lake Champlain between 1830-1930. Introductory essay "Lake Champlain Shipping" by the author. Illus., charts, maps.

579. Glenn, Morris F. *Glenn's History of Lake Champlain: Volume 3; Steam Navigation.* Alexandria, VA., Glenn, 1980. Unpaged.

Reference work consists of copy of Gideon Lathrop's diary concerning steam navigation on Lake Champlain.

580. Glenn, Morris F. *Glenn's History of Lake Champlain: Volume 5; Lozier Launches.* Alexandria, VA., Glenn, 1980. Unpaged.

Short history of the Lozier Motor Company. Most of work is advertisements, manuals, and written material about the company and Lozier family. Very limited. ed.

581. Glenn, Morris F. *Glenn's History of Lake Champlain: Volume 6; Lake Champlain Sailabouts and Cape Cod Knockabouts.* Alexandria, VA., Glenn, 1980. 30p.

History of two varieties of pleasure craft used on Lake Champlain.

582. Glenn, Morris F. *Glenn's History of Lake Champlain: Volume 7; Power Boats.* Alexandria, VA., Glenn, 1980. Unpaged.

Reference work on power boats. Reprinted list of boat builders in New York and Vermont from 1918.

583. Glenn, Morris F. *Glenn's History of Lake Champlain: Volume 8; Sail Canoes and Skiffs.* Alexandria, VA., Glenn, 1980. Unpaged.

Collected information from Adirondacks and Lake Champlain on these kinds of crafts. Mention made of J.H. Rushton as well as of the St. Lawrence skiff.

584. Lozier Motor Company. *Lozier Marine Gas Engines.* Plattsburgh, Lozier Motor Co., 1901; reprint, Vestal, N.Y., Vestal Press, 1984. 48p.

Reprint of 1901 catalog of Plattsburgh-based company. Thoroughly illustrated description of company's 2 cycle engines.

# Architecture

585. Domblewski, Mary Ellen. *The Adirondack Camp of the Last Quarter of the Nineteenth Century: A Wilderness Architecture.* Ithaca, N.Y., Cornell University, 1974; Ithaca, N.Y., Cornell University Photo Service, 1977. vi, 181 lvs.

Places the Adirondack camp in the milieu of American summer camp architecture. Discusses how camp architecture reflected American attitudes towards wilderness in late 19th century. Focuses on the Durant camps and their influence locally, regionally, and nationally. Appendix entitled "Social History and Life Styles of the Late Nineteenth Century Adirondack Camp." Bibliography.

586. Everest, Allan S. *Our North Country Heritage: Architecture Worth Saving in Clinton and Essex Counties.* Plattsburgh, N.Y., Tundra Books, 1972. 143p.

Pictorial work. This volume builds upon work of 'Pioneer Homes' and is more inclusive, covering the period 1740-1910. Excellent photos. Glossary of architectural terms.

587. Everest, Allan S. *Pioneer Homes of Clinton County 1790-1820.* Plattsburgh, N.Y., Clinton County Historical Association, 1966, 1971. 96p.

Pictorial work. Each of the 178 photos of a pioneer home is accompanied by a short, written description, including location.

588. Gallos, Philip L. *Cure Cottages of Saranac Lake: Architecture and History of a Pioneer Health Resort.* Saranac Lake, N.Y., Historic Saranac Lake, 1985. xi, 186p.

Architecture and history of cure cottages and health industry in Saranac Lake, New York. Photos and short essays describe the residences. Index, bibliography.

589. Hadden, Jean, & Peter LaGrasse & Carol LaGrasse. *An Enduring Heritage: A Study of Prominent Buildings in Stony Creek Center.* Stony Creek, N.Y., Stony Creek Community Association, 1989. 46p.

Architectural study of Stony Creek, New York; prominent buildings, residences, churches highlighted with construction history and architectural commentary. Illus.

590. Howard, Hugh. *The Preservationist's Progress: Architectural Adventures in Conserving Yesterday's Houses.* New York, N.Y., Farrar, Straus, and Giroux, 1991. 272p.

Second chapter about Essex Community Heritage Organization, a local preservation group and its role in protecting one of the community's old Victorian homes. Illus.

591. McGowan, Robert H. *Architecture from the Adirondack Foothills: Folk and Designed Architecture of Franklin County, New York.* Malone, N.Y., Franklin County Historical and Museum Society, 1977, 1988. 112p.

Excellent book on architecture of Franklin County, New York. Mostly northern sections of county outside the Park boundary. Some are in southern Franklin County; Great Camps and Litchfield Castle as well as houses, cabins, churches and barns. Excellent map of westward migration through northern N.Y. in nineteenth century. Illus., bibliography.

592. McNulty, George F. and Margaret Schein. *Essex, The Architectural Heritage.* Burlington, VT., Queen City Printers, 1971. 52p.

Architectural highlights of the village of Essex in Essex County, New York. Essex lies just outside of the boundary of the Adirondack Park. Contains an essay on architectural styles: Colonial, Federal, Greek Revival, and Victorian. Illus.

# Life and Manners

## General

593. Alibrandi, Tom with Frank Armani. *Privileged Information.* New York, N.Y., Dodd, Mead & Co., 1984. 215p.; reprint, New York, New York, HarperPaperbacks, 1991. xiii, 318p.

Frank H. Armani was defense attorney for murderer, Robert Garrow. Garrow told Armani where 2 of his victims were buried. Armani refused to divulge information because it would have violated client-lawyer confidentiality. Paperback ed. in 1991.

594. Bartholomew, Paul, et al. *Monsters of the North Woods.* Whitehall, N.Y., Bartholomew, 1980. 5,

118p.; 1st thus, Utica, N.Y., North Country Books, 1992. 136p.

Bigfoot lore and sightings in the Adirondacks and Green Mountains. Dozens of accounts of sightings from Colonial to contemporary times. Illus.

595. Bentley, Sudjai N. *Oriental Cooking in the Adirondacks.* Tupper Lake, N.Y., Bentley, 1992. 169p.

596. Betters, Fran. *Adirondack Fish & Game Recipes.* Wilmington, N.Y., Adirondack Sports Publications, 1993. 92p.

597. Blue Mountain Lake United Methodist Church. *Blue Mountain Lake's Favorite Recipes.* Blue Mountain Lake, N.Y., United Methodist Church, 1982. 132p.

598. Blue Mountain Lake United Methodist Church. *Blue Mountain Lake's Favorite Recipes No. 2.* Blue Mountain Lake, United Methodist Church, 1990. 146p.

599. Brandon, Craig. *Murder in the Adirondacks: An American Tragedy Revisited.* Utica, N.Y., North Country Books, 1986. 380p.

Detailed account of Grace Brown and Chester Gillette murder case in 1906. Follows the case from Gillette and Brown's relationship in Cortland to Grace Brown's death in Big Moose Lake to Chester Gillette's trial and execution. Well researched book based on newspaper accounts and letters. Index and bibliography.

600. Brownell, Joseph W. & Patricia Wawrzaszek. *Adirondack Tragedy: The Gillette Murder Case of 1906.* Interlaken, N.Y., Heart of the Lakes Publishing, 1986. 216p.

Chester Gillette murder case. Follows Gillette's life from early years to his execution in 1907. Bibliography.

601. Clinton County Historical Museum. *Clinton Prison at Dannemora.* Plattsburgh, N.Y., Clinton County Historical Museum, 1987. 52p.

Catalog for exhibit about Clinton Correctional Facility. Prison was founded in 1845. It is now a maximum security prison for 2,700 inmates with 1,400 workers. Exhibit included photos and objects from nineteenth and twentieth centuries.

602. Colton Neighborhood Center. *Adirondack Country Cookbook.* Colton, N.Y., Colton Neighborhood Center Advisory Board, 1968. 206p.

603. Committee for Economic Development of Essex County. *The Adirondack Collection of Edible Inspirations.* Keeseville, N.Y., The Committee, 1992. 98p.

604. Crowell, Marnie Reed. *Greener Pastures.* New York, N.Y., Funk and Wagnells, 1973; paper, Canton, N.Y., Greener Pastures, Inc., 1983. ix, 242p.

About rural life in the northern Adirondack foothills, Pierrepont, New York, just outside the Blue Line. Crowell writes about rural life without romanticizing it. Each chapter covers the activities of a month of the year.

605. DeGarmo, Todd. *Festival of the Adirondacks: Celebrating Living Cultural Traditions.* Glens Falls, N.Y., Crandall Library, 1990. 30p.

Catalog for festival held on September 15, 1990. Lists numerous artists and their crafts, with photo and brief information on each individual. In addition, there are four articles based on presentations: DeGarmo on folk tradition and regional tourism; Varick A. Chittenden on food; Bruce G. Cole on the oral tradition; Ellen McHale on country music in the Adirondacks.

606. Essex County Adirondack Garden Club. *Food, Flowers, and Fireworks: Bicentennial Cookbook.* s.l., The Club, 1975. 192p.

607. Everest, Allan S. *Rum Across the Border: The Prohibition Era in Northern New York.* Syracuse, N.Y., Syracuse University Press, 1978. ix, 172p.

A fascinating history of bootlegging in northern New York around Plattsburgh and Champlain. Much of the information was obtained through interviews with participants. Paper ed. in 1991.

608. Fickbohm, Beverly. *Top of the Woodstove Cookbook.* Lowville, N.Y., Beverly Fickbolm, 1981. 50p.

609. Hill, Donna M. *The Neighborhood Cookbook.* Saranac Lake, N.Y., Hill, 1985.

610. Hoffman, Nancy. *Canaras Cookbook.* Canton, N.Y., St. Lawrence University Conference Center, n.d. 72p.

611. Hopkinton Bicentennial Committee. *Hopkinton Maple Festival Cookbook*. Hopkinton, N.Y., Hopkinton Bicentennial Committee, 1976. 82p.

612. LaBastille, Anne. *Women and Wilderness*. San Francisco, CA, Sierra Club Books, 1980. xi, 310p.

Study of women and wilderness with background discussion of frontier women by Adirondack guide, writer and conservationist. Part II profiles a dozen women and their wilderness-related roles and activities. Two chapters with Adirondack content. Bibliography, index, afterword. Paper edition in 1984.

613. League of Women Voters, Plattsburgh. *Plattsburgh: A Citizen's Handbook; A Description of Government in Clinton County, the Town of Plattsburgh and the City of Plattsburgh*. Plattsburgh, N.Y., League of Women Voters, 1973. 64p.

Brief look at important social and political structures in Plattsburgh in early 1970s. Information on town, county and city government, municipal services; police and fire services as well as health, education, recreation, zoning. Maps, charts, illus.

614. Manthei, George. *Wild & Famous: Fish and Game Cookbook; A Treasury of Fish and Game Recipes and Stories*. Plattsburgh, N.Y., Schildge Publishing Co., 1990. 130p.

615. Morrisonville Methodist Church. *Morrisonville Cookbook*. Morrisonville, N.Y., Morrisonville Methodist Church, 1948; reprint, Plattsburgh, N.Y., Clinton County Historical Association, 1975. 68p.

616. National Association of Retired Federal Employees, Tupper Lake. *Rhubarb & Sauerkraut Recipes*. Tupper Lake, N.Y., Adirondack Mountain Chapter, 1986.102p.

617. Old Forge Library. *Old Forge Library Cookbook*. Old Forge, N.Y., The Old Forge Library, 1987. 98p.

618. Orcutt, Georgia. (comp.). *The Best Recipes from New York State Inns*. Dublin, N.H., Yankee Books, 1987. 319p.

619. Ortloff, George C. *A Lady in the Lake: The True Account of Death and Discovery in Lake Placid*. Lake Placid, NY: With Pipe and Book, 1985. 51p.

Mabel Douglas drowned in Lake Placid in September 1933, but her body was not recovered until 30 years later. Story of the recovery, autopsy and coroner's ruling of accidental death, based on interviews. Illus.

620. Phillips, Judy. *Reflections and Confections of the Adirondacks*. s.l., s.n., 1982, 1986. 71p.

621. Ratner, Shanna E. *Diversified Household Survival Strategies and Natural Resource Use in the Adirondacks: A Case Study of Crown Point, New York*. Ithaca, N.Y., Cornell University, 1984. 255 lvs.

Study of natural resource use in economically depressed area of rural New York. Based on a random survey of 60 households. After wages and social security, resource use was third largest source of income. Ratner estimates the gross value of annual resource production in Crown Point at that time at over $900,000. Ratner also outlines ways to improve contribution of resource based activities to local economies. Bibliography.

622. Retired Senior Volunteer Program of Franklin County. *The Blueberry Cookbook*. Malone, N.Y., Retired Senior Volunteer Program, 1981. 48p.

623. Retired Senior Volunteer Program of Franklin County. *The Zucchini Cookbook*. Malone, N.Y., Retired Senior Volunteer Program, 1977. 178p.

624. Runyon, Linda. *Lawn Food Cook Book (Groceries in the Backyard)*. Warrensburg, N.Y., Runyon Institute, 1985. 46p.

625. Runyon, Linda. *A Survival Acre: 50 Northeastern Wild Foods & Medicines: A Basic Guide*. Saranac Lake, N.Y., The Chauncy Press, 1985. 43p.

Guide book to regional wild foods. Each entry is accompanied by a small drawing by the author. Information provided: name, Latin name, history, and present uses. Book also contains wild food recipes and information on medicinal uses of plants. Author has ties to Adirondack region.

626. St. Lawrence County Historical Association. *Landmarks and Lemon Crackers*. Canton, N.Y., St. Lawrence County Historical Association, 1981. 212p.

627. Schildge, Sue. *Famous Adirondack Restuarants and Recipes*. Plattsburgh, N.Y., Schildge Publishing, 1984, 1986, 1989; rev. ed., 1992. 212p.

628. Schildge, Sue. *Tastes of the Adirondack Restaurants.* Plattsburgh, N.Y., Schildge Publishing Co., 1985, 1988. xi, 236p.

629. Senior Citizen Group II. *Bicentennial Heritage Cooks.* Plattsburgh, N.Y., Town of Plattsburgh, 1985.

630. Stillwater Hunting Club. *The Stillwater Cookbook.* Canton, N.Y., The Stillwater Hunting Club, 1989.

631. Tupper Lake Business and Professional Women's Club. *The Bear Cupboard Cookbook.* Tupper Lake, N.Y., The Club, 1987. 90p.

632. V.F.W. Ladies Auxiliary. *Best Ever Palate Pleasers,* Warrensburg, N.Y., The Auxiliary, 1986. 76p.

633. Women's College Scholarship Club. *Classic Cookbook.* Saranac Lake, N.Y., The Club, 1988.

## Folklore and Ballads

634. Aber, Ted. *Adirondack Folks.* Prospect, N.Y., Prospect Books, 1980, 1982. xii, 218p.

Nearly 80 short stories, tales and anecdotes of people and their way of life in Hamilton County, New York. Aber was a well-known figure in the preservation and interpretation of Hamilton County history.

635. Bethke, Robert D. *Adirondack Voices, Woodsmen and Woods Lore.* Champaign, Ill, University of Illinois Press, 1981. 148p.

Storytelling and folk music of people who worked in the woods, mostly in southern St. Lawrence County. Recalls lumber camps and working in the woods. Discusses Sunday Rock. Ham Ferry, Ted Ashlaw, and others.

636. Carr, Harvey. Edited by Vaughn Ward. *I Was On the Wrong Bear: Adirondack Tall Tales.* Greenfield Center, N.Y., Greenfield Press, 1992. 165p.

Over five dozen stories and yarns. Nicely illus. by Deborah Delaney.

637. Peck, James Glenn. *High Country Pathways: Tales of the Adirondacks, Book 1.* Amsterdam, N.Y., Noteworthy, 1978. 88p.; reprint, *Night Camp: Tales of the Adirondacks.* Utica, N.Y., North Country Books, 1987. 119p.

A collection of stories, folklore from southeastern Adirondacks. Rev. enhanced ed. of *High Country Pathways,* first published in 1978. Fifteen additional stories and anecdotes. Peck's style is simple, direct, almost conversational. Illustrated by John Mahaffy.

638. Sawyer, Donald J. *Shoo-Fly and Other Folk Tales from Upstate.* Gloversville, N.Y., Mayfield Books, 1984. xiii, 152p.

Folklore of Fulton County, Mohawk Valley uplands and southern Adirondack foothills.

639. Smith, Adeline. *The Gentle Land.* s.l., s.n., 1965; reprint, 1980. 80p.

Reminiscences, local history and yarns about Jay, Upper Jay, Keene, Ausable Forks, and Clintonville. No illus.

640. Stiles, Fred Tracy. *From Then till Now: History and Tales of the Adirondack Foothills.* Hudson Falls, N.Y., Washington County Historical Society, 1978, 1980. 207p.

Family and oral history as well as anecdotes from Washington County. Chapters and photos on smaller settlements and their residents, Lake Champlain and Lake George. Bibliography.

641. Tyler, Helen Escha. *In Them Thar Hills: Folk Tales of the Adirondacks.* Saranac Lake, N.Y., Currier Press, 1968. 104p.

Brief stories, most based on real happenings, about 30 in number. Illustrated by Suzanne Tubby Batra.

642. Tyler, Helen Escha. *Log Cabin Days: Folk Tales of the Adirondacks.* Saranac Lake, N.Y., Currier Press, 1969. 110p.

Mostly anecdotes based on actual happenings in the Adirondacks. The balance are 'tall tales'. Titles such as "A Hard Winter," "Spring Thaw," and "A Logging Operation" reflect Adirondack themes.

643. Tyler, Helen Escha. *Mountain Memories: Folk Tales of the Adirondacks.* Saranac Lake, N.Y., Currier Press, 1974. 118p.

Third book of folk stories by Tyler, many of which first appeared in her columns in the *Adirondack Daily Enterprise.*

644. Tyler, Helen Escha. *This 'n' That: Folk Tales of the Adirondacks*. Saranac Lake, N.Y., Currier Press, 1983. 102p.

Twenty-three folktales. Anecdotal accounts of real events; some tall tales, which are indentified as fictional. Illus. by Suzanne Tubby Baker.

645. Vinton, John. *A Treasury of Great Adirondack Stories*. Utica, N.Y., North Country Books, 1991. 155p.

Thirty stories. Each story is preceded by brief passage identifying the location where the story occurred, its source and occasionally a brief description. Map at back of book identifies location of each story. Vinton has also provided a list of sources by original author. Illus. by Larry Miller. Contains some Seneca Ray Stoddard visual work. Intro. by George D. Davis.

646. Ward, Vaughn. *I Always Tell the Truth (Even If I Have to Lie to Do It!)*. Greenfield Center, N.Y., Greenfield Review Press, 1990. 114p.

Tall tales from the Adirondacks by contemporary storytellers. Illus. by Deborah Delaney. Bibliography.

647. Warner, Anne. *Traditional American Folk Songs from the Anne & Frank Warner Collection*. Syracuse, N.Y., Syracuse University Press, 1984. xxiii, 501p.

Discography. Authors spent time in Adirondacks over the years and collected regional songs. Chapter 2 highlights songs of New York State, and comprises about one-sixth of the book. Also in paper in 1985.

648. Wells, Leila. *Memories of the Good Old Days*. Essex, N.Y., Museum of Poke-O-Moonshine, 1969. 24p.

Short vignettes about daily life while author was growing up in the late nineteenth century in northern New York. Illus. by Sister Mary Felicitas Wells.

649. Wells, Leila. *Once Upon a Time*. Elizabethtown, N.Y., Denton Publications, 1971. 48p.

Short reminiscences about daily life in the late nineteenth and early twentieth century in Essex County, N.Y. Illus. by Sister Mary Felicitas Wells.

650. Wells, Leila. *Times Have Changed*. Elizabethtown, N.Y., Denton Publications, 1973. 48p.

Reminiscences of life in Keene Valley and Lake Placid in the Adirondacks. Offers insights into daily life for rural residents in the early 20th century. Illus. by Sister Mary Felicitas Wells.

651. Zarzynski, Joseph W. *Champ: Beyond the Legend*. Port Henry, N.Y., Bannister Publications, 1984. 224p.; reprint, Wilton, N.Y., M-Z Information, 1988. 240p.

"Champ" refers to the Lake Champlain monster. Book pulls together existing information on Champ as of the early 1980s. Details on sightings, photos, biology of Lake Champlain, and possible explanations make for interesting reading. Maps, illus., bibliography.

652. Zarzynski, Joseph W. *Monster Wrecks of Loch Ness and Lake Champlain*. Wilton, N.Y., M-Z Information, 1986. 111p.

Reveals other mysteries and interesting facts discovered about Lake Champlain and Loch Ness in the course of searching for their respective monsters. Bibliography.

## Printing and Publishing

653. Fowler, Barney. *Adirondack Album*. Schenectady, N.Y., Outdoor Associates, 1974. 200p.

A photo-journalistic look at past events in the Adirondack region as well as more recent happenings. Focuses on interesting people and places. Good section on Adirondack wildlife. Book contains over 300 illus.

654. Fowler, Barney. *Adirondack Album: Volume II*. Schenectady, N.Y., Outdoor Associates, 1980. 200p.

Second volume by Fowler. The Adirondack Mountain region as seen through the eyes of a newspaper writer. Fowler concentrates on human interest stories. Numerous photos. Entertaining and informative book.

655. Fowler, Barney. *Adirondack Album: Volume III*. Schenectady, N.Y. Outdoor Associates, 1982. 192p.

Volume III continues Fowler's earlier format and the themes of the earlier two works. Human interest stories and photos of Adirondack people, places and wildlife. Fowler died in 1986.

656. Gallos, Phil. *By Foot in the Adirondacks*. Saranac Lake, N.Y., Adirondack Publishing Co., Inc., 1972. 142p.

Selected newspaper columns that first appeared in the *Adirondack Daily Enterprise* and *Lake Placid News*. Not a guidebook in the formal sense, but an almanac of sorts. Precursor of the successful format used in the *Discover the Adirondacks Series*, based on Russell Carson's approach. Includes history and natural history. Focuses on specific areas: Ampersand, Cascades, Heart Lake, Keene Valley, Lake Placid, McKenzie, St. Huberts, Saranac Inn, and Saranac Lake.

657. Hall, Robert F. *Pages from Adirondack History*. Fleischmanns, N.Y., Purple Mt. Press, 1992. 152p.
Collected newspaper pieces by Hall on Adirondack history; mostly about eastern Adirondack people and places.

658. Metivier, Donald. *Metivier on: Saratoga, Glens Falls, Lake George and the Adirondacks*. Champaign, IL., Sagamore, 1993. x, 228p.
Collected newspaper columns from Glens Falls papers with Adirondack content.

659. Munsell, Joel. *Bibliotheca Munselliana: A Catalogue of the Books and Pamphlets Issued from the Press of Joel Munsell from the Year 1828 to 1870*. Albany, N.Y., Munsell, 1872; reprint, New York, N.Y., Burt Franklin, 1969. 191p.
Reprint of a catalog of the books and pamphlets from the press of Joel Munsell. Munsell was an important nineteenth century publisher of northern New York materials, such as Houghs' numerous histories. Munsell lived and worked in Albany, N.Y.

660. Parks, O.Kenneth. *Maple Sugar Sticks*. Lake Placid, N.Y., Parks, 1975. 67p.
Recollections of the Adirondacks. Collected newspaper columns from the *Lake Placid News*.

661. Rice, Seaver. *Along the Quinebaug: Tales*. Bethesda, MD., Vandergriff Research, 1976. iii, 56p.
Rice was born in Saranac Lake, New York and is a descendant of the town's founder. Collected newspaper columns that first appeared in Southbridge, MA. *Evening News*. Some Adirondack content.

662. Rice, Seaver. *The Apple Butter Winter and Other New England Tales*. Millersville, MD, Vandergriff Research, 1982. 29p.
Articles by Saranac Lake native, descended from that village's founder, Pliny Miller. Illus. Some Adirondack content.

663. Taylor, Daniel T. *The Shores of Champlain*. Collected from *The Champlain Counselor*, Rouses Point, N.Y., 1892; reprint, *The North Countryman*, 1937; reprint, Champlain, N.Y., Moorsfield Press, 1979. 43p.
Collected newspaper columns about the towns along the New York side of Lake Champlain and their residents in the late 19th century. Taylor was a native of Rouses Point. 150 copy edition printed but not issued in 1937.

# *Health and Medicine*

664. Caldwell, Mark. *The Last Crusade: The War on Consumption 1862-1954*. New York, N.Y., Atheneum, 1988. 336p.

Chronicles the fight against tuberculosis and the "sanitarium culture" it fostered. Much information on role of Saranac Lake and Edward Livingston Trudeau. Bibliography.

665. Mooney, Elizabeth. *In the Shadow of the White Plague: A Memoir*. New York, N.Y., Crowell, 1978. 196p.

A memoir about the author's mother who had tuberculosis in the early 1920s and went to recover in Saranac Lake. TB was still a killer disease and the impact on the patient's family was often devastating. In an age when there is renewed concern over TB, Mooney's book is a poignant reminder.

# *Religious Life and History*

666. Becker, Martin Joseph. *A History of Catholic Life in the Diocese of Albany, 1609-1864*. New York, N.Y., Fordham University, 1973; New York, N.Y., U.S. Catholic Historical Society, 1975. 353p.

Doctoral thesis done in 1973. Scholarly study of Catholic Church in northern New York from time of Champlain to eve of the Civil War. Relies upon primary sources to chronicle history of Albany Diocese. Maps, bibliography.

667. Bodine, Sam & William Hurd. *Church of the Ascension: The First 100 Years*. Saranac Inn Post Office, N.Y., Church of the Ascension, 1984. 37p.

Based on earlier booklet updated to celebrate the centennial of this unique church building constructed from logs. Map of Upper Saranac Lake, New York on the inside of the front and back cover. Information on church, rectory, clergy and church organ. Appendices on Church Committee, marriages, baptisms, and memorials.

668. Bullock, Mary and Helen Arthur. *History of the United Congregations Church 1821-1971*. Elizabethtown, N.Y., Denton Publications, 1971. 39p.

Church history, mostly text. Picture of church on cover.

669. Engel, Herbert M. *Shtetl in the Adirondacks: The Story of Gloversville and Its Jews*. Fleischmanns, N.Y., Purple Mountain Press, 1991. 220p.

History of the Jewish congregation in this Fulton County community. Highlights the congregation's adaptability to a small town environment and its role in the glove making industry. Illus., index, notes.

670. First Presbyterian Church of Plattsburgh. *175th Anniversary, October First 1797-1972*. Plattsburgh, N.Y., First Presbyterian Church, 1972. 31p.

History of church, list of pastors, program for anniversary service, chronological listing of important church dates. Letters of commendation from President Nixon and Governor Rockefeller. Poem on inside of back cover written by late Thomas John Carlisle. Illus., portraits.

671. Koppe, Ellie Reed. *The Big Moose Community Chapel: First Fifty Years*. Big Moose, N.Y., Trustees of the Big Moose Community Chapel, 1981. 138p.

Story of the construction of Big Moose Chapel made possible by the community's ecumenical spirit. Appendices include lists of charter members, by-laws, ministers, trustees and officers, gifts of furnishings, etc. For related information see *The Earl Covey Story* in Reprint Section.

672. McKenna, Rusty Hovey. *St. Agnes, Lake Placid, New York: An Informal History of the Catholic Community of the Olympic Village, 1894-1984*. s.l., s.n., 1984. 116p.

Pictorial work. Chronology of Catholic parish in Lake Placid.

673. St. Bernard's Church. *St. Bernard's Church*. Saranac Lake, N.Y., Currier Press, 1969. Unpaged.

Pictorial work. About rebuilding of St. Bernard's after 1967 fire. Pictures of new church, its adornments as well as previous buildings.

674. St. John the Baptist Church. *St. John the Baptist Church, Plattsburgh, N.Y.: The First Century 1875-1975*. Plattsburgh, N.Y., St. John the Baptist Church, 1975. 40p.

Centennial publication of church and its parish. History, centennial calendar. Profiles of parish, its societies, councils and other affiliations. Parish membership list, photos.

675. Swarthout, Paul F. *The Hills Beyond the Hills: 400 Years in the Ministry*. Lakemont, N.Y., North Country Books, 1971. 327p.

Eight ministers describe their ministries. In Chapter 8 Frank Reed describes his years of serving as a minister in the Adirondack Region. Illus.

676. Taylor, Sister Mary Christine. *A History of Catholicism in the North Country*. Camden, N.Y., A. M. Farnsworth Sons, Inc., 1972. xii, 282p.

History of Diocese of Ogdensburg which was established in 1872 when it was separated from the Diocese of Albany. The Ogdensburg Diocese includes St. Lawrence, Franklin, Clinton, Jefferson, Lewis, and Essex County. Numerous appendices include lists of past and present priests, defunct parishes, missions, Catholic hospitals, schools, schools of nursing and other institutions.

677. Taylor, Sister Mary Christine. *A History of the Foundations of Catholicism in Northern New York.* St. Louis, MO., St. Louis University, 1967. 441 lvs.; reprint, New York, N.Y., United States Catholic Historical Society, 1976. xi, 440p.

History of Catholicism in Northern New York from an Indian mission to a modern diocese, comprised of Essex, Franklin, Jefferson, Lewis, and St. Lawrence County as well as parts of Herkimer and Hamilton Counties. This work covers the years 1642-1891. The first chapter establishes the historical background and geographical setting, then traces the development of Catholicism in northern New York, era by era. The presence of Catholic churches, schools, nursing programs and other church-related facilities were important to the lives of the region's inhabitants. Bibliography.

678. Whiteface Community United Methodist Church. *200 Years of Methodism 1784-1984: 150 Years of the Whiteface United Methodist Church, Wilmington, N.Y., 1834-1984.* s.l., s.n., 1984. 28p.

Brick church was built in 1834. Brief history of Methodism, but mostly about Wilmington Church. Chronological list of ministers.

# *Education*

679. Adirondack Park Agency. *An Environmental Education Resource Manual for Adirondack Schools.* Ray Brook, N.Y., Adirondack Park Agency and Department of Environmental Conservation, 1979, 1981. 141p.

Teaching guide for outdoor education for Adirondack region. Chapter on the natural history of the region.

680. Bonney, Bruce F. and Jack K. Drury. *The Backcountry Classroom: Lesson Plans for Teaching in the Wilderness.* Merrillville, IN., ICS Books, 1992. xi, 272p.

Wilderness education handbook. Drury is Director of Wilderness Education Leadership Program at North Country Community College in Saranac Lake, N. Y. Contains 40 chapters for use as lesson plans on all aspects of taking wilderness trips. Index.

681. Garrison, Guy G. and Barbara O. Slanker. *Library Resources in the North Country Area of New York State.* Urbana, IL., University of Illinois, Library Research Center, 1966. 104p.

Survey results on library resources in mid-1960s. Done as part of preliminary work for Reference & Research Resources plan in New York State. Attempts to document needs for reference/research services and materials. Discusses aims of survey, major regional libraries, faculty questionnaire on libraries, and identification of reference materials. Numerous tables.

682. Gilborn, Craig A. & Alice Gilborn. *Museum of the Adirondacks.* Blue Mountain Lake, N.Y., Adirondack Museum of the Adirondack Historical Association, 1984; rev. ed., 1991. 64p.

Brief, colorful overview of the Adirondacks and the Adirondack Museum. Short essays and photos delineate major themes of the region and its people. Livelihood, crafts, travel, outdoor recreation and the museum discussed.

683. Kaemmerlen, Mea. *Blooms on Bedrock: The Story of a Mountain Garden.* Blue Mountain Lake, N.Y., Adirondack Museum, 1992. 76p.

Story of gardens and landscaping at Adirondack Museum. Color photos of gardens and museum grounds by Craig Gilborn. Index.

684. Office of Planning, Research and Support Services. *Condition of Education in the Adirondack Park School Districts.* Albany, N.Y., State University of New York, Department of Education, 1992. 59p.

Describes school districts, elementary and secondary education (including BOCES), and lifelong learning in the Adirondacks. Statistical tables. Draft in May 1992.

685. Robinson, Julia. *Back to School: A Look at the Past.* Plattsburgh, N.Y., Clinton County Historical Association, 1987. 157p.

History manual on local education for school teachers. Contains ideas for bulletin boards, schools, school work, compositions and letters.

686. Robinson, Julia. *What's In a Name.* Plattsburgh, N.Y., Clinton County Historical Association, 1985. 82p.

A teaching manual with suggested activities and worksheets using personal and place names.

687. Snitzer, Herb. *Today is for Children: Numbers Can Wait.* New York, N.Y., Macmillan, 1972. 238p.

Foreword by A.S. Neill. Story of Wadhams-Lewis School in Essex County, based on Summerhill. Photos. Text written as journal entries.

688. Taub, Bruce R. *A Description of the Seven A.W.A.R.E. Counties with Special Attention to the Educational and Culture Posture Thereof.* s.l., n.p., 1967. 114p.

Statistics for Clinton, Essex, Franklin, Hamilton, Saratoga, Warren and Washington Counties compiled from other sources about cultural and educational topics. Also contains survey of school principals and college presidents. Copy of survey instrument included.

689. Woods, James R. *Paul Smith's College 1937-1980, A Saga of Strife, Struggle, and Success.* Paul Smiths, N.Y., The College, 1980. viii, 275p.

History of Paul Smiths College from its difficult early years to more stable recent times. Today Paul Smiths reflects its Adirondack surroundings with a unique and practical approach to higher education. Illus., charts, index, bibliography.

# Recreation in the Adirondacks

## General

690. Adirondack Park Association. *Off-The-Beaten-Path; Scenic Roads in the Adirondack Park Area of N.Y. State.* Lake George, N.Y., Adirondack Resorts Press, 1972. 27p.

Back roads guide to Adirondack region. Includes 3 or 4 suggested jaunts for each county.

691. Allen Organization. *Comprehensive Park and Recreation Plan, City of Plattsburgh, New York.* Bennington, Vt., Allen Organization, 1971. 60 lvs.

Long term recreation plan for Plattsburgh. Describes city, current park and recreation administration, budget. Prioritizes development of recreation facilities.

692. Carman, Bernard R. *Adirondack Places and Pleasures.* Keene, N.Y., Adirondack Life, 1978. 91p.

Introduction by Carman. Regional sampler of Adirondack Mountains through articles and photography from *Adirondack Life* magazine. Thirteen articles. Illus. by Lucretia Romey.

693. Division of Audits and Accounts. *Financial and Related Practices, Department of Environmental Conservation, Lake George Recreation Facilities and Campsites, August 31, 1979.* Albany, N.Y., The Division, 1980. 25 lvs.

NAR

694. Folwell, Elizabeth. *The Adirondack Book: A Complete Guide.* Stockbridge, MA., Berkshire House, 1992. 344p.

Nineties guide to the Adirondacks with chapters on history, transportation, lodging, culture, restuarants, and recreation. Adirondack region divided into 5 separate areas. Lodging and restuarant index. Maps.

695. Foulke, Patricia & Robert Foulke. *Daytrips, Getaway Weekends and Budget Vacations in the Mid-Atlantic States.* Chester, CT., Globe Pequot Press, 1986. 480p.

Authors are from Lake George. Short sections on Adirondacks and Thousand Islands. Brief descriptions of various sights and places to visit.

696. Horton, Robert. *The Great Green Cathedral: An Adirondack Adventure.* East Greenbush, N.Y., GAN Press, 1976. viii, 276p.

The Great Green Cathedral is the Adirondack Park. Author has been an outdoor columnist who has written about backpacking, hunting, fishing, and hiking. Both entertaining and informative. Photos.

697. Howland, John Jr. ed. *Exploring Lake Champlain and its Highlands.* Burlington, VT., Lake Champlain Committee, 1981. 224p.

Glossy travel guide including both New York and Vermont locations in Champlain Valley region. Lists various recreation-related services. Advts.

698. Martin, J. Peter. *Adirondack Golf Courses: Past and Present.* Lake Placid, N.Y., Adirondack Golf, 1987; reprint, 1993. 112p.

Pictorial work. Highlighting 64 Adirondack region golf courses. Excellent historical photos. Brief glossary; maps locating the golf courses in and around the park.

699. New York State. Office of Parks and Recreation. *North Country Bicycle Touring Guide.* Albany, N.Y., The Office, 1979. 182p.

Pocket-size guide book. County-by-county guide to roads, landmarks and attractions, plus natural history and description of Adirondack Region. Comprehensive touring map, suggested routes.

700. New York Vacation. *Adirondack Regional Guide 1988-89.* Lake Clear, N.Y., Vacation N.Y., 1988. 91p.

Information on lodging, restuarants, tourist attractions, camping.

701. Randall, Willet. *Wilderness Patchwork.* Bradford, Pa., Hounds and Hunting, 1968. 147p.; 2nd ed., 1993.

Story of raising hounds at Beaver Meadow Farm near North Creek in southeastern Adirondacks.

702. Rechlin, Michael. *Recreational Impact in the Adirondack High Peaks Wilderness.* Ann Arbor, MI, University of Michigan, 1973. 64 lvs.

Masters thesis. Attempts to address the question of how to protect the High Peaks while still affording people the opportunity to experience the wildernesss. Describes the facilities, history and natural history of the High Peaks region. Maps, figures, color plates. Study used an on-site survey.

703. Reiger, John F. *American Sportsmen and the Origins of American Conservation.* New York, N.Y., Winchester, 1975; rev. ed., Norman, OK., University of Oklahoma Press, 1986. 316p.

Author's thesis is that people who hunt for sport have made an important contribution to the conservation movement in the U.S. Author cites Adirondacks in developing his main ideas. Notes, bibliography.

704. Scheller, William G. *New York: Off the Beaten Path.* Chester, CT., Globe Pequot Press, 1987. 58p.; 2nd ed., 1990. 150p.

Chapter 2 covers the Adirondacks. Brief descriptions of nineteen places complete with location, phone number, and information on charges, facilities, features.

705. Shafer, Elwood L. *Effects of Sampling Location, Period, and Method on Camper Survey Results.* Syracuse, N.Y., State University College of Forestry, 1966. xv, 245 lvs.

Doctoral thesis. Study concluded that individual campgrounds had distinctive characteristics in terms of economic class of the camper, their uses or activities and their recreational goals. These characteristics also varied from month to month during the camping season. Based on surveys and interviews. Charts, graphs, b and w photos. Includes literature cited and sample survey instrument. Rollins Pond, Fish Creek Ponds, Rogers Rock and Hearthstone Point camp sites in the Adirondacks were among those used for this study.

706. Warren County Bicentennial Commission. *A Heritage Guide to the Historic Towns and Byways of Warren County, N.Y.* s.l., Warren County Bicentennial Commission, 1975. 43p.

Lists points of interest for the following Warren County towns: Bolton, Chester, Hague, Horicon, Johnsburg, Town of Lake George, Town of Lake Luzerne, Queensbury, Stony Creek, Warrensburg and City of Glens Falls. Pocket-size. Contains small map of each locale.

707. Waterman, Laura & Guy Waterman. *Forest and Crag: A History of Hiking, Trail Blazing and Adventuring in the Northeastern Mountains.* Boston, Ma., The Appalachian Mountain Club, 1989. 960p.

Comprehensive guide on hiking in the Northeastern states. Chapters 2, 16, 17, 21, 33, 37 specifically about the Adirondacks. Some other chapters provide valuable general history, background information. Figures, tables, maps, bibliography, index, illus.

708. Woodruff, Charles B. *An Appraisal of Potential Outdoor Recreational Developments in Clinton County, New York.* Plattsburgh, N.Y., Clinton County Soil and Water Conservation Office, 1969. 58p.

Overview of a wide variety of recreation resources in Clinton County. Inventory includes vacation homes, campgrounds, fishing spots, golf courses, picnic places, scenic sites, riding stables, shooting ranges, vacation farms, water and winter sports, wild game, and historic sites. Appendix.

# Canoeing

709. Davidson, James West & John Rugge. *The Complete Wilderness Paddler.* New York, N.Y., Knopf, 1976. xiv, 259p.; reprint, New York, N.Y., Vintage, 1983. xiv, 260p.

A thorough look at wilderness canoeing. Rugge practices medicine in the Adirondacks. Bibliography.

710. Jamieson, Paul F. *Adirondack Canoe Waters North Flow.* Glens Falls, N.Y., Adirondack Mountain Club, Inc., 1975. 299p.

Canoeing guide that has gone through several printings. Information about the Oswegatchie, Grass, Raquette, St. Regis, Salmon, Chautegay, Great Chazy, Saranac, and Ausable Rivers as well as Lake Champlain and Lake George. Classification of difficulty of canoe trips and a chapter on camping. Additional printings and editions in 1977, 1981, 1984, 1986, 1988, and 1991. Var. pag. Index. Recent ed. done with the assistance of Paul Morris.

711. New York State. Department of Environmental Conservation. *Adirondack Canoe Routes*. Albany, N.Y., Department of Environmental Conservation, 1969, 1974. Var. pag.

Recreational circular published over the years.

712. Niemi, Judith & Barbara Weiser (eds.). *Rivers Running Free: Stories of Adventurous Women*. Minneapolis, MN., Bergamot Books, 1987. 287p.

Brief excerpt about canoeing near Saranac Lake.

713. Proskine, Alec C. *Adirondack Canoe Waters: South and West Flow*. Glens Falls, N.Y., Adirondack Mountain Club, Inc., 1985. xix, 139p.; second ed., 1989. xix, 150p.

Canoe guide to 3 major watersheds of southern and western Adirondacks: Black River, Upper Hudson, and the Mohawk. Some Tug Hill waters included as well. Specifically covers Boreas River, Cedar River, East Canada Creek, Fish Creek, Hudson River, Indian River, Moose River, Sacandaga River, Salmon River, Schroon River and West Canada Creek. Intended to complement Adirondack Canoe Waters North Flow. Maps, bibliography.

714. Proskine, Alec C. *No Two Rivers Alike: 50 Canoeable Rivers in New York and Pennsylvania*. Trumansburg, N.Y., Crossing Press, 1980. 221p.

First 40 pages is a "How-to" section. Balance of book describes canoe waters. For those interested in the Adirondacks, Proskine includes sections on Moose River, the Oswegatchie, Raquette River, Sacandaga River, Saranac River, and West Canada Creek. Short informative descriptions of each river.

# Hiking, Climbing and Camping

## Hiking Guides

715. Adirondack Park Agency. *Hiking and Backpacking in the Adirondack Park*. Ray Brook, N.Y., The Agency, 1976, 1978. 23p.

Written descriptions of 47 camping and backpacking opportunities in the Adirondack Park. Each entry includes information on location, description, statistics and access. Divided into four sections: Wild Forest, Primitive, Wilderness, and Canoe Paddles. Profile of Adirondack Park on the inside cover. Map of Adirondack Park, list of required topographic maps, list of maps and guides. Brief section on safety precautions for being in the mountains as well as backpacking and hiking etiquette. Slightly revised in 1978.

716. Dunn, John M. *Winterwise: A Backpacker's Guide*. Lake George, N.Y., Adirondack Mountain Club, 1989. 1988. 182p.

How-to book on winter backpacking in northeastern U.S. Author lives in Keene, N.Y. Chapters on weather, food, clothing, shelters, sleeping, equipment, finding the way, safety and first aid.

717. Ehling, Dr. William P. *Fifty Hikes in Central New York: Hikes and Backpacking Trips from the Western Adirondacks to the Finger Lakes*. Woodstock, VT., Backcountry Publications, 1984. 286p.

Book covers approximately 20 hikes in Adirondack foothills, Tug Hill, Eastern Lake Ontario hills, and Black River Valley. In addition to a written description, distances, hiking times, vertical rise and appropriate U.S. Geologic Survey maps are listed. Plates, bibliography.

718. Haberl, Arthur. *Guide to Adirondack Trails: West-Central Region*. Glens Falls, N.Y., Adirondack Mountain Club, 1980, 1984, 1987, 1989. Var. pag.

Trail guide to Independence River, Big Moose, Raquette Lake, Blue Mountain Lake, Brantingham, Old Forge-Thendara, Moose River recreation area, plus others. Appendices on state campgrounds, lean-tos and highest 100 peaks. Includes other information on campgrounds, history, fishing tips, etc. Bibliography, index. Map in pocket inside back cover. Forest Preserve Series, Vol. V.

719. Healy, Trudy. *A Climber's Guide to the Adirondacks: Rock and Slide Climbs in the High Peaks Region*. Glens Falls, N.Y., Adirondack Mountain Club, 1967, 1971. 108p.

Introduction about geology, history and technique of rock climbing. Rock climbs described include Chapel Pond, St. Huberts, Keene Valley, Cascade Lakes, Heart Lake, Pitchoff Mt., Poke of Moonshine and Haystack Mt. The following rock slide climbs are mentioned: General, Macomb,

East Dix, Giant, Wright Peak, Mount Colden and Seymour. Out of print. Illustrated by the author.

720. Jaffe, Howard & Elizabeth Jaffe. *Geology of the Adirondack High Peaks: A Hiker's Guide*. Glens Falls, N.Y., Adirondack Mountain Club, Inc., 1986. 201p.

Brief geological history of high peaks. Description of three dozen hikes in ten different locations. Illus., tables, bibliography, glossary, and index.

721. Laing, Linda. *Guide to Adirondack Trails: Southern Region*. Glens Falls, N.Y., Adirondack Mountain Club, 1988. 172p.

Each hike contains written description with distances. Appendices include glossary of terms, lists of lean-tos and state campgrounds. Index. Map in rear pocket. Divided into sections: Stony Creek, Hadley & the Eastern section; Wilcox Lake Wild Forest, Baldwin Spring section; Benson, Wells, Silver Lake Wilderness; Canada Lake, Caroga, Pawley and Piseco sections. Forest Preserve Series, Vol VII.

722. McMartin, Barbara. *Adventures in Hiking: A Young People's Guide to the Adirondacks*. Utica, N.Y., North Country Books, 1993. 110p.

Introduction is general overview of hiking. Contains 28 hikes throughout the Adirondack region. Directed at children in the 8-12 year range. Illus. Bibliography, index. Includes directions to Adirondack trailheads.

723. McMartin, Barbara, et al. *Discover the Adirondack High Peaks*. Woodstock, VT., Backcountry Publications, 1989. 258p.

150 hikes in sixteen areas in or near the High Peaks. Map in back pocket. Each hike includes time required, vertical climb, time necessary for hike, as well as written description. Photos, bibliography. Discover the Adirondacks Series, Vol. 11.

724. McMartin, Barbara. *Discover the Adirondacks, 1: From Indian Lake to the Hudson River, A Four Season Guide to the Out-of-Doors*. Somersworth, N.H., New Hampshire Publishing Co., 1979; reprint, *Discover the South-Central Adirondacks: Including the Siamese Ponds Wilderness Area*. Woodstock, VT., Backcountry Publications, Inc., 1986, 1990. Var. pag.

Ninety-one entries for the Siamese Pond Wilderness Area. Includes location, description of trails, and appropriate uses and activities for each trail or trip described. Information regarding plant life, geology etc. References. Updated ed. of work which was first printed in 1979. Discover the Adirondacks Series, Vol. 1.

725. McMartin, Barbara. *Discover the Central Adirondacks: Four Season Adventures in the Heart of the North Woods*. Woodstock, VT, Backcountry Publications, Inc., 1986; second ed., 1992. Var. pag.

Sixty-seven hikes and outings in the central Adirondacks. Photos with short written description of each hike. Includes uses for each route, distances, and time needed. Index, bibliography. Discover the Adirondacks Series, Vol. 3.

726. McMartin, Barbara. *Discover the Eastern Adirondacks: Four-Season Adventures Near Lake George, Pharoah Lake, and Beyond*. Woodstock, VT., Backcountry Publications, 1988; rev. ed., 1991. 224p.

With the assistance of Edythe Robbins. Rev. ed. of *Guide to the Eastern Adirondacks*. Discover the Adirondacks Series, Vol. 4.

727. McMartin, Barbara. *Discover the Northeastern Adirondacks Four-Season Adventures from Lake Champlain to the Rock-Crowned Eastern Slopes*. Woodstock, VT., Backcountry Publications, 1987. 225p.

Contains information about 90 hikes in the northeastern Adirondacks. Each description indicates type of activities suitable to the trail, plus time and distance where appropriate. Flora, fauna, and geologic features mentioned often. Hikes grouped in chapters by access points. Each chapter begins with a general description of the area and a map. Prepared with the assistance of Dennis Conroy. Discover the Adirondacks Series, Vol. 10.

728. McMartin, Barbara. *Discover the Northern Adirondacks: Four-Season Excursions from Lake Placid, Saranac Lake, and Points North*. Woodstock, VT., Backcountry Publications, 1988. 255p.; rev. ed., 1994.

Describes 98 hikes in 19 different geographic subdivisions. Each written description accompanied by suggested appropriate activities, length of hike in distance and time, changes in elevation, which geologic survey map to use. Plates, maps, index. Prepared with the assistance of E.H. Ketchledge. Discover the Adirondacks Series, Vol. 9.

729. McMartin, Barbara. *Discover the Northwestern Adirondacks: Four Season Adventures in the Broad Forest and the Park's Frontier Region.* Woodstock, VT., Backcountry Publications, 1990 224p.; rev. ed., 1994.

Over 100 outdoor excursions in northern and western Adirondacks. Region divided into geographic sections. Each outing includes physical description, appropriate activities, directions for getting to each location. Plates, maps. Discover the Adirondacks Series, Vol. 8.

730. McMartin, Barbara. *Discover the Southwestern Adirondacks: Four Season Adventures in the Wild-Forested Foothills.* Woodstock, VT., Backcountry Publications, 1987. 192p.; 2nd ed., 1993.

Over 100 hikes in Southwestern Adirondacks where terrain is better suited for nature walks than mountain hiking. Photos. Each hike includes a description of the walk, distances, time necessary, and appropriate activities. Topographic maps with trails added are useful. Discover the Adirondacks Series, Vol. 7.

731. McMartin, Barbara. *Discover the West-Central Adirondacks: A Guide to the Western Wilderness and Moose River Plains.* Woodstock, VT., Backcountry Publications, 1988. 297p.

Descriptions of over 170 hikes in various wilderness areas around Canada Lakes, Big Moose Plains, Fulton Chain, Old Forge, Eagle Bay, etc. Photos, maps, and references. Descriptions of each hike include information on appropriate activities and length of the walk. Discover the Adirondacks Series, Vol. 2. Prepared with the assistance of Lee M. Brenning, Sandy Edwards, and Dennis Conroy.

732. McMartin, Barbara. *Fifty Hikes in the Adirondacks.* Somersworth, N.H., New Hampshire Pub. Co., 1979, 1980; reprint, Woodstock, VT., Backcountry Publications, 1988, 1990. 253p.

Hiking Guide. Hikes from every corner of the Adirondack Park. Each hike offers the following information: distance, vertical rise, hiking time, and what USGS map to use, as well as a written description of hike.

733. McMartin, Barbara. *Old Roads and Open Peaks.* Glens Falls, N.Y., Adirondack Mountain Club, 1977. o.p. from Adirondack Mountain Club Books; reprint, *Discover the Southeastern Adirondacks: Four-season Adventures on Old Roads and Open Peaks.* Woodstock, VT., Backcountry Publications, Inc., 1986. 144p.; rev. ed., 1994

Seventy-five hikes in the southeastern Adirondacks. Each hike has a brief written description and tells what quadrangle map to use. Illus, Map in paper pocket. Updated edition prepared with the assistance of Willard Reed. Sixty-seven hikes and daytrips in the southeastern Adirondacks, principally the Wilcox Lake Forest. Photos, maps, and references. As in other works in the series, each hike is thoroughly described and includes time required to make the trip, and appropriate activities. Prepared with the assistance of Willard Reed. Discover the Adirondacks Series, Vol. 5.

734. O'Shea, Peter. *Guide to Adirondack Trails: Northern Region.* Glens Falls, N.Y., Adirondack Mountain Club, Inc., 1986, 1988, 1990. Var. pag.

Trail guide to Grasse River, Star Lake, Cranberry Lake, Wanakena, Tupper Lake, and St. Regis/Paul Smiths region. Appendices include glossary of terms, lean-to locations, and state campgrounds. Maps in pocket inside back cover. Forest Preserve Series, Vol. II.

735. Patterson, Barbara McMartin. *Walks and Waterways: An Introduction to Adventure in the East Canada Creek and the West Branch of the Sacandaga River Sections of the Southern Adirondacks.* Glens Falls, N.Y., Adirondack Mountain Club, 1974. 171p.; reprints, *Discover the Adirondacks 2: Walks, Waterways, and Winter Treks in the Southern Adirondacks.* Somersworth, N.H., New Hampshire Publishing Co., 1979; *Discover the Southern Adirondacks: Walks, Waterways, and Winter Treks.* Woodstock, VT, Backcountry Publications, 1988. 193p.

Out of print from Adirondack Mountain Club Books. Hiking guide and canoeing guide book for the southern Adirondacks. Twice revised in 1979 and 1988. Updated descriptions of hikes and new hikes. Includes photos, maps, index of list of sources. References. Discover the Adirondacks Series, Vol VI.

736. St. Lawrence County. *Trail Guide for St. Lawrence County.* Canton, N.Y., St. Lawrence County, 1992. 46p.

Spiral bound typescript. Maps and brief written descriptions of 20 hiking and skiing trails in St. Lawrence County. Several are within the Blue Line. Trails listed by type of use as well as alphabetically.

737. Tisdale, Betsy. *Guide to Adirondack Trails: Eastern Region.* Glens Falls, N.Y., Adirondack Mountain Club, 1981, 1986, 1987, 1989. Var. pag.

Hiking guide for area from Lake Champlain to Lake George. Pocket-size with folded map inside back cover. North Hudson, Moriah, Pharoah Wilderness, Putnam Pond, Crown Point, Wardsboro, Schroon Lake, Brant Lake are some of the areas covered. Forest Preserve Series, Vol. VI.

738. Wadsworth, Bruce. *An Adirondack Sampler: Day Hikes for All Seasons.* Glens Falls, N.Y., Adirondack Mountain Club, 1979, 1986, 1988; 3rd ed., Lake George, N.Y., 1991. Var. pag.

Hiking guide. Fifty day hikes in all corners of the Adirondacks. Each hike described begins with a brief summary, including length of time the hike could take, round trip distance, elevation covered, summit elevation, difficulty and what quadrangle map to use. The summary is followed by a page-length description of the trail. Occasional black and white photos make the reader want to get out on the trail. Second edition in 1988.

739. Wadsworth, Bruce. *An Adirondack Sampler II: Backpacking Trips.* Glens Falls, N.Y., Adirondack Mountain Club, 1981, 1986, 1989. Var. pag.

Describes a dozen selected backpacking trips in the Adirondack Park. Each hike is described in detail: difficulty, length of hike, time required and what USGS map to use. Photos, and general information on hiking and use of this book have also been provided.

740. Wadsworth, Bruce. *Guide to Adirondack Trails: Central Region.* Glens Falls, N.Y., Adirondack Mountain Club, 1986. Var. pag.

Trail guide for area surrounding Blue Mt. Lake, region east of Newcomb, and an area from Indian Lake to Speculator to North Creek. Pocket-size. Maps, descriptions of hikes, photos. Appendices have glossary of terms, list of high peaks, list of campgrounds and lean-tos, and index. Map in pocket. Forest Preserve Series, Vol. III.

### Camping

741. Mulholland, William D. *Public Campsites in the Forest Preserve Park Region.* Albany, N.Y., Conservation Dept., 1966, 1968. 36p.

Over 3 dozen campsites in the Adirondacks. Some Catskills listings too. Photos, short description of each campsite.

742. Scheib, John. *State Parks and Campgrounds in Northern New York.* Woodstock, VT., Backcountry Publications, 1987. x, 214p.

Covers Adirondack Park, Thousand Islands, eastern shore of Lake Ontario. Lists over 5 dozen campgrounds. Each entry contains address, phone number, directions to the campground. Services and activities offered are listed and explained. Illus., maps.

## Hunting and Fishing

743. Alsheimer, Charles J. & Larry C. Watkins. *A Guide to Adirondack Deer Hunting.* Dolgeville, N.Y., Beaver Creek Press, 1987. xvii, 219p.

Thorough guide on subject. Information on Adirondacks and deer as well as practical information on New York State laws. Where to hunt, where to stay, hunting techniques, field dressing, meat processing, and photographing trophies are some of the topics covered. Illus. Bibliography. Also a paper ed.

744. Aprill, Dennis. *Good Fishing in the Adirondacks.* Tarrytown, N.Y., Northeast Sportsman's Press, 1989. 222p.; reprint, *Good Fishing in the Adirondacks: from Lake Champlain to the Streams of Tug Hill.* Woodstock, VT., Backcountry Publications, 1992. 238p.

Essays by a number of authors about fishing in various bodies of water throughout Northern New York. Maps by Larry Boutin and Jim Capossela. Illus.

745. Betters, Francis. *Fish Are Smarter in the Adirondacks.* Wilmington, N.Y., Adirondack Sports Pub-

lications, 1983. 101p.

Tales and articles about fishing in the Adirondacks, some are true, others tall. Seven poems by Betters. Illus. by Terrance Young.

746. Betters, Francis. *Fishing the Adirondacks.* Wilmington, N.Y., Adirondacks Sporting Publications, 1982; rev. 1987. vi, 118p.

Guidebook to fish and waters of the Adirondacks. Illus. of 20 species of fish common to Adirondack waters. Lists of locations of species organized by county. Endpapers contain tribute to West Branch of the Ausable River. Maps, illus.

747. Betters, Francis. *Fran Betters' Fly Fishing, Fly Tying and Pattern Guide.* Wilmington, N.Y., Adirondack Sports Publications, 1986. 108p.

Most of book on tying flies. Introductory section on equipment, types of trout streams, and insects trout consume. Wildlife drawings by Francis Davis, plus photos of flies. Ed. by Craig Woods.

748. Cole, N. B. *Guide to Trout Waters in Adirondack Lakes.* Ithaca, N.Y., Outdoor Publications, 1974. 48p.

Short guide to trout species and trout waters of the Adirondacks. Brief description of major trout lakes and streams. Illus., charts, maps.

749. Engels, Vincent. *Adirondack Fishing in the 1930s: A Lost Paradise.* Syracuse, N.Y., Syracuse University Press, 1978. viii, 155p.

Fishing stories of the central Adirondacks in the 1930s. Not a how-to book but an ode to the Adirondacks and people who like to fish. Afterword by Charles Todd touches upon some of the issues that led to the decline of Adirondack trout waters: acid rain, too many motorboats on small lakes, and manipulation of water levels to support other types of recreation.

750. New York State. Conservation Department. *Fish and Fishing in New York.* Albany, N.Y., Conservation Department, 1967. 36p.

Color booklet on a variety of fishing experiences: trout streams and ponds, hatcheries, lists of record holders as of 1968, fresh and salt water fishes. Color plates of various species.

751. Schoonmaker, Peter R. *Primitive Pursuit: Stories Afield of Muzzleloader Rifle Hunting.* Greenville, PA., Beaver Pond, 1992. 140p.

Collection of hunting articles by Gloversville resident. Most written in 1980s. Art work by Walt McCurdy.

752. Thompson, Harvey W. *The Spooners.* Dearborn, MI., Eppinger Manufacturing, 1979. 39p.

Story of Buel Co., Whitehall, N.Y.

753. Wharton, Donald. *Adirondack Forest and Stream: An Outdoorsman's Reader.* South Glens Falls, N.Y., Pine Mountain Press, 1992. 131p.

Stories on a variety of outdoor and sporting activities. Author is fisherman, hunter, hiker and canoeist. Over 90 photos.

# Winter Sports

## General

754. Burnett, Jim. *Adirondack Snow Flurries.* Cranberry Lake, N.Y., Halstead Pub. Co., 1987. 106p.

Reminscences of life in northern Adirondack foothills and adjacent St. Lawrence Valley near Cranberry Lake. Chapters on snowmobiling. Illus.

755. Posen, I. Sheldon. *You Hear the Ice Talking: The Ways of People and Ice on Lake Champlain.* Plattsburgh, N.Y., Clinton-Essex-Franklin Library System, 1986. 62p.

Engrossing book on ice, Lake Champlain when it's frozen, with chapters on ice fishing, ice harvesting, recreational activities and ice-related lore. Bibliography.

## Olympic Games

756. Baker, Eugene H. *XIII Olympic Winter Games: Lake Placid 1980.* Wilmette, IL., Ice Skating Institute of America, 1979; var. ed., Chicago, IL., Rand McNally, 1979. xxv, 230p.

Pictorial work. History, results of past Winter Olympic games. Information on figure skating, speed skating, hockey, alpine skiing, nordic skiing, biatholon, luge, and bobsledding. Lake Placid 1932 and 1980.

757. Becker, Jonathan. *The Games of Lake Placid in 1932: Collecting the Memories.* Cos Cob, CT., Becker, 1991. 31p.
Lists and photos of memorabilia; publicity material, official estimated value of the items pictured. 100 copies.

758. Brennan, Gale. *The XIII Winter Olympic Games, Lake Placid, 1980.* Milwaukee, WI., Ideals Publishing Corp., 1979. 79p.
Guide book to 1980 Winter Olympic games, organized by event. Winners of each event through 1976 listed. Color photos.

759. Grombach, John V. *The 1980 Olympic Guide: Complete Sport by Sport History with Records of Every Event.* New York, N.Y., Times Books, 1980. 351p.
General guide. History and origins of Olympic Games. Chapter 17 on winter sports and Chapter 22 on the future of the games. Last chapter lists daily schedule for 1980 games.

760. Hollander, Zander. *The Complete Handbook of the Olympic Winter Games: Lake Placid 1980.* New York, N.Y., New American Library, 1979. 224p.
Preview of 1980 Winter Olympic Games in Lake Placid, N.Y. from t.v. guide to world records in each event to history and background of each sporting event.

761. Kilianan, Michael Morris. *The Olympic Games: 80 Years of People, Events, and Records.* Don Mills, Ont., Collier Macmillan Canada, 1976; reprint, *The Olympic Games 1980: Moscow and Lake Placid.* New York, N.Y., Macmillan Publishing Co., 1979; rev. ed., New York, Collier Books, 1980. 319p.
History of modern Olympics and the International Olympic Committee. Section on Winter Olympics mentions Lake Placid in 1932, lists famous Olympians and medal winners.

762. Lake Placid Organizing Committee. *Final Report: XIII Olympic Winter Games Lake Placid, N.Y. February 13-24, 1980.* s.l., Ed Levine Associates, 1982. 223p.
Bilingual, French and English, printing of Final Report for 1980 Winter Olympics in Lake Placid. Components of Final Report include: History, Sports, Protocol, Marketing, Construction, Operations, Press, Legal-Financial. Plates.

763. Podolsky, Sherwin. *Postal History and Vignettes of the Xth Olympiad and the III Winter Olympic Games.* Cleveland, OH., Sports Philatelists, 1976. viii, 196p.
Includes stamps and postcards commemorating XIII Winter Olympic Games in Lake Placid, N.Y. in 1932. Definitely has appeal for philatelists, but the drawings on stamps and postcards depicting Lake Placid themes and winter sporting events would interest others as well. The majority of the book, however, is about postal materials commemorating the 1932 Los Angeles Summer Games.

764. Powers, John & Arthur Kaminsky. *One Goal: A Chronicle of the 1980 U.S. Olympic Hockey Team.* New York, N.Y., Harper and Row, 1984. x, 257p.
U.S. Gold Medal in Hockey at Lake Placid in 1980 serves as focal point for discussion of hockey in the U.S. and the players who were members of that team.

765. Spallek, Edgar P. *Olympic Winter Games, USA 1980: The Official Pictorial Record of the XIII Olympic Winter Games.* s.l., Spallek, 1980. 150p.
Pictorial work. Photo album that conveys the speed, grace and dramatic action of Winter Olympic Sports. Vividly captures the human element; the generosity and the goodwill that is the Olympic spirit.

766. Sports and Culture U.S.A. *Lake Placid '80.* Salt Lake City, UT., Sports and Culture USA, 1980; var. ed., Colorado Springs, CO., United States Olympic Committee, 1980. 205p.
Pictorial work. Text in both French and English. These are two variations of same item with minor differences in layout and content. "The Official Olympic Book of the United States Olympic Committee."

767. Wendel, Tim. *Going For the Gold: How the U.S. Won at Lake Placid.* Westport, CT.., L. Hill, 1980. xi, 131.
Human interest story about team members and reviews the games the U.S. Olympic Hockey team played en route to winning the Gold Medal in 1980.

## Winter Mountain Climbing and Rock Climbing

768. Danielsen, John A. *Winter Hiking and Camping.* Glens Fall, N.Y., Adirondack Mountain Club,

1972, 1977, 1982, 1986. Var. pag.

Introductory book on winter hiking and camping that presents preparations and safety steps necessary for winter outings. Basic first aid, ski touring and winter survival information provided.

769. Mellor, Don. *Climbing in the Adirondacks: A Guide to Rock and Ice Routes in the Adirondack Park.* Lake Placid, N.Y., Lake Placid Climbing School, 1983. 170p.; *1986 Supplement: Climbing the Adirondacks.* New York, N.Y., s.n., 1986. 72p.; reprint, including supplement, Lake George, N.Y., Adirondack Mountain Club, 1989. 320p.

Seventy-plus hikes and ice climbs in 7 different regions of the Adirondacks. Chapters on wilderness ethics, history of climbing in the Adirondacks. Maps, photos of various climbs, annotated with climbing routes. Describes over 50 rock and ice climbs in the Adirondacks. Black and white photos, with suggested route marked, accompany each description. Essay entitled "A History of Climbing in the Adirondacks," Supplement to 1983 edition, with 72 pages adds 175 new climbs. Superseded by the 1989 edition.

770. Rosencrans, Thomas R. *Adirondack Rock and Ice Climbs.* Lake George, N.Y., Rosencrans Outing and Climbing Klub, 1976. xiii, 124p.

Pocket-size paper. Brief overview of rock climbing includes grading, geology, and history. Ensuing sections cover rock climbing, ice climbing and slide climbing. Each climb is graded for difficulty and offers a short climbing strategy. Some have maps or photos to illustrate recommended approach.

## Skiing

771. Adirondack Ski Touring Council. *Adirondack Ski Tours: A Guide to Sixteen Ski Tours in the Adirondack Park Including the Jack Rabbit Trail.* Lake Placid, N.Y., Adirondack Ski Touring Council, 1989. 37p.

Abridged version of 1982 ed. of *Northern Adirondack Ski Tours* by Tony Goodwin. Distances, difficulty, what US Geologic Survey map to use and a brief written description provided for each ski tour. Bibliography.

772. Adler, Allen. *New England & Thereabouts: A Ski Tracing.* Barton, VT., Netco Press, 1985. xii, 138p.

Several pages in Chapter 6 about Lake Placid in 1930s and the 1932 Winter Olympics.

773. Coggeshall, Almy & Anne Coggeshall. *25 Ski Tours in the Adirondacks: Cross-Country Skiing Adventures in the Southern Adirondacks, the Capital District and Tug Hill.* Somersworth, N.H., New Hampshire Publishing Co., 1979. 143p.

Twenty-five cross-country ski tours, 20 of which are north of the Thruway and south of a line that extends from Watertown through Blue Mountain Lake to Rt. 74. For each tour information on distance, which US Geologic Survey map to use, and type of terrain is followed by a written description and photos.

774. Cohen, Stan. *Pictorial History of Downhill Skiing.* Missoula, Mont., Pictorial Histories Publishing Co., 1985. ix, 246p.

History of skiing. Chapter 5 on the Winter Olympics covers information on Lake Placid in 1932 and 1980.

775. Conroy, Dennis with Shirley Matzke. *Adirondack Cross Country Skiing A Guide to Seventy Trails.* Woodstock, VT., Backcountry Publications, 1992. 283p.

Descriptions of almost 6 dozen cross-country ski trips in Eastern Adirondacks, mostly central and southern areas. Initial chapter is on skiing, equipment, keeping warm and winter outdoor safety, using maps. Index, suggested reading list.

776. Goodwin, Tony. *Northern Adirondack Ski Tours: 30 Selected Tours for the Novice to the Expert Skier.* Glens Falls, N.Y., Adirondack Mountain Club, 1981, 1992. xiii, 146p.

Thirty cross-country ski trips in northern New York between Lake Champlain and the northwestern Adirondacks. Vary from afternoon outings to extended winter camping trips.

# *Clubs, Private Preserves and Great Camps*

777. Adirondack League Club. *Fishery Management Report.* s.l., s.n., 1979. 1, 42p.

Details management strategies for Adirondack League Club-owned lakes. Addresses issues such as effect of trash fish, acid precipitation, beaver control and re-stocking programs.

778. Adirondack Trail Improvement Society. *ATIS, 1897-1972: Seventy-Fifth Anniversary.* St. Huberts, N.Y., Adirondack Trail Improvement Society, Inc., 1972. 32p.

Highlights of organization's history plus timeline, ledger of 1971-72 members, and a list of trails then marked by ATIS. Illus.

779. Comstock, Edward Jr., (ed.) *The Adirondack League Club.* Old Forge, New York, The Adirondack League Club, 1990. 287p.

Thorough history of the Adirondack League Club. Chapters written by various individuals, chronology of the Club's development, checklist of imprints by and about the club, and lists of members and officers. Plates, maps, bibliography. 1250 copies. Prepared with assistance of Mark C. White.

780. DuBois, Gaylord. *Reflections on the Eyrie.* Alexandria, VA., Glenn, 1984. 38 lvs.

Poems about Eyrie, Morris and Ellin Glenn's camp on Whallons Bay, New York, which was once part of the Crater Club. Illus., maps.

781. DuFort, Rene. *Not Far from Land: A Chronicle of the Valcour Sailing Club 1966-1986.* Plattsburgh, N.Y., The Club, 1987. xii, 138p.

Edited by Alice Connor. Foreword and commentary by David B. McDowell. History of Valcour Sailing Club on Lake Champlain. Information about club, its buildings, members, committees, and boat races.

782. Fisher, Lewis (ed.). *Old Hollywood: The Story of the Jordan Club 1890-1960.* Hollywood, N.Y., The Jordan Club 1965. 107p; reprint, *Old Hollywood: The Story of the Jordan Club 1890-1980.* Canton, N.Y., St. Lawrence County Historical Association, 1980. 102p.

Refers to the Jordan Club located at the juncture of the Jordan and Raquette Rivers in Hollywood, Town of Colton, N.Y. Once a summer colony in the Adirondack foothills. Hollywood is "Faraway" in Philip Wylie's *The End of the Dream.* Reprint edited by Paul Jamieson.

783. Garden Club of America. *Sixtieth Annual Meeting, Lake Placid, May 21-24. 1974.* Elizabethtown, N.Y., Garden Club, 1973. 35p.

Program for meeting and directory of Garden Club officers. Mostly short vignettes on various aspects of regional life and history: Lake Placid, the mountains; Lake Champlain, the climate; the Adirondack Park Agency, the Adirondack Park, and cultural life. Illustrated by Martha Wardenburg.

784. Gill, Brendan & Dudley Witney. *Summer Places.* New York, N.Y., Metheun, 1978. 223p.

Photos of two of the Great Camps as well as of Saratoga.

785. Glenn, Morris F. *American Authors' Summer Retreat on Lake Champlain.* Alexandria, VA., Glenn, 1979. 138p.

A history of the Crater Club and its importance to American Literature between 1908 and 1935. The Crater Club was formed in 1899; its surroundings, both the Adirondacks and Lake Champlain, influenced the writers who came there according to Glenn.

786. Glenn, Morris F. *Glenn's History of the Adirondacks: Volume 4; A Forgotten Summer Retreat for American Authors.* Alexandria, VA., Glenn, 1980. 32p.

About Crater Club. Selected photos 1900-1980. Very limited ed.

787. Glenn, Morris F. *Glenn's History of the Adirondacks: Volume 5; Documents Relating to the Cra-*

*ter Club, Essex, New York.*Alexandria, VA., Glenn, 1980. Unpaged.

Collected documents, records, advertisments for Crater Club. Mostly from between the two World Wars.

788. Gonino, Vincent J. *The Huntington Memorial Camp.* Dubuque, Iowa, Kendall/Hunt Pub. Co., 1974. 187p.

Book about outdoor education as exemplified by SUNY Cortland's acquisition and running of Huntington Memorial Camp. Background chapters on the Adirondacks, Raquette Lake, and early settlers. A study of outdoor education and the role of Huntington Memorial Outdoor Education Center. Bibliography.

789. Hudowalski, Grace L. *The Adirondack High Peaks and The Forty-Sixers.* Albany, N.Y., Peters Print., 1970, 1971. 357p.

The Forty-sixers refers to individuals who have climbed all 46 high peaks. The story of the Forty-sixers and the identification of the peaks. Information on natural history, folklore, birds, mammals, and geology included by various contributors. Illustrated by Trudy Healy. 1,200 copies.

790. Kaiser, Harvey H. *Great Camps of the Adirondacks.* Boston, MA., D.R. Godine, 1981, 1982, 1986, 1991. xv, 240p.

Comprehensive book on great camps. Discusses camps individually, as well as history, background, contemporary problems and future. Bibliography, index, illus. Hard cover and paper ed.

791. Kirschenbaum, Howard. *The Story of Sagamore.* Raquette Lake, N.Y., Sagamore Institute, 1990. 72p.

Brief account of one of the Adirondack great camps from its construction in the last century to the establishment of the Sagamore institute. Illus.

792. Peterson, Paula. *Coming Home: An Intimate Glance of a Family Camp in the Adirondack North Country.* Utica, N.Y., North Country Books, 1993. 64p.

Pictorial work. About an Adirondack camp and the meaning and value of the camp experience.

793. Pilcher, Edith. *Up the Lake Road: The First Hundred Years of the Adirondack Mountain Reserve.* Keene Valley, N.Y., Adirondack Mountain Reserve, 1987. 192p.

The Adirondack Mountain Reserve, founded in 1887 to protect Upper Ausable Lake and surrounding vicinity from extensive logging, contains 40,000 acres. Publication honors anniversary of the Reserve.

794. Piseco Company. *Life at an Adirondack Inn: The Story of One Hundred Years of the Irondequoit Club Inn and Its Owner, the Piseco Company.* Piseco, N.Y., Piseco Club, 1992. 235p.

History of one of the Adirondack's better known clubs with emphasis on important and colorful personalities.

795. Stevens, Dennis W. *The History of Whiteface Mountain Lodge 789, Free and Accepted Masons.* Saranac Lake, N.Y., The Lodge, 1992. 95p.

Typescript. Minutes of meetings. Illus.

796. Tefft, Tim, ed. *Of the Summits, Of the Forests.* Morrisonville, N.Y., Adirondack Forty-Sixers, 1991. 352p.

Successor volume to *The Adirondack Forty-sixers* and *The Adirondack High Peaks and the Forty-sixers.* Numerous contributors writing about all aspects of the High Peaks region. Bibliography, index, illus.

797. Wilson, Leila Fosburgh. *The North Woods Club 1886-1986: One Hundred Years in the Adirondack Wilderness.* s.l., s.n., 1986. 32p.

History and development of North Woods Club which had earlier been known as Baker's Clearing.

# Biography

## Collective

798. Brown, Henry A.L. & Richard J. Walton. *John Brown's Tract: Lost Adirondack Empire*. Canaan, N.H., Phoenix Pub., 1988. xv, 366p.

Role of the Browns, a renowned Providence R.I. family, in the Adirondacks between 1770 and 1850, as they tried to forge an economic empire based on farming and mining. Based on family letters. Family holdings consisted of 200,000 acres in Hamilton, Herkimer, and Lewis Counties. Introduction by William McLoughlin. Bibliography, index.

799. Burdick, Virginia M. *Love & Duty: Letters and Diaries of the Delord-Webb Women 1794-1913*. Plattsburgh, NY, Wiki Publications for Kent-Delord House, 1987. xiv, 161p.

Story of three generations of women from a prominent Plattsburgh family. Material comes from primary sources such as letters and diaries. Family tree, bibliography. Plates.

800. Byrne, Margaret Myers. *The Plattsburgh Platts: A Genealogy of the Four Platt Brothers Who Settled Plattsburgh, New York, Beginning in 1785*. Plattsburgh, N.Y., Clinton County Historical Association, 1991. 82p.

Family history. Four Platt brothers, Zephaniah, Nathaniel, Charles and Daniel were original settlers of Plattsburgh, New York, following Revolutionary War. Descendants organized by each brother. Surname index.

801. Clarkson, Elisabeth Hudnut. *An Adirondack Archive: the Trail to Windover*. Utica, N.Y., North Country Books, 1993. x, 262p.

Hudnut family history from late nineteenth century to present, its ties to Adirondack region in North Creek and the southeastern Adirondacks.

802. Curth, Louis C. *The Forest Rangers: A History of the New York Forest Ranger Force*. Albany, N.Y., New York State Department of Environmental Conservation, 1987. 245p.

Centennial history of New York State Forest Rangers from 1885-1985. Topics mentioned are rangers, job descriptions, big fires, fire districts, training. Eleven appendices on subjects related to Forest Rangers plus others on railroads in the Forest Preserve, Civilian Conservation Corp. and standard plans for an Adirondack lean-to.

803. Douglas, Geoffrey. *Class: The Wreckage of an American Family*. New York, N.Y., H. Holt, 1992. 253p.

Story of decline of an "old money" family due to alcoholism. Douglas family spent summers in the Northern Adirondack region during the late 1940s and early 1950s. Describes camp and camp life.

804. Everest, Allan S. *Henry Delord and His Family*. Plattsburgh, N.Y., Kent-Delord House, 1979. viii, 112p.

Short work on Henry Delord, prominent Clinton County settler. Chapter on Delord House in contemporary times. Pocket-size book with bibliography, illus.

805. Gilborn, Craig A. *Durant: The Fortunes and Woodland Camps of a Family in the Adirondacks*. Sylvan Beach, N.Y., North Country Books, 1981. 176 p.; reprint, Blue Mountain Lake, N.Y., Adirondack Museum, 1986. 170p.

Story of Durant's financial activities and great camps in the Central Adirodacks in the last quarter of the nineteenth century. Short histories and descriptions of several great camps. Illus.

806. Greene, Evelyn. *The Schaefer Expeditions 1953-1956: Climbing in the High Peaks*. s.l., privately printed, 1989. 142p.

Accounts of family outings in the high peaks. Photos by Mary Schaefer. Map of high peaks region on endpapers.

807. Harris, H. Russell. *Harrisena: A Settlement Near Lake George, New York 1775-1985*. Glens Falls, N.Y., Glens Falls-Queensbury Historical Society, 1985. 158p.

Local history of Queensbury-Fort Ann region south of Lake George, with special attention to Harris family genealogy. Ports.

808. Harrison, Crockett Allen. *Thomas Seavy & Robert Irwin: Their Descendants and Connecting Lines.* Baltimore, MD., Gateway Press, 1988. xii, 486p.
Family history with ties to Saranac, Plattsburgh, and Peru in Clinton County, New York. Name index.

809. Jones, Mabel. *Some Other Joneses: Descendants of Increase Jones of Minerva, N.Y.* Minerva, N.Y., Mabel Jones, 1967. 267p.
Genealogy of Jones family from Newcomb-Minerva area. Index, illus., charts, maps, family ports.

810. Kozma, Ethel. *In the Beginning: Wadhams 1820-1970.* s.l., s.n., 1970. 42p.
Story of Wadhams family and their role in the development of the Town of Westport, Essex County. Family ports., maps.

811. Offensend, Dorothy. *The Sexton Boatbuilders of Hague, Lake George, N.Y.* Pawlet, VT., D.B. Offensend, 1982. 144p.
Sexton family history and memorabilia. Some early family members were boat builders. Bibliography, illus., notes.

812. Parker, Marjorie F. *Memoirs of the Lewis King Parker Family.* Saranac Lake, N.Y., Currier Press, 1973.
Malone family history. Information on recent family members and farm, as well as genealogy. Ports.

813. Pilcher, Edith. *The Constables: First Family of the Adirondacks.* Utica, N.Y., North Country Books, 1992. 160p.
Recounts story of 5 generations of prominent Adirondack family, their role and impact in Western Adirondacks, Boonville and Raquette Lake. Most of the book is about the Constables through the 1880s. Ports, illus., maps, bibliography.

814. Rose, Alexander G. *The Durant Genealogy.* Baltimore, MD., privately printed, 1966. 2 v.
Two volume Durant Family history, compiled by Rev. William Durant to 1890 and added to by Rose.

815. Saxton, Kermit. *Life's Book of Recollections 1825-1975.* Brushton, N.Y, Saxton, 1975. 84p.
Family histories of early settlers along the Gale Rd. in the town of Brushton, N.Y. in northern Franklin County.

816. Sherman, Gordon C. & Elsie L. Sherman. *The Sherman Genealogy, Six Hundred, Seventy-One Years of Generations (1300-1971).* Drucila Sherman, 1971. 36p.
Sherman family history-one branch of family has ties to Clinton County, New York.

817. Smith, Dorothy. *The Wilder Family Story.* Malone, N.Y., Franklin County Historical and Museum Society, 1972. 36p.
Information about the Wilder family in Burke, near Malone in northern New York State, in Wisconsin and on the prairies. Later printing in 1975, 1980, and 1985.

818. Wynn, Michelle Balliett. *The North Country Fiddlers.* Saranac Lake, N.Y., Association of North Country Fiddlers, 1992. 61p.
Photos and short biographical essays on over 40 regional men and women fiddlers.

# Individual

819. Alkalay-Gut, Karen. *Alone in the Dawn: The Life of Adelaide Crapsey.* Athens, GA., University of Georgia Press, 1988. x, 364p.
Biographical work about literary figure who contracted tuberculosis and spent time in Saranac Lake, New York. She died at age 36. Final chapter includes some of her poetry. Illus. Lengthy bibliography.

820. Armour, Marylee. *Heartwood: The Adirondack Homestead Life of W. Donald Burnap.* Old Forge, N.Y., Wildwood, 1988. 322p.
Story of Adirondack homestead at Fourth Lake in the Fulton Chain of Lakes from its rustic beginnings in the early 20th century to its latter days as a resort. Burnap also ran the Fulton Chain mail boat for many years. Illus.

821. Baigell, Matthew. *Thomas Cole.* New York, N.Y., Watson-Guptill Publications, 1981, 1985. 84p.
Landscape paintings of nineteenth century artist Thomas Cole, who many consider to be the founder of the Hudson River School of painting.

Contains two Adirondack works; Schroon Mountain, Adirondacks and Schroon Lake. Besides paintings, an essay on Cole, and a chronology of his life. Notes, bibliography.

822. Best, Tharratt Gilbert. *Early Memoirs of a Country Gentleman.* Lakemont, N.Y., North Country Books, 1976. ix, 258p.
Based on letters and diaries of a man who spent his teen-age years in Boonville, and Utica, N.Y. Edited by Virgina Best Clarenden.

823. Blanchard, Ralph R. *Bits and Pieces of a Man's LIfe.* New York, N.Y., Vantage, 1985. 56p.
Anecdotes and stories by native of Franklin County. Blanchard worked as an auto mechanic.

824. Bransom, Paul (as told to Helen Ireland Hays). *All Unplanned: Memoirs of the Golden Age of Illustration.* s.l., sn., 1983. 287p.
Memoirs about Paul Bransom, a wildlife artist who spent his summers in the Canada Lake region. Each chapter preceded by a Bransom drawing or painting.

825. Butterfield, Bruce A., ed. *Bicentennial of William Beaumont, M.D. 1985-1853.* s.l., s.n., 1985. 114p.
Collection of papers presented in honor of nineteenth century Plattsburgh physician who was a pioneer in physiology of the human stomach. Presentations took place at 4th Champlain Valley Proceedings, 1985 and focused on Beaumont's life, formative influences and his contribution to the medical field. Papers include citations.

826. Carr, Blanche G. *Memories of Yesterday, Prayers For Tomorrow.* s.l., s.n., 1982. 44p.
Autobiographical work by woman from Malone area. Carr's maiden name was Castle. Ports.

827. Coffin, Rosemary H. *A Ministry of Grace: An Account of the Life of Reverend Frederica Mitchell.* Exeter, N.H., Academy Press (Phillips Academy), 1983. 116p.
Biography of minister who served in Keene Valley.

828. Costa, Richard Hauer. *Edmund Wilson: Our Neighbor from Talcottville.* Syracuse, N.Y., Syracuse University Press, 1980. 173p.
Wilson was a writer and literary critic, author of *Upstate*, who had a strong attachment to Talcottville in southern Lewis County. A personal account of Wilson's last ten years.

829. Crapsey, Adelaide. *The Complete Poems and Collected Letters of Adelaide Crapsey.* Albany, N.Y., State University of New York Press, 1976. 288p.
Poetry and personal correspondence. An upstate New York native, Adelaide Crapsey was treated for tuberculosis in Saranac Lake. Edited by Susan Sutton Smith, who also wrote the introduction and notes.

830. De Sormo, Maitland C. *Joe Call: The Lewis Giant.* Saranac Lake, N.Y., Adirondack Yesteryears, 1981. 81p.
Biography of legendary Essex County muscle man. Endpapers contain illustration of region surrounding Lake Champlain on the New York side entitled "Joe Call Country." Illus. by Bill McLaughlin.

831. De Sormo, Maitland C. *John Bird Burnham-Klondiker, Adirondacker, and Eminent Conservationist.* Saranac Lake, N.Y., Adirondack Yesteryears Inc., 1978. 272p.
Biographical sketch of Burnham, resident of Willsboro and conservationist. His farm in northern New York was operated as a game preserve. In the early 1900s he served in New York State government as chief game protector and Commissioner of Fish and Game. He worked hard for migratory bird protection laws and treaties. Also a section about Burnham in Alaska. Illus., bibliography.

832. De Sormo, Maitland C. *Noah John Rondeau: Adirondack Hermit.* Saranac Lake, N.Y., North Country Books, 1969, 1970, 1970; Utica, N.Y., 1983, 1988. Var. pag.
Edited by Maitland C. De Sormo. Classic about this well known Adirondack resident. With permission from the family, DeSormo was able to edit material from Rondeau's personal letters, journals, and poetry. Autobiographical piece by Rondeau entitled "Recollections of 60 Years."

833. De Sormo, Maitland C. *Seneca Ray Stoddard: Versatile Camera Artist.* Saranac Lake, N.Y., Adirondack Yesteryears, 1972. 190p.
DeSormo makes his case for the proper recog-

nition of this accomplished nineteenth century photographer. Photos of Adirondack places and people.

834. Dean, Illamay Toland. *As I Look Back*. Blacksburg, VA., author, 1975.78p.

Reminiscences. Author's parents were natives of Franklin County. First 50 pages are about growing up in Burke, N.Y. in the early 20th century. Burke is in northern Franklin County, just outside of the Blue Line. Ports.

835. Everest, Allan S. *The Military Career of Alexander Macomb and Macomb at Plattsburgh*. Plattsburgh, N.Y., Clinton County Historical Association, 1989. 85p.

Two part work documenting the career of Alexander Macomb, an American military figure who played an important role in land fighting at the Battle of Plattsburgh in the War of 1812. Part I briefly outlines Macomb's military career. Part II is a journal of Macomb at Plattsburgh. Index.

836. Everest, Allan S. *North Country Pioneer: Pliny Moore of Champlain, New York*. Plattsburgh, N.Y., Clinton County Historical Association, 1990. 136p.

Story of prominent Clinton County individual and his family. Illus., ports., index.

837. Flexner, James Thomas. *Mohawk Baronet: Sir William Johnson of New York*. New York, N.Y., Harper, 1959. 400p.; reprint, *Lord of the Mohawks: A Biography of Sir William Johnson*. Boston & Toronto, Little Brown & Co., 1979; Syracuse, N.Y., Syracuse University Press, 1989. xviii, 400p.

A detailed and comprehensive biography of the flamboyant Sir William Johnson whose accomplishments included frontiersman, millonaire, diplomat, Indian chief, general, and English noble. He was as comfortable in Native American culture as he was in white society of Colonial America and served as a bridge between the two worlds. Bibliography.

838. Glover, James M. *A Wilderness Original: The Life of Bob Marshall*. Seattle, WA., Mountaineers, 1986. 323p.

Biography of wilderness advocate and conservationist. Marshall spent summers as a youth in the Adirondacks near Saranac Lake, New York. This experience was a formative one. Bibliography.

839. Gurley, Ralph Randolph. *Life of Jehudi Ashmun, Late Colonial Agent in Liberia*. Washington, D.C., J.C. Dunn, 1835; reprint, New York, N.Y., Negro University Press, 1969. 396p., 106.

Biography of Clinton County native, born in mid-1790s.

840. Hamilton, Milton W. *Sir William Johnson and the Indians of New York*. Albany, N.Y., Office of State History, 1967. 47p.

Iroquois were a significant force in Colonial and Revolutionary eras in New York State. Johnson was important in dealing with Iroquois- he was fair, honest and skillful in doing so. Also mentions French and Indian War, and Battle of Lake George, which earned Johnson much recognition. Illus. Bibliography.

841. Hochschild, Adam. *Half the Way Home: A Memoir of Father and Son*. New York, N.Y., Viking, 1986. 197p.

Harold Hochschild was a powerful businessman, chief of a multinational corporation. Adam, his son, was an anti-war activist, and co-founded *Mother Jones*. The elder Hochschild wrote *Township 34* and had a long-standing interest in and commitment to the Adirondack region. Also in paper, 1987, Large print ed. in 1986.

842. Hochschild, Adam. *Harold K. Hochschild*. Dexter, MI, s.n., 1982. 133p.

Part I is edited writings of Harold Hochschild; reminiscences, letters and poems. Part II consists of writings of others *about* Hochschild, including an essay "HKH and the Adirondacks." Remembrances of Hochschold by Patricia Hochschild Labalme and article about HKH as a businessman by F. Taylor Ostrander.

843. Hodges, Willis Augustus. *Free Man of Color: The Autobiography of Willis Augustus Hodges*. Knoxville, TN., University of Tennessee Press, 1982. lxxiii, 97p.

Introduction by Willard B. Gatewood Jr. Autobiography of free Black man who was part of an Afro-American colony in the Adirondacks during the late 1840s. Community named Blacksville was in Franklin County near Loon Lake. Bibliography.

844. Hoy, Ralph L. *An Adirondack Boyhood Remembered*. Santa Barbara, CA., Pilgrim Press, 1978;

revised ed., Santa Barbara, CA., Mendicus Press, 1978. 82p.

Edited by Joanne H. O'Roarke. Hoy's reminiscences of growing up in Brainardsville, N.Y. before WW I. Family ports.

845. Hoy, Ralph L. *Heritage of the Adirondacks: Frosty Peaks, Warm Hearts*. Santa Barbara, CA., Mendicus Press, 1979. 92p.

Second volume of Hoy's memoirs on northern Adirondacks, discussing life in the 1920s and during the Depression. Picks up the life of the author as a young man. Recollections of Lake Placid's development for the 1932 Olympics. Illus.

846. Jamieson, Paul F. *Uneven Ground*. Canton, N.Y., Friends of Owen D. Young Library, St. Lawrence University, 1992. vi, 232p.

Well-written autobiography by Adirondack author, scholar, and conservationist.

847. Johnson, Fridolf, ed. *Rockwell Kent: An Anthology of His Work*. New York, N.Y., Knopf, 1982. 358p.

Commemorates 100th anniversary of Kent's birth. Kent lived on a farm near AuSable Forks in the Adirondacks. Biographical essay by Johnson. Many illus. by Kent as well as reproductions of his paintings. Folio. Bibliography, index.

848. Keller, Betty. *Black Wolf: The Life of Ernest Thompson Seton*. Vancouver, B.C., Douglas & McIntyre, 1984. 240p.

Biography of naturalist and writer. Seton wrote ROLF IN THE WOODS, an Adirondack classic. Bibliography.

849. Kellogg, David S. *A Doctor at All Hours: The Private Journal of a Small-Town Doctor's Varied Life 1886-1909*. Brattleboro, VT., Stephen Greene Press, 1970. vii, 229p.

Journal of a Plattsburgh physician who lived in the late 19th century, edited by Allan S. Everest. Besides insights into the life of physician during that time, Kellogg was also keenly interested in folklore, local history, and natural history. Editor's notes introducing each year and ending each chapter enhance the journals. Illus.

850. Kelsay, Isabel Thompson. *Joseph Brant 1743-1807, Man of Two Worlds*. Syracuse, N.Y., Syracuse University Press, 1984, 1986. xii, 775p.

Biography of well-known American Indian, based on primary sources. Illus., bibliography.

851. LaBastille, Anne. *Beyond Black Bear Lake*. New York, N.Y., W.W. Norton and Company, 1987. 251p.

Feeling the infringements of people, planes and developers Anne LaBastille moved deeper into the woods. This work tells of the circumstances that led her to move and how she did it.

852. LaBastille, Anne. *Woodswoman*. New York, N.Y., E.P. Dutton, 1976; reprint, New York, N.Y., Penguin Books, 1991. xi, 277p.

This volume chronicles LaBastille's early years in the Adirondack woods. Professionally, she works as a biologist, conservationist, writer, and lecturer. Personally, she has a strong desire to live in the wilderness. This book tells how she went about building her cabin in the woods.

853. Levine, Ed. *The Adventures of Red Perkins: Remembrances of an Adirondack Guide*. Lakemont, N.Y., North Country Books, 1976. 66p.

Reminiscences of Adirondack guide and Old Forge, N.Y. native Red Perkins. He worked as a lumberjack and guide, and was involved in the construction of McCauley Mt. ski area. Pictures span several decades.

854. Longstaff, George H. *From Heyday to Mayday*. St. Petersburg, FL., Valkyrie Publishing House, 1983. 215p.

Reminiscences. Provides some insight into rise and decline in Central Adirondacks. Describes development of children's summer camps. Part II is author's remedy for America's economic, social and educational disintegration.

855. Lynn, Robert L. *Who Was Nessmuk?*. Wellsboro, PA., Wellsboro Chamber of Commerce, 1971. 28p.

Background and biographical information on nineteenth century Adirondack outdoorsman George Washington Sears whose nickname was Nessmuk. Published for the Nessmuk Sesquicentennial celebration.

856. Mackay, Margaret. *The Violent Friend: The Story of Mrs. Robert Louis Stevenson*. Garden City, N.Y., Doubleday, 1968. 566p.

Story of Stevenson's American wife. Mention

of Saranac Lake where Stevenson went in 1889 for his tuberculosis and where he wrote *The Master of Ballantrae*. Illus., bibliography, index.

857. Manley, Atwood. *Rushton and His Times in American Canoeing*. Syracuse, N.Y., The Adirondack Museum/Syracuse University Press, 1968, 1977. xiii, 203p.

Rushton was born in the Adirondacks and later located in Canton, N.Y. He was a canoe builder and a promoter of canoeing who built lightweight craft, including the *Sairy Gamp* for George Washington Sears. Appendices about Rushtons's method of construction, line drawing of Rushton Boats, a reprint of article by George Washington Sears on Rushton's smaller crafts. Paul Jamieson assisted Manley on this project. Illus.

858. Manley, Atwood and Margaret Manley Mangum. *Frederic Remington and the North Country*. New York, N.Y., Dutton, 1988. xxviii, 272p.

Biographical work about Remington emphasizing his North Country roots. Based on diaries of his wife Eva Caten Remington which have not been available until recently. Best known for his western art, Remington also produced a body of paintings and drawings with North Country subjects. Bibliography.

859. McFadden, John Jersey. *The Diary of John Jersey McFadden in the Year 1872*. Plattsburgh, N.Y., A.L. Shields, 1983. ix, 40p.

First person account of a Scottish immigrant. Annotated by Addie Shields, Clinton County Historian. Illus., maps, index.

860. Mitchell, Roger. *Clear Pond: The Reconstruction of a Life*. Syracuse, N.Y., Syracuse University Press, 1991. 230p.

Engrossing biographical and historical case study of the life of Adirondacker Israel Johnson. Roger Mitchell grew up in Saranac Lake, New York.

861. Murphy, Eloise C. *Theodore Roosevelt's Night Ride to the Presidency*. Blue Mountain Lake, N.Y., Adirondack Museum, 1977. 35p.

Theodore Roosevelt was vacationing in the Adirondacks in 1902 when President McKinley was assassinated. Story of his trip from Lake Tear of the Clouds to rail station in North Creek, on his way to assume the presidency. Illus.

862. Nelson, Rodney B. *Beaumont, America's First Physiologist*. Geneva, Ill., Grant House Press, 1990. 379p.

Biography of Plattsburgh physician. 500 copies.

863. Pelkey, Rosemary. *The Life and Times of Robert Codgell Gilchrist: Adirondack Bridgebuilder from Charleston*. Utica, N.Y., North Country Books, 1993. 161p.

NAR

864. Schiff, Leonard J. & Joseph F. Schiff. *Edward Payson Baird: Inventor, Industrialist, Entrepreneur*. Plattsburgh, N.Y., Clinton Press, 1975. ix, 61p.

Story of Baird clock works, which operated for several years in the late nineteenth century in Plattsburgh, N.Y. Numerous photos of old clocks will please buffs and collectors.

865. Severance, Charles R. *Recollections of a Country Boy*. Minerva, N.Y., Minerva Historical Society, 1991. 73p.

Author grew up in North Creek. Provides view of life in the Adirondacks around the time of the Great Depression. Text only.

866. Shanahan, Glenna. *Muster to the Drum: A True Story*. Ozark, MO., Yates Publishing Co., 1984. 188p.

Story of author's ancestor who fought in the Revolutionary War in Eastern Adirondacks. Bibliography.

867. Shields, Addie L. *Account Book for the Farmer "1876": Amos Barber II (1828-1889)*. Plattsburgh, N.Y., Clinton County Government Center, 1984. 126p.

Edited by Shields. Financial records of West Chazy farmer. Old Barber family ports. Maps, deeds and other miscellaneous information.

868. Smith, Vivian G. *With Hand and Heart: The Courtship Letters of Franklin B. Hough and Mariah Kilham: January Through May 1849*. Utica, N.Y., North Country Books, 1993. 124p.

Two dozen letters. Franklin B. Hough is best known in northern New York for his various county histories. These letters and Hough's early diaries belong to Lewis County Historical Museum in Lyons Falls, N.Y.

869. Splete, Allen P. and Marilyn D. Splete. *Frederic Remington, Selected Letters.* New York, N.Y., Abbeville Press, 1987. 487p.

Collected letters of Remington compiled by former North Country residents. Important insights into Remington as a person, in his own words. Accompanied by many ink drawings by Remington. Intro. by late Atwood Manley. Bibliography.

870. Stanton, Rev. E. Lester. *Souvenirs of the Adirondack Mountains: Blue Mountain Lake; My Boyhood Home in Poetry/Prose/ Pictures.* s.l., s.n., 1982. 100p.

Reminiscences of Blue Mountain Lake and poetry by the author. Numerous photos, many of which are courtesy of the Adirondack Museum.

871. Stevenson, Gordon & Judith Kramer-Greene. *Melvil Dewey: The Man and the Classification, A Seminar.* Albany, N.Y., Forest Press, 1983. ix, 210p.

Edited proceedings of seminar on Dewey. Information on Lake Placid Club which Dewey established in early 1900s. Sponsored by Lake Placid Education Foundation.

872. Teall, Edna West. *Adirondack Tales: A Girl Grows Up in the Adirondacks in the 1880s.* Willsboro, N.Y., Adirondack Life, 1970. 191p.

Short essays on a wide variety of daily topics intermixed with 40 color paintings by the author. 82 woodcuts that depict life in the late 1800s. A nicely done book, limited to 1,000 copies.

873. Thomas, Howard. *Joseph Brant (Thayendanegea).* Prospect, N.Y., Prospect Books, 1973; reprint, Utica, N.Y., North Country Books, 1984. 176p.

Biography of important Native American figure in New York State history. Fought at Battle of Lake George in 1755 as an ally of Sir William Johnson.

874. Torrance, Fred A. *Fred A. Torrance: His Life, Times and Philosophy; Including His Early Articles on the Town of Jay 1878-1948.* Troy, N.Y., Prout Press, 1982. 118p.

Personal writings about Jay, New York. Early history and politics of Jay as well as personal letters, philosophy, speeches. List of town officials and maps of township in appendix.

875. Traxel, David. *An American Saga: The Life and Times of Rockwell Kent.* New York, N.Y., Harper & Row, 1980. 248p.

Biography of Rockwell Kent. Deals with his personal life and political activity. Brief mention of the Adirondacks. Bibliography.

876. Tuckerman, Bayard. *Life of General Philip Schuyler 1733-1804.* New York, N.Y., Dodd and Mead & Co., 1903; reprint, Freeport, N.Y., Books For Libraries Press, 1969. 277p.

Based on Schuyler's papers and letterbooks. Provides insight into this prominent Colonial New York State family and individual. Schuyler's role in Revolutionary War effort in eastern Adirondacks (Ticonderoga, Burgoyne's campaign).

877. Tuttle, Charles Henry. *A Supplement: With Father Time's Collaboration, To My Family "Memorabilia" of April 21, 1969.* Lake George, N.Y., Halcyon Press, 1970. 94p.

Personal reminiscences and memorabilia of Lake George.

878. Tyler, Helen Escha. *Born Smart: The Story of Paul Smith.* Utica, N.Y., North Country Books, 1988. 182p.

Biography of Paul Smith, businessman and Franklin County hotel owner. Illus. by Bruce John.

879. Welch, Fay. ed. *The Old Guide's Story of the Northern Adirondacks: Reminiscences of Charles E. Merrill.* Burlington, VT., The George Little Press, 1973. 224p.

Reminiscences of Charles E. Merrill, Adirondack guide, 1863-1935, about the Chateaugay Lake region. Front endpapers contain Colvin drawing of Chateaugay Lake region. Back endpapers have a map of "The Old Guide's Country." Illustrated by Tom Welch.

880. Whitney, C.V. *High Peaks.* Lexington, KY., University of Kentucky Press, 1977. x, 127p.

Autobiographical work of Cornelius Vanderbilt Whitney. Adirondack connection is that Whitney has a a camp near Long Lake in the Adirondacks.

881. Williams, Donald R. *Oliver H. Whitman, Adirondack Guide and Other Adirondack Stories: Based on the 1882-1920 Journals of Oliver Wesley Whitman.* Wells, N.Y., Haderondack House, 1979. 186p.

Whitman journals cover 38 years and are revealing about the daily life of an Adirondack farmer and guide in the late nineteenth century and early twentieth century. Whitman family ports.

882. Williams, Donald R. *The Saga of Nicholas Stoner Or, A Tale of the Adirondacks*. Wells, N.Y., Adirondack Books, 1969. 159p.

Biography of Nicholas Stoner, a Fulton County hunter and trapper.

883. Wilson, Edmund. *The Fifties: from Notebooks and Diaries of the Period*. New York, N.Y., Farrar, Straus, & Giroux, 1986. xxxii, 663p.

Diaries and journals of writer Edmund Wilson, edited by Leon Edel. Reflects his wide-ranging activities including his interest in the Iroquois of Northern New York and his family home in Talcottville, in southern Lewis County.

884. Wilson, Edmund. *Upstate: Records and Reflections of Northern New York*. New York, N.Y., Farrar, Straus, and Giroux, 1971. 386p.

Wilson was a prolific writer and a literary critic. *Upstate* is his reminiscences about Talcottville in southern Lewis County, New York.

885. Wolf, Ben. *Harold Weston*. Philadelphia, PA., Art Alliance Press, 1978. 96p.

Works of Harold Weston. Early career spent at St. Hubert's near Keene Valley in the High Peaks, known as his "private man" period. Many of his works from this period were inspired by the beauty of the Adirondack wilderness. Interview with his wife, Faith, is interesting and insightful.

886. Wyld, Lionel D. *Walter Edmonds, Storyteller*. Syracuse, N.Y., Syracuse University Press, 1982. xii, 154p.

Biography of Black River valley regional writer Walter Edmonds, who was born in Boonville in 1903. Best known for *Drums along the Mohawk*. Wyld focuses on Edmond's fiction. Bibliography, index.

# Adirondacks in Art and Literature

## General

887. Bruchac, Joseph. *Hoop Snakes, Hide-Behinds and Side-Hill Winder: Tall Tales from the Adirondacks.* Freedom, CA., Crossing Press, 1991. 115p.
Many of the stories about Bill Greenfield who lived in the Southern Adirondacks and died in 1903.

888. Bruchac, Joseph. *Iroquois Stories: Heroes and Heroines, Monsters and Magic.* Trumansburg, N.Y., Crossing Press, 1985. 198p.
Traditional Iroquois stories. Bruchac is of Native American ancestry, and was raised in foothill community of Greenfield Center. Illustrated by Daniel Burgevin.

889. Bruchac, Joseph. *New Voices from the Longhouse: An Anthology of Contemporary Iroquois Writing.* Greenfield Center, N.Y., Greenfield Review Press, 1989. 292p.
Approximately 15 of artists are Mohawk. Poetry and prose. Illus. Paper edition in 1990.

890. Bruchac, Joseph, ed. *North Country: An Anthology of Contemporary Writing from the Adirondacks and the Upper Hudson Valley.* Greenfield Center, N.Y., Greenfield Review Press, 1986. xii, 458p.
Contains works by 50 different Adirondack writers. Photo of each writer, biographical sketch, and partial list of publishing credits.

891. Bruhns, Walter C. *An Adirondack Affair: Photography and Poetry of the Waters and Mountains.* Lake Placid, N.Y., Bruhns, 1988. 45p.
Poetry, color photos of the Adirondack region. Intro. by Maitland C. De Sormo.

892. Cadbury, Warder & Henry F. Marsh. *Arthur Fitzwilliam Tait: Artist in the Adirondacks; An Account of His Career, a Checklist of His Works.* Newark, DL., University of Delaware Press, 1985. 344p.
Divided into 2 parts. Part I by Warder H. Cadbury recounts Tait's career. Three chapters specifically discuss Tait in the Adirondacks and his works. Part II is a checklist of Tait's art. Appendices, bibliography, indexes. Photos of Tait's paintings.

893. Carpenter, Teresa. *Missing Beauty: A True Story of Murder and Obsession.* New York, N.Y., Norton, 1988. 478p.; New York, N.Y., Kensington Publishing, 1989. 605p.
True account of a young prostitute who was murdered by Prof. William Douglas, who was an Adirondack native and attended college in northern New York. Douglas worked at Tufts as a research scientist. British editions in 1989 and 1991.

894. Cooper, Helen A. *Winslow Homer Watercolors.* Washington, D.C., National Gallery of Art; New Haven, CT.,Yale University Press, 1986. 259p.
Chapter on Homer in the Adirondacks (1889-1900) contains almost 3 dozen paintings portraying world of Adirondack woodsman.

895. Foster, Jeanne Robert. *Adirondack Portraits: A Piece of Time.* Syracuse, N.Y., Syracuse University Press, 1986. xli, 172p.
Stories of people of Essex, Warren, and Hamilton Counties in the late 1800s. Biographical essay about Jean Robert Foster by Noel Riedinger-Johnson. Prose and poetry about Adirondacks. Photos of the region and the author. Foreword by Alfred Kazin. Bibliography.

896. Frederic Remington Art Museum and the Adirondack Museum. *Artist in Residence: the North Country Art of Frederic Remington: an Exhibition.* Ogdensburg, N.Y., Frederic Remington Art Museum, 1985. 96p.
Sixty-seven paintings and illus. with North Country/Adirondack content. Written contributions by David Tatham and Atwood Manley.

897. Glenn, Ellin & Morris F. *The Adirondack Art of Homer Dodge Martin.* Alexandria, VA., Glenn, 1979. 26p.
Work stresses Martin's connection to the Adirondacks. He was most closely associated with the region between 1865 and 1878. Contains many

of Martin's Adirondack works. Foreword by Maitland C. De Sormo.

898. Goeldin, Michel. *A l'Ouest de Lake Placid.* Roman, Vevey, Editions Bertil Galland, 1979. 194p.

Written in French. This is the story of a young photographer of international renown and his fight to prevent the takeover of Camp Woodridge by a corporation that wants to use it to build a giant factory. (This annotation provided by Christian Verlaque, Canton, N.Y.)

899. Halpern, Sue. *Migrations to Solitude.* New York, N.Y., Pantheon, 1992. 213p.

Book on solitude and privacy by Adirondack resident.

900. Homer, Winslow. *Winslow Homer Illustrations.* New York, N.Y., Dover Publications, 1983. 43p.

Forty-one wood engravings and illus. by Homer. Only one specifically Adirondack in content, "Camping out in the Adirondack Mountains," appeared in *Harpers Weekly*, November 7, 1874.

901. Howat, John K. *The Hudson River and Its Painters.* New York, N.Y., Viking Press, 1972. 207p.; reprint, New York, N.Y., American Legacy, 1983. 208p.

Preface by James Biddle. Foreword by Carl Carmer. 100 paintings of Hudson River. Only about 25% are from Albany north—a handful by Winslow Homer and Homer Dodge Martin. Plates are followed by a short description of each painting.

902. Jamieson, Paul F. *Adirondack Pilgrimage.* Glens Falls, N.Y., Adirondack Mountain Club, Inc., 1986. 238p.

Writings of Jamieson on the Adirondack region. Topics include geology, geography, well-known people, four 19th century literary classics on the Adirondacks, and several 20th century writers. Bibliography. First printing limited to 500 copies. Also in paper.

903. Jones, Louis C. *Things That Go Bump in the Night.* New York, N.Y., Hill and Wang, 1959. 208p., 1967. xii, 208p.; reprints, Mattituck, N.Y., Aeonian Press, 1978. 208p.; Syracuse, N.Y., Syracuse University Press, 1983. xiv, 208p.

Ghost stories and haunted tales. Some regional references. Illus. by Erwin Austin. Index.

904. LaBastille, Anne. *The Wilderness World of Anne LaBastille: A Selection of Never Before Published Poems, Plus Her Finest Nature Essays, Short Stories and Color Photographs.* Westport, N.Y., West of the Wind Publications, 1992. 119p.

Foreword by Clarence Petty. Poetry plus reprints of some of her essays. Cover notes "In Celebration of the Adirondack Park Centennial."

905. MacDonald, John D. *The House Guests.* New York, N.Y., Doubleday & Co., 1965; reprint, New York, N.Y., Fawcett Gold Medal, 1988. 182p.

About author's cats, Roger and Geoff. Part of the book set in Piseco.

906. McKibben, Bill. *The Age of Missing Information.* New York, N.Y., Random House, 1992. 261p.

Discussion of social aspects of television. Uses experiences of climbing a mountain near his home in the Adirondacks for sake of comparison and contrast.

907. McKibben, Bill. *The End of Nature.* New York, N.Y., Random House, 1989. 226p.

Books discusses environmental consequences of man's technological domination of nature. McKibben now lives in the Adirondacks and refers to the region in developing his ideas.

908. Oppel, Frank comp. *New York: Tales of the Empire State.* Secaucus, N.J., Castle, 1988. 480p.

Seven of 32 entries relate to the Adirondacks. Reprints of periodical articles first published in late nineteenth and early twentieth century.

909. Rankin, Nicholas. *Dead Man's Chest: Travels After Robert Louis Stevenson.* Boston, MA., Faber & Faber, 1987. xi, 366p.

Contains chapter on Saranac Lake. Rankin traced Stevenson's travels, adding his own comments and perpectives. Stevenson wrote *The Master of Ballantrae* during his stay at Saranac Lake in 1887.

910. Roth, Richard Patrick. *The Adirondack Guide (1820-1919): Hewing out An American Occupation.* Syracuse University, Syracuse, N.Y., 1990. 330 lvs; also, Ann Arbor, MI., University Microfilm Dissertation Services, 1990.

Doctoral thesis. Study of portrayal of the legendary Adirondack Guide in arts and letters. Discusses works of Tait, Murray, Homer, Colvin, Remington, Stoddard, Bacheller, Keith and Fay Welch.

911. Samuels, Peggy & Harold Samuels. *The Collected Writings of Frederic Remington.* Garden City, N.Y., Doubleday, 1979. xx, 649p.

Along with sculpting and painting, Remington also wrote between 1887 and 1906. Over 100 articles and stories by Remington appeared in periodicals of the day. The Samuels' work contains over 130 illus. A substantial work. Bibliography.

912. Schweizer, Paul D. (comp.). *The Art of Trenton Falls 1825-1900.* Utica, N.Y., Museum of Art, Munson-Williams-Proctor Institute, 1989. 72p.

Trenton Falls lies just outside the southwestern corner of the Blue Line.

913. Smith, David. *David Smith by David Smith: Sculpture and Writings.* New York, N.Y., Holt, Rinehart, Winston, 1968.; reprint, 1988. 176p.

Edited by Cleve Gray. Works of David Smith who lived and worked near Bolton Landing until his death in 1965. Artist worked in steel and was also a writer. Illus.

914. Tovell, Rosemarie L. *David Milne: Painting Place.* Ottawa, Ont., National Gallery of Canada, 1976. 40p.

Essay on David Milne. Mention of Big Moose Lake where he lived for a time in the 1920s. Contains photos of a few of Milne's works and a bibliography. Bi-lingual in English and French.

915. Winn, Wesley George. *Art of the Adirondack Mountains.* Detroit, MI., Wayne State University, 1988. ii, 126 lvs.

Masters thesis. Concentrates on the nineteenth century and discusses painting, literature and some folk traditions. Concludes Hudson River School of painters showed the most interest in the region. Writers were interested primarily hunting and fishing. Only canoe builders and log cabin builders were residents of the region. Bibliography.

916. Winter, Kate H. *The Woman in the Mountain: Reconstruction of Self and Land by Adirondack Women Writers.* Albany, N.Y., State University of New York Press, 1989. ix, 208p.

Chapters on 7 women writers, including such contemporaries as Jean Rikhoff, Alice Wolf Gilborn, and Anne LaBastille. Lists Adirondack-related books by women. Bibliography. Also in paper.

# Exhibit Catalogs

917. Adirondack Museum. *A.F. Tait, Artist in the Adirondacks.* Blue Mountain Lake, N.Y., Adirondack Museum, 1974. 73p.

Exhibit catalog of popular 19th century artist A.F. Tait. Known for his wildlife paintings, he also lived in the Adirondacks and many of his painting reflect regional subjects.

918. Bourcier, Paul G. *History in the Mapping: Four Centuries of Adirondack Cartography; A Catalog of the Exhibition, June 12, 1984-October 15, 1985.* Blue Mountain Lake, N.Y., Adirondack Museum, 1986. 69p.

Catalog for exhibit of 66 maps and atlases from Adirondack Museum. Essay places the exhibit in historical context and describe three eras of regional development.

919. Brainerd Art Complex. *Robert Plumb: A Memorial Exhibition, December 14, 1985-January 19, 1986.* Potsdam, N.Y., State University College at Potsdam, 1986. 30p.

Exhibit catalog. Features black and white photographs of 20 Plumb paintings with North Country/ Adirondack content. Essay discusses Plumb as painter, teacher and photographer. He died in 1985 at age 52.

920. Burdick, Virginia M. and Katherine Lochridge. *Portraits and Painters of the Early Champlain Valley, 1800-1865.* Plattsburgh, N.Y., State University of New York, 1975. 40p.

Catalog for exhibit of regional painters and portraitures. Photos of over 50 paintings with information on the author, the size, and medium used. Brief biographical information on person in portrait. Selected bibliography.

921. Chittenden, Varrick & Herbert W. Hemphill. *Found in New York's North Country: The Folk Art of a Region.* Utica, N.Y., The Institute, 1982. 72p.

Essays by Varrick Chittenden and Herbert W. Hemphill. Folk art of northern New York. Various media: beadwork, decoys, signs, weather vanes, figurines. Chittenden's essay, "New York's North Country: A Way of Life," is a definitive essay on the region.

922. Clinton County Historical Museum. *Reflections: The Story of Redford Glass*. Plattsburgh, N.Y., Clinton County Historical Museum, 1979. 38p.

Redford Glass was produced in Clinton County between 1831 and 1851. Part of "South Jersey" tradition. Essay about the company by Bruce Stark. Photos and notes on each glass object that was in the exhibit.

923. Cone, Jane Harrison. *David Smith, 1986-1965: A Retrospective Exhibition*. Cambridge, MA., s.n., 1966. 107p.

Catalog of exhibit done shortly after Smith's death in 1965. He lived in Bolton Landing, N.Y. at the time. Book also contains chronology of Smith's life. Selected bibliography on Smith and his work, plus 4 articles by Smith. Interview by Katherine Kuh. Introductory essay by Cone. Plates.

924. Crowley, William. *Seneca Ray Stoddard: Adirondack Illustrator*. Blue Mountain Lake, New York, Adirondack Museum, 1981. vii, 64p.

Exhibit took place June 15-October 15, 1981 and 1982. Catalog has a chronology of Stoddard's life and a checklist of exhibited works. Illus. Essays on Stoddard's career and landscape photography. 2,000 copies.

925. Everson Museum of Art. *Winslow Homer in the 1880s: Watercolors, Drawings and Etchings*. Syracuse, N.Y., Everson Museum of Art, 1983. 32p.

Features eighty works by Homer in the 1880s when he lived in Prout's Neck. Only a few with Adirondack content.

926. Hoopes, Donelson F. *Winslow Homer Watercolors*. New York, N.Y., Watson-Guptill Publications, 1969. 87p.

Handful of illus. are connected to the Adirondacks. Excellent outline chronology of Homer's career. Bibliography. Paper edition in 1976.

927. Hyde Collection. *Artists of Lake George 1776-1976*. Glens Falls, N.Y., The Hyde Collection, 1976. 56p.

Published in association with exhibit of the same name. Seventeen individual and institutional lenders contributed. Works on Lake George and by artists of Lake George in a variety of media: painting, watercolors, drawings, photography, prints and sculpture. Nineteenth century landscape paintings of Lake George are particularly striking.

928. Katonah Museum of Art. *Forever Wild: The Adirondack Experience; In Celebration of the Centennial of the Adirondack Park*. Katonah, N.Y., The Museum, 1991. 40p.

Exhibit catalog plus 5 essays by Craig Gilborn, Anthony N.B. Garvan, Paul Malo, Paul Jamieson. Lists items in exhibit.

929. Jones, Barbara. *Nature Staged: The Landscape and Still Life Paintings of Levi Wells Prentice*. Blue Mountain Lake, N.Y., Adirondack Museum, 1993. 95p.

Catalog for exhibit at Adirondack Museum during 1993 season. Prentice was born near the Adirondacks and painted nearly 70 regional works during the last third of the nineteenth century. Essay and check list by Barbara L. Jones. Bibliography and index.

930. Lake George Arts Project. *The Prospect Mountain Sculpture Show: An Homage to David Smith*. Lake George, N.Y., The Project, 1979. 54p.

Exhibit Catalog. Eighteen artists participated in an art show on Prospect Mountain, near Lake George, honoring David Smith, 1906-1965. Smith was a well known American sculptor who lived and worked in Bolton Landing, N.Y. Chronology of Smith's life. Illus.

931. Mandel, Patricia. *Fair Wilderness: American Paintings in the Collection of the Adirondack Museum*. Blue Mountain Lake, N.Y., Adirondack Museum, 1990. 175p.

Check list with photos of paintings in Adirondack Museum. Introductory essay by editor entitled, "What is Adirondack in Adirondack Art?" Bibliography.

932. McGrath, Robert L. *Wild Sort of Beauty: Public Places and Private Visions*. Blue Mountain Lake, N.Y., Adirondack Museum, 1992. vi, 56p.

Essay by McGrath entitled, "A Central Park for the World: Nature and Self in the Adirondacks." Photos of landscape paintings on exhibit.

933. Orchard, Harry Frederick. *Charles Lanman: Landscapes and Nature Studies.* Morristown, N.J., Morris Museum of Arts and Science, 1983. 28p.
Several paintings of Lake George area. Essay on Lanman by Orchard. Bibliography.

934. Owens, Gwendolyn. *Nature Transcribed: The Landscapes and Still Lifes of David Johnson (1827-1908).* Ithaca, N.Y., Herbert F. Johnson Museum of Art, Cornell University, 1988. 87p.
Works of David Johnson, a landscape artist, who used Lake George as his subject. Lists of paintings, photos of displayed works, and selected bibliography.

935. Owens, Gwendolyn. *The Watercolors of David Milne.* Ithaca, N.Y., Herbert F. Johnson Museum of Art, Cornell University, 1984. 56p.
Milne was a Canadian artist who lived at Darts Lake and Big Moose Lake in 1921 and 1922. Book contains photos of 40 paintings and an essay chronicling Milne's career. Chronology of author's life and selected bibliography.

936. Tovell, Rosemarie L. *Reflections in a Quiet Pond: The Prints of David Milne.* Ottawa, Ont., National Gallery of Canada, National Museum of Canada, 1980. xvi, 244p.
Milne, a Canadian artist, lived in the Adirondacks in the 1920s, producing many paintings of the region (Chapter 3). Bibliography.

937. Van Lent, Peter C. *The Hidden Heritage: The French Folk Culture of Northern New York.* Malone, N.Y., Malone Arts Council, 1988. 113p.
Plates of French American arts and crafts. Foreword by by Varrick Chittenden. Text discusses work, religion, home life, language, community folk literature. Personal profiles of French Americans in northern New York.

# Essays

938. Bergmann, Frank ed. *Upstate Literature: Essays in Memory of Thomas F. O'Donnell.* Syracuse, N.Y., Syracuse University Press, 1985. 222p.
Chapter entitled "North Country Voices" written by Kate H. Winter discusses Bacheller, Deming and Edmonds. References. Also in paper.

939. Coolidge, William III. *Mountains and Memories.* Elizabethtown, N.Y., Denton Publication, 1987. 80p.
Twenty-three essays and some poems on North Country living; sugaring, weather, Christmas, gardening, snowshoes and other similiar subjects. Book II in Woodsmoke Series.

940. Coolidge, William III. *Woodsmoke and Mountain Ways.* Elizabethtown, N.Y., Denton Publications, 1985. 80p.
Collection of 14 written pieces by regional author. Some Adirondack content. Woodsmoke Series.

941. Hall, Robert F. *The Empty Nest: Adirondack Essays and Other Reflections.* Willsboro, N.Y., Adirondack Yesteryears, 1984. 108p.
Illustrated by Charles Hawley. Mr. Hall was a former publisher of the *Warrensburg-Lake George News* and founder of *Adirondack Life.* From 1971-1976 Hall edited *The Conservationist.*

942. Hall, Robert F. *North Country Almanac: Journal of the Adirondack Seasons.* Fleischmanns, N.Y., Purple Mountain Press, 1990. 134p.
Collected nature essays by Hall which originally appeared in other publications. Organized by seasons. Chapter on nature writers, past and present.

943. Hays, Helen Ireland. *Heritage.* Francestown, N.H., N. Jones Co., 1979. 218p.
Collection of stories, several are about southern Adirondacks.

944. Reid, Edwin A. *Adirondack Reidings.* Saranac Lake, N.Y., Reid Publications, 1987. 100p.
Short essays and anecdotes about hunting in the Adirondacks. A few poems. Illus. by P. Teale.

945. Reid, Edwin A. *Reach For the Wilds.* Wanakena, N.Y., Reid Publications, 1989. 120p.
Illus. by Penny Teale and Paula Joy. Short essays and writings about the outdoors and "the wilds" of the Adirondacks.

946. Reid, Edwin A. *This is...Packbasket Country.* Wanakena, N.Y., Reid Publications, 1990. 112p.
Essays and poetry on woodsmen and woods lore. Ink drawings.

947. Schaefer, Paul. *Adirondack Cabin Country*. Syracuse, N.Y., Syracuse University Press, 1993. xxvii, 195p.
Well-known conservationist's memoirs of the Adirondacks from the 1930s.

948. Schaefer, Paul. *Defending the Wilderness: The Adirondack Writings of Paul Schaefer*. Syracuse, N.Y., Syracuse University Press, 1989. xxiii, 250p.
Foreword by Charles Calison. Collected articles, essays, and 5 dozen photos of the Adirondacks by conservationist, Paul Schaefer, cover almost 60 years. Essays are about the Adirondack wilderness itself, or the need to protect it. Award-winning book. An earlier version privately printed in 1986 was entitled, *The Adirondacks: Pathways to Wilderness*, 270p.

949. Weston, Harold. *Freedom in the Wilds*. St. Huberts N.Y., Adirondack Trail Improvement Society, 1971, 1972. 232p.
Artist Weston's personal testimonial to the Adirondack Region and the inspirational power of the natural world. He lived at Ausable Club. Many photos from the 1920s, or earlier, plus reproductions of Weston's paintings. Illus.

950. Zahniser, Edward (ed.) *Where Wilderness Preservation Began: Adirondack Writings of Howard Zahniser*. Utica, N.Y., North Country Books, 1992. 88p.
Writings of late Howard Zahniser, who was former Executive Director of Wilderness Society. Added material by other wilderness advocates George Davis, Paul Schaefer, and Douglas Scott. Illus.

# Fiction

951. Allen, Sybel. *Explanation Please!* Elizabethtown, N.Y., Denton Publications, 1967. 96p.
Extrasensory perception stories with sizeable section on North Country occurrences.

952. Andrus, Dyckman. *Days When the House Was Too Small*. New York, N.Y., Scribner, 1974. 226p.
Novel plus seven short stories set in the Adirondacks. Book takes its title from the novel and is about a married couple and a 17-year old boy coping with the constraints of a harsh Adirondack winter.

953. Banks, Russell. *The Sweet Hereafter: A Novel*. New York, N.Y., Harper Collins Publishers, 1991. 257p.
Novel set in the Adirondacks that explores individual and community responses to a fatal school bus accident.

954. Betters, Fran. *Adirondack Tall Tales and Short Stories*. Wilmington, N.Y., Adirondack Sports Publications, 1991. 112p.
Thirty tales/stories based on author's personal experiences or handed down to Betters by family and friends. Many are about domestic animals or wild life. Illus. by Sybil Hedricks.

955. Betters, Fran. *The Collection*. Wilmington, N.Y. Adirondack Sports Pulblications, 1992. 156p.
Mystery about fishing set in the Adirondacks.

956. Bonsack, Cornelia pseud. *The Parody Murder Case*. New York, N.Y., Vantage, 1987. 240p.
Murder mystery with a funny edge set in Keene Valley, New York.

957. Conners, Bernard F. *Dancehall*. Indianapolis, Bobbs-Merrill, 1983. 359p.
Murder mystery set in Lake Placid.

958. Cooper, Frank Albert. *Yankee Yankee*. New York, N.Y., Carlton Press, 1990. 128p.
Novel about War of 1812 that takes place in the history-rich Lake Champlain-Albany corridor.

959. Crane, Caroline. *The Third Passenger*. New York, N.Y., Dodd, Mead, 1983. 224p.
Novel about a plane crash and the struggle to survive during the winter in the Adirondacks.

960. Davis, Christopher. *Dog, Horse, Rat*. New York, N.Y., Viking, 1990. 244p.
Novel about Vietnam era of early 1970s set in Warren County area.

961. DeCamp, L. Sprague. *The Purple Pterodactyls*. Huntington Woods, MI., Phantasia Press, 1979; reprint, New York, N.Y., Ace Books, 1980. 228p.
Science Fiction with an Adirondacks setting.

962. Degen, Everett R. *Autumn on the Hudson*. Westport, N.Y., ENR Publications, 1989. 333p.
Author lives in Westport, N.Y. Partially set in Champlain Valley.

963. Doctorow, E.L. *Loon Lake*. New York, N.Y., Random House, 1979, 1980. 258p.
Novel partly set in the Adirondack community of Loon Lake during the Depression.

964. Eckert, Allan W. *Wilderness Empire: A Narrative*. Boston, MA., Little, Brown, 1969. xiv, 653p.
Historical fiction of mid-half of 18th century about conflict of French and English in Iroquois country, including New York State. Based on primary materials. Bibliography, index, and "List of Indian Characters."

965. Edwards, Page. *Peggy Salté*. New York, N.Y., Marion Boyars, 1983. 215p.
Novel set in Keene Valley, N.Y. Traces life of main character Peggy Salté from childhood to her death in 1970s. Story of a woman trying to maintain her independence within the constraints of a rural community.

966. Fosburgh, Lacey. *Old Money*. New York, N.Y., Pocket Books, 1983; 377p.; Garden City, N.Y., Doubleday & Co., 1983. 425p.
Novel about decline and disillusionment among old money family. Fosburgh's father wrote about the Adirondacks.

967. Frey, James N. *Winter of the Wolves*. New York, N.Y., H. Holt, 1992. 307p.
Suspense novel involving ex-intelligence officer who has resigned and retreated to fictional Adirondack community of Amber.

968. Godwin, Gail. *Violet Clay*. New York, N.Y., Knopf Books, 1978, 1986. 324p.
Novel. Violet Clay's life is in crisis. Her trip to Schroon Lake in the eastern Adirondacks to settle an estate also becomes a personal journey in which she re-examines her identity, and her abilities.

969. Goldrick, Emma. *King of the Hill*. New York, N.Y., Harlequin Books, 1987. 187p.
Adirondack Mountains provide setting for this fictional work. Family feud provides the story's plot.

970. Gorog, Judith. *No Swimming in Dark Pond and Other Chilling Tales*. New York, N.Y., Philomel Books, 1987. 111p.
Thirteen scary stories. Three of the tales: Dr. Egger's Favorite Dog, Hookman, and No Swimming in Dark Pond had their roots in stories told around a campfire in the Adirondacks.

971. Knott, Bill. *White Death*. New York, N.Y., SMP, 1993. 172p.
Tale of diamond smuggling, murder and blizzards in Adirondacks. Hero sets up villain in the end.

972. Lathen, Emma, (pseud.). *Going for the Gold*. New York, N.Y., Simon & Schuster, 1981. 251p.
Murder mystery set in Lake Placid during the Olympics.

973. Levon, Fred (pseud.). *The Manx Cat*. New York, World Publishing Co., 1970. 144p.
One of the main characters is from Saranac Lake.

974. MacDonald, John D. *Cinnamon Skin*. New York, Harper & Row, 1982. 275p.
Travis McGee novel with one chapter set in southern Adirondacks.

975. Michael, Judith. *A Ruling Passion: A Novel*. New York, N.Y., Poseidon Press, 1990. 574p.
Novel about broadcasting industry. Partially set in the Adirondacks. Opening chapter features a dramatic plane crash.

976. Oates, Joyce Carol. *Angel of Light*. New York, N.Y., Dutton, 1981. 434p.
Part of the action occurs near Saranac Lake, N.Y. Murder mystery about fictional descendants of John Brown.

977. Oates, Joyce Carol. *Bellefleur*. New York, N.Y., E.P. Dutton, 1980. 558p.
Bellefleur is the name of an Adirondack family. Book traces 6 generations. Received good reviews at the time of publication.

978. Oates, Joyce Carol. *Childwold*. New York, N.Y., Vanguard Press, 1976. 295p.
Title is taken from the name of a small Adirondack hamlet in southern St. Lawrence County. Main character falls in love with a 14-year old girl from Childwold.

979. P., B. *The Borderman #1-5*. s.l., s.n., n.d.
Five short works of varying lengths, 15-40 pp. Setting is Prohibition and the 1920s in northern

New York. Titles are: Case of Slimey Mike, In the Case of the Ring of Three, In the Case of the Crooked Sheriff, The Case of the Injured Frenchman, The Case of the Barefoot Boy.

980. Pronzini, Bill & Barry Malzberg. *The Running of Beasts*. New York, N.Y., Putnam, 1976. 319p.; Berkeley, New York, N.Y., Black Lizard Books, 1988. 316p.

Suspense novel. Essex County provides setting for murder mystery.

981. Rauch, Constance. *A Deep Disturbance*. New York, N.Y., St. Martin's Press, 1990. 202p.

Novel about a woman who relocates with her two small children to a small Adirondack town, but does not escape the difficulties she left behind.

982. Rawlings, Louisa. *Forever Wild*. New York, N.Y., Warner Books, 1986. 418p.

Romance novel. Setting is based on author's knowledge and research of Long Lake/Clear Pond vicinity in Hamilton County in the central Adirondacks.

983. Rikhoff, Jean. *Buttes Landing*. New York, N.Y., Dial Press, 1973. 440p.

A historical novel set in the mid-nineteenth century. Follows the lives of three generations of an Adirondack family. Action of the story ends around the Civil War.

984. Rikhoff, Jean. *One of the Raymonds*. New York, N.Y., Dial Press, 1974. 370p.

Rikhoff's sequel to Buttes Landing. Partially set in the 19th century Adirondacks. Story of the coming of age of Mason Raymond and his mentor Worth Hart. Hart seems to have been inspired by the Adirondack guides and woodsmen of the last century.

985. Sanford, John. *Adirondack Stories*. Santa Barbara, CA., Capras Press, 1976. 107p.

Adirondack short stories. Written during a stay one summer near Warrensburg. Notes on stories explain their various origins. Stories are distinguished by their simple direct language.

986. Sawyer, Donald J. *They Came to Sacandaga: The Story of Godfrey Shew: Fish House Patriot*. Prospect, N.Y., Prospect Books, 1976. ix, 220p.

Historical fiction about the ancestors of the author. Action spans two generations and the events of the colonial and Revolutionary War eras. Illus. by John D. Mahaffy

987. Sheffer, Roger. *Lost River*. Boonville, N.Y., Night Tree Press, 1988. 133p.

Lost River is the name given to a fictional Adirondack community that serves as the setting for the stories in the book. Sheffer attempts to offer a realistic rather than romantic portrayal of the contemporary Adirondacks.

988. Shulman, Alix Kates. *Memoirs of an Ex-Prom Queen*. New York, Knopf, 1972; 274p.

Small part of the action set in the Adirondacks. Main character spends a month waitressing in Lake Placid. Other printings in 1973, 1979, and 1985.

989. Stevens, Elisabeth. *Horse and Cart: Stories from the Country*. Washington, D.C., Wineberry Press, 1990. 99p.

Stories with rural subjects. Two have Adirondack setting. Illus.

990. Trezise, "Scuzzer." *Safari So Good*. s.l., s.n., 1989. 88p.

Humorous treatment of camping in the Adirondacks. Illus. by Tim Tresize.

991. VanHoevenbergh, Henry. *Told Around the Campfire*. Old Forge, N.Y., North Country Books, 1967; Saranac Lake, N.Y., Adirondack Yesteryears, 1986. viii, 102p.

Edited by Maitland C. De Sormo. Several stories or tales attributed to VanHoevenbergh, early Adirondack settler and hotel owner. Illus. Introductory biographical essay by De Sormo.

992. Volk, Patricia. *White Light*. New York, N.Y., Antheneum, 1987. 226p.

Urban career woman escapes to Adirondack resort to get away and gain perspective on her stress-filled life.

993. Westlake, Donald E. *Help I Am Being Held Prisoner*. New York, N.Y., M. Evans, 1974. 275p.; reprints, New York, N.Y., Ballantine, 1975. 213p.; New York, N.Y., Mysterious Press, 1989. 213p.

Humorous book with a far-fetched plot. Main character is a practical joker who ends up in a state penitentiary, presumably Dannemora in Clinton County.

994. Wilder, Laura Ingalls. *Farmer Boy*. New York, N.Y., Harper and Row, var. ed.
Story of Almanzo Wilder growing up near Malone in the 1800s.

995. Wilson, Sloan. *All the Best People*. New York, N.Y., Putnam, 1970, 1971. 501p.
Novel about the disturbing success of the American upper middle class. The parents of the two main characters own a resort in Lake George. Considered good fiction.

996. Wilson, Sloan. *Small Town*. New York, Arbor House, 1978. 514p.
Setting is modeled after an Adirondack community. Novel about a love triangle and the conflicts and rivalries that underlie the seemingly placid appearances of life in a small town.

997. Wood, Bari. *Light Source*. New York, New American Library, 1984. 310p.
Suspense novel with Adirondack setting.

998. Wright, H. W. *Running for the Exit: An Autobiographical Novel of the Early 1920s*. San Francisco, CA., Strawberry Hills Press, 1979. 152p.
Novel set in "Scotch Lake," the Adirondack community of Loon Lake in the 1920s.

999. Wright, T. M. *The Island*. New York, N.Y., Doherty Associates, 1988; New York, N.Y., St. Martin's Press, 1988. 208p.
Horror story with Adirondack setting.

1000. Wright, T. M. *The Playground*. New York, N.Y., Tom Doherty Associates, 1982. 315p.
Suspense novel set in the Adirondacks.

1001. Wylie, Philip. *The End of the Dream*. Garden City, N.Y., Doubleday, 1972. 206p.
Introduction by John Brunner. Futuristic story with an Adirondack setting. Capitol of District 2 in the book (formerly U.S. and Canada) is located in the Adirondacks, north and west of Saranac Lake.

# Poetry

1002. Betters, Francis. *Something's Fishy in the Adirondacks*. Wilmington, N.Y., Adirondack Sports, 1985. 89p.
Fifty-plus poems on fishing. Printed in blue ink. Author is from Wilmington, N.Y. and has written other works about fishing.

1003. Bruchac, Joseph. *Near the Mountains*. Fredonia, N.Y., White Pine Press, 1987. 63p.
Poetry with some Adirondack content. Author has produced a number of works related to the Adirondacks and Native Americans.

1004. Cornwell, George. *Year of the Golden Moon: An Adirondack Book*. New York, N.Y., Vantage Press, 1975. 54p.
Poetry inspired by Lake George region.

1005. Edson, James Stuart. *Trails to the Summit: A Collection of Adirondack Poems*. Skaneateles, N.Y., Lakeside Printing, 1986. 53p.
Four dozen poems with Adirondack content.

1006. Harrison, Jeffrey. *The Singing Underneath*. New York, E.P. Dutton, 1988. xii, 68p.
Poetry—some Adirondack content. National Poetry Series. Selected by James Merrill.

1007. Heitz, Ken. *Flickering Free*. s.l., s.n., 1972. 44p.
Poetry with Adirondack themes. Illus. by Linda Heitz.

1008. Heitz, Ken. *A Glimpse of Peace from the Adirondack Wilds*. Saranac Lake, N.Y., Adirondack Yesteryears, 1973. 43p.
Adirondack-inspired poetry by Heitz. Drawings by Linda Heitz.

1009. Kenny, Maurice. *Between Two Rivers: Selected Poems 1956-1984*. Fredonia, NY, White Pine Press, 1987. 168p.
Collected poems by Maurice Kenny. Title refers to where Kenny grew up—between Black and St. Lawrence Rivers. Some poems have Adirondack content.

1010. Kenny, Maurice. *Black Robe: Isaac Jogues*. Saranac Lake, N.Y., North Country Community College Press, 1982. xi, 69p.
Poems about Isaac Jogues, Jesuit priest who was a missionary to the Iroquois and was tortured and killed by them. Kenny is a Native American from northern New York and until recently served as poet in residence at North Country Community

College in Saranac Lake, New York.

1011. Kenny, Maurice. *Dancing Back Strong the Nation.* Buffalo, N.Y., White Pine Press, 1979, 1981. 24p.
Poetry. Some northern New York content. Kenny is an Native American originally from Northern New York.

1012. Kenny, Maurice. *Humors and/or Not So Humorous.* Buffalo, N.Y., Swift Kick Press, 1988. 43p.
Recent poetry by Kenny. Some northern New York content.

1013. Kenny, Maurice. *Is Summer This Bear.* Saranac Lake, N.Y., Chauncy Press, 1985. 54p.
Poems by northern New York poet. Unifying theme is to remind people that they are just a part of creation—and not necessarily the dominant part.

1014. Kenny, Maurice. *Tekonwatonti/Molly Brant.* Fredonia, N.Y., White Pine Press, 1992. 209p.
NAR

1015. Knox, Ann B. *Stonecrop.* Washington, D.C., Washington Writers Publishing House,1988. 63p.
Poetry collection. Some of these works first appeared in *Blueline*. Knox is a summer resident of the Central Adirondacks.

1016. Kuzma, Greg. *Adirondacks.* Ann Arbor, MI., Bear Claw Press, 1978. 57p.
Poems with Adirondack content. Drawings by Tom Pohrt.

1017. Lape, Walter, John Quirk, & Lawrence Allen. *Three Adirondack Poets: Walter Lape, John Quirk, Lawrence Allen.* Glens Falls, N.Y., Loft Press, 1982. 32p.
Poems with some Adirondack content. Drawings and cover by Paul Chapman.

1018. Larom, Henry V. *Backtrail: Selected Poems.* s.l., s.n., 1974. 67p.
Poems by Saranac Lake native. Some Adirondack content.

1019. Longacker, Warren F. *Green Are the Mountains: Poems and Portraits of the Adirondacks.* Schenectady, N.Y., Acme Press, 1975. 85p.
Collection of poetry with Adirondack content. Part I is about the land and places. Part II contains poems about various well-known Adirondack people.

1020. Mitchell, Roger. *Adirondack.* Kansas City, MO., BkMk Press, 1988. 61p.
Thirty-three Adirondack-inspired poems. Some with historical themes. Illus.

1021. Mitchell, Roger. *A Clear Space on a Cold Day.* Cleveland, OH., Cleveland State University Poetry Center, 1986. 80p.
Poetry. Some Adirondack content. Adirondack native who has reconnected with the region through his writings.

1022. Reid, Edwin A. *Adirondack We Celebrate.* Wanakena, N.Y., Reid Publications, 1992. 100p.
Approximately 40 poems celebrating Adirondack Park Centennial.

1023. Reid, Edwin A. *Hello...Adirondacker.* Wanakena, N.Y., Reid Publications, 1992. 96p.
Reid's first volume of poetry. Drawings by author.

1024. Seltzer, Joanne. *Adirondack Lake Poets.* Glens Falls, N.Y., Taft Press, 1985. 27p.
Twenty-six poems with Adirondack content. Full-page black and white photographs by Alan Cederstrom accompany poetry.

1025. Viva, Gayle H. *Forests, Fields, and Folks.* s.l., Viva, 1981. 48p.
Poems written around the themes of woods, farms, and individuals. Some Adirondack content.

1026. West, Henry Scott. *The Dawn.* Glens Falls, N.Y., Rist-Frost Associates, 1971, 1972. 62p.
Poetry. Author raised in the Adirondack Mountains.

1027. Wikoff, Jack. *Complete Works: Adirondack Portfolio/Penelope.* Barrytown, N.Y., Open Book Publications, 1983. 236p.
Two vol. in one. Author ran a ski lodge in Lake Placid for 25 years. *Adirondack Portfolio*, poems with Adirondack content. *Penelope*, an unrelated work based on legend of Penelope and Odysseus.

1028. Zahniser, Ed. *The Way to Heron Mountain.* Boonville, N.Y., Night Tree Press, 1986. 76p.

Poetry about a man who travels to an Adirondack retreat and his spiritual journey. Illus. by Grace E. Oesher.

## Photography

1029. Cannon, Barrie Rolleston & George Cannon. *Coming into the Light: An Invitation.* Atlanta, GA., Voyageur, 1979. 91p.

Inspirational photographic essay with quotes from Thoreau, Emerson and others. About a dozen photos of the Adirondacks, mostly of Blue Mountain Lake and vicinity.

1030. Clifton, Carr. *New York: Images of the Landscape; Photography by Carr Clifton.* Englewood, CO., Westcliffe Publishers, 1988. 160p.

Wonderful color prints from throughout New York State, three dozen of which are of the Adirondacks.

1031. Farb, Nathan. *The Adirondacks.* New York, N.Y., Rizzoli International Publications, 1985. 183p.

Recent Adirondack classic. Seventy-seven beautiful, full page photos of Adirondacks. Introductory essay by Paul Jamieson. Also done as a special edition limited to 50 copies, signed, numbered and in portfolio boxes with five press proofs.

1032. Farb, Nathan. *100 Views of the Adirondacks.* New York, N.Y., Rizzoli, 1989. 168p.

Foreword by Governor Mario Cuomo. Full page photos of the Adirondacks divided into sections: morning views, mountain views, winter views, wetland views, autumn snow. Accompanied by occasional quotes from written works on the Adirondacks.

1033. Glenn, Morris F. *Lake Champlain Album: Volume 1.* Alexandria,VA., Glenn, 1978. 38p.

Photos and drawings. Some text on Essex and Westport, N.Y. as well as on the Crater Club. Illus.

1034. Glenn, Morris F. *Lake Champlain Album: Volume 2.* Alexandria, VA., Glenn, 1979. 256p.

Photographic essay. Mostly Lake Champlain but also chapters on the Adirondacks. Some photos of windmills and water mills in the region.

1035. Harris, Bill. *New York State.* New York, N.Y., Crescent Books, 1987. 96p.

Color photos of Lake Champlain-Hudson River corridor and Lake Placid.

1036. Healy, William M. *The Adirondacks: A Special World.* Utica, N.Y., North Country Books, 1986, 1992. 126p.

Photo essay on Adirondacks. Beautiful full-page color photos.

1037. Hope, Jack. *A River for the Living: The Hudson and Its People.* Barre, MA., Barre Publishers, 1975. 224p.

A photographic essay on the Hudson River from Lake of the Tears to New York City. First 66 pages deal with Adirondack section of the Hudson.

1038. Kantor, MacKinley & Tim Kantor. *Hamilton County.* New York, N.Y., Macmillan, 1970. 288p.

Pictorial work about people and landscape of 10 U.S. counties bearing the name Hamilton. One of these is in the heart of the Adirondack Mountains. Plates of Hamilton County, New York.

1039. Oppersdorff, Mathias T. *Adirondack Faces.* Syracuse, N.Y., Syracuse University Press/Adirondack Museum, 1991. xxi, 111p.

Text by Alice Wolf Gilborn. Foreword by Adam Hochschild. Portraits of Adirondack residents, well known and unknown. Each photo accompanied by short passage about the individual. Smaller photos of each person appear on front and back endpapers.

1040. Porter, Eliot. *Forever Wild: Photographs.* Blue Mountain Lake, N.Y., Adirondack Museum, 1966. Unpaged.

Color nature photos of the Adirondack. Captions from the works of William Chapman White. Introduction by Harold Hochschild.

1041. Ryder, Ron. *The Way It Was: Saved by the Camera!.* Boonville, N.Y., Country Books, 1975. 110p.

Photos starting from the turn of the twentieth century. Some of the Adirondacks, the rest of eastern central New York State. Advts.

1042. Shangle, Robert & Craig Ryan. *Beautiful New York.* Beaverton, OR., Beautiful American Publishing Co., 1979. 71p.

Pictorial of New York State. Approximately 15 photos of the Adirondack region.

1043. Smith, Clyde H. *The Adirondacks.* New York, N.Y., Viking Press, 1976. 64p.

Pictorial. A real cross section of the Adirondacks; not just scenery, but many action shots of outdoor activities: white water canoeing, hiking, skiing, rock climbing, boating. Some wildlife photos. Captures the vitality of the region.

1044. Smith, Clyde H. *New York.* Portland, OR., Graphic Arts, 1977. 160p.

Color plates of Adirondack region.

1045. Smith, Clyde H. *New York: The State.* Dublin, N.H., Foremost Publishers, 1986. 128p.

Thirty-five pages of color plates of wildlife and scenery in Adirondacks and northeastern New York.

1046. Stillman, William J. *Poetic Localities: Photographs of the Adirondacks, Cambridge, Crete, Italy, Athens.* Boston, MA., J.R. Osgood & Co., 1876; reprint, New York, N.Y., Aperture Foundation, 1988. 126p.

Some photos of Adirondacks from 1859. Biographical essay on Stillman.

1047. Taylor, Kip. *Wild Side of the Adirondacks: Winter/Spring.* Saranac Lake, N.Y., Taylor, 1991. 136p.

Color nature photos.

1048. Weber, Bruce. *Bear Pond.* Boston, MA., Little Bear Press, 1990; New York, N.Y., Bullfinch Press, 1990. 201p.

Title is double entendre. Photo book of male nudes taken in Adirondack settings.

1049. Wuerthner, George. *The Adirondacks: Forever Wild.* Helena, MT., American Geographic Publishers, 1988. 104p.

Over 150 beautiful color photos of Adirondack scenery and wildlife.

# *Juvenile Works*

1050. Adler, C.S. *Caryl's Buck.* New York, N.Y., Clarion Books, 1987. 167p.

Caryl is living with her aunt and uncle in the Adirondacks after the death of her mother and ensuing estrangement from her father. Her interest in a particular deer provides a distraction from her own problems. When the deer is accidentally shot, she is provided with a chance to grow.

1051. Amsel, Sheri. *Cecil's Adirondack Adventure.* Elizabethtown, N.Y., Pine Tree Press, 1991. 32p.

Puzzles, mazes and coloring activities centered around the Adirondacks for children.

1052. Baird, Thomas. *Where the Time Ends: A Novel.* New York, N.Y., Harper and Row, 1988. 230p.

Two teenage boys are camping in the Adirondacks when Soviet missles attack the U.S.

1053. Blackwood, Gary L. *Wild Timothy.* New York, N.Y., Atheneum, 1987. 153p.

Survival story of thirteen-year-old boy who becomes lost in the Adirondack wilderness while camping with his father.

1054. Blake-Allen, Mary and Meg Bernstein. *The Wood Spirits Story.* s.l.,s.n., 1989. 24p.

Coloring and activity books for children with Adirondack content.

1055. Campbell, Hope. *Looking for Hamlet: A Haunting at Deep Lake.* New York, N.Y., Macmillan, 1987. 238p.

Ghost story set at a large Victorian Hotel in the Adirondacks.

1056. Casey, Jack. *Lily of the Mohawks.* New York, N.Y., Bantam Books, 1984. 309p.

Story of Kateri Tekakwitha, a young Mohawk woman who converted to Christianity. The Roman Catholic church canonized her in 1980.

1057. Clark, Margaret Goff. *Adirondack Mountain Mystery.* New York, N.Y., Funk and Wagnells, 1966. 158p.

Adventures of thirteen-year-old Andy Scott in Keene Valley. Andy helps capture two bank robbers and climbs mountains. Based on more than casual knowledge of the region.

1058. Collier, James Lincoln. *When the Stars Begin to Fall.* New York, N.Y., Delacorte Press, 1986, 1989. 160p.

Young adult fiction. Fourteen-year-old boy from a poor Adirondack family attempts to blow whistle on an industry he suspects is polluting a local river.

1059. Danzinger, Jeff. *The Champlain Monster.* Plainfield, VT., Lanser Press, 1981; reprint, Shelburne, VT., New England Press, 1983. 91p.

About the legendary Lake Champlain creature. Illus. by author.

1060. Fosburgh, Liza. *Summer Lion.* New York, N.Y., Morrow, 1987. 184p.

Young adult ficiton. Setting is the Adirondacks. A teenage boy's parents operate a resort inn. His summer job, which brings him into contact with rich summer people, provides a contrast to his own way of life. He learns to appreciate his family and values.

1061. French, Michael. *Us against Them.* Toronto, Ont., Bantam Books, 1987. 151p.

Setting is the Adirondacks. Story of a teenage club whose members are involved in the accidental shooting of a local man. Crisis creates dilemmas and conflicts that become tests of the teens' characters. Paper in 1989.

1062. Fritz, Jean. *Traitor: The Case of Benedict Arnold.* New York, N.Y., Putnam, 1981. 192p.; New York, N.Y., Puffin, 1989. 191p.

Award-winning biography of Benedict Arnold for young readers. Bibliography.

1063. Helms, Marion. *Peter's Folks: What Treasures Do These Adirondacks Hold for Peter?.* Elizabethtown, N.Y., Denton Publications, 1975. 119p.

Historical fiction. Story based on letters received by a family from Chesterfield, N.Y. during the second half of the nineteenth century.

Main character in Helms' fiction is the recipient of these letters. Using the letters as a point of departure Helms aims to capture the flavor of the times in Essex County, New York, in the late nineteenth century.

1064. Hiscock, Bruce. *The Big Rock.* New York, N.Y., Atheneum, 1988. 32p.
Geology for children based on an Adirondack rock. Illus. by author.

1065. Judson, William. *Cold River.* New York, N.Y., Mason & Lipscomb, 1974. 182p.; New York, N.Y., New American Library, 1976. 213p.
Set in the Adirondacks in 1921. After the death of their father during a camping trip, two teen-agers fight for survival during a harsh winter in the wilderness. Also a large type edition in 1976.

1066. June, David. *Mitchell.* North Syracuse, N.Y., June Enterprises, 1977. 90p.
Short novel about Sabattis Boy Scout Camp. Book focuses on the wild and not-so-responsible side of adolescent boys.

1067. Lonergan, Carroll V. *Brave Boys at Old Fort Ticonderoga.* Interlaken, N.Y., Empire State Books, 1987. 143p.
Story of two teenage boys in eastern New York at the time of the American Revolution. Illustrated by Christoper Wolff.

1068. Maguire, Gregory. *The Lightning Time.* New York, N.Y., Farrar, Straus, Giroux, 1978. 247p.
Children's literature. Set in the fictitious Adirondack community of Canaan Lake. Daniel goes to his Grandmother's when his mother goes into the hospital for surgery. He and a friend discover a magical world on a nearby mountain.

1069. Maguire, Gregory. *Lights on the Lake.* New York, N.Y., Farrar, Straus, Giroux, 1981. 244p.
Set in the fictional Adirondack community of Canaan Lake. Daniel solves the mystery of the lights on the lake and the illness of a poet who lives in Canaan Lake.

1070. Mott, Michael. *Master Entrick, 1754-56: An Adventure.* New York, N.Y., Dell Publishing Co., 1965, 1969, 1986; also New York, N.Y., Delacorte, 1966. 190p.
Historical novel about a teenage English boy kidnapped and taken to Colonial America as a bond servant during the French and Indian War. He escapes his harsh master during an Indian raid and is befriended by an Indian youth.

1071. Murtaugh, Beverly. *For Kids Only: An Adirondack Mountain Book.* Utica, N.Y., North Country Books, 1987. 148p.
Juvenile. Adirondack-oriented coloring book; animals, plants and outdoor activities with short text or captions.

1072. Peck, Robert Newton. *Fawn.* Boston, MA., Little, Brown, 1975. xiii, 143p.; New York, N.Y., Dell, 1977. 128p.
Historical fiction set at the time of the French and Indian War near Fort Ticonderoga. Action seen through the eyes of a teen-age boy (Fawn) who is of mixed French and Indian parentage.

1073. Peck, Robert Newton. *Jo Silver.* Englewood, FL., Pineapple Press, 1985. 132p.
Young adult fiction about sixteen-year-old boy who climbs Adirondack mountain seeking a Native American who lives there. Peck spent his early adulthood in the Adirondacks.

1074. Schuyler, Doris E. *The Adirondack Princess.* Brookfield, N.Y., Worden Press, 1982. 139p.
Historical novel set in the Adirondacks.

1075. Schuyler, Doris E. *The Adirondack Princess: Book II.* Little Falls, N.Y., Canal Place Publishers, 1990. 128p.
Sequel continues the story of Emmie.

1076. Scott, John Anthony & Robert Alan Scott. *John Brown at Harper's Ferry.* New York, N.Y., Facts On File Publications, 1988. viii, 184p.
Abolitionist John Brown had North Country connections. References to Brown and family presence at North Elba, New York. Bibliography.

1077. Steinberg, Michael. *Our Wilderness.* Lake George, N.Y., Adirondack Mountain Club, 1992. 118p.
History of Adirondack Region for young readers. First ADK work specifically written for a young audience. Illus.

1078. Tolan, Stephanie S. *The Great Skinner Homestead.*

New York, N.Y., Four Winds Press, 1988. 159p.
Story about a family who spends a summer roughing it in the Adirondacks.

1079. Tripp, Valerie. *Samantha Saves the Day: A Summer Story*. Madison, WI., Pleasant Co., 1988. 68p.
Adirondack setting. Story of young girl who visits an island frequented by her family in the past. Caught in a severe storm, Samantha helps her companions. Pictures from the Adirondack Museum set a north country mood for this book. Illus. by Robert Grace and N. Niles. Also in paper in 1988.

1080. Turbek, Joan. *The Little River and the Big, Big Bridge*. Utica, N.Y., North Country Books, 1993. 48p.
Children's story about replacement of a covered bridge by large steel one. What happens when "progress" comes. Based on events in Jay, N.Y.

1081. Veeder, Millicent & Virginia Westervelt. *Guns on the Heights*. Redlands, CA., Beacon Printer, 1976. 120p.
Historical fiction for young readers on American Revolutionary activity in eastern N.Y. Story is about a Quaker family living nearby during the Saratoga campaign and Burgoyne's invasion. Maps, illus. used in telling this story.

1082. Woods, George A. *Catch A Killer*. New York, Harper, 1972. 248p.
Young adult fiction. Murder suspense novel by author born in the Adirondacks.

1083. Woods, George A. *Vibrations*. New York, N.Y., Harper, 1970. 164p.
Paradox Lake, in eastern New York is setting for part of the story of a seventeen-year-old boy going through the pains of growing up. Woods was born in the Adirondacks.

# *Reprints of Items with "Plum" Numbers*

Abbott, Henry. *The Birch Books of Henry Abbott.* Harrison, N.Y., Harbor Hill Books, 1980. 254p.

Reprint of 19 works originally published between 1914 and 1932, each with a different theme. Each essay recounts an excursion into the woods. The original birch books are very scarce.

Aber, Ted and Stella King. *Tales from An Adirondack County.* Prospect, N.Y., Prospect Books, 1961, 1978, 1981. 208p.

A collection of tales and stories from Hamilton County in the central Adirondacks.

Adirondack Mountain Club. *The Forest Preserve of New York State.* Gabriels, N.Y., Adirondack Mountain Club, 1964; reprint, 1966. 36p.

Describes forest preserve: its character, acquisition, how it is protected by New York State Constitution and the law, its proper use and future protection. Contains bibliographic essay and a copy of Article 14, section 1-4 as of 1964, which protects Forest Preserve. Mostly Adirondack, some Catskills.

Allen, Ethan. *A Narrative of Col. Ethan Allen's Captivity.* Burlington, VT., H. Johns and Co., 1838. 50p.; reprint, Bowie, MD., Heritage Books, 1987. 122p.

Allen fought in the battle for Ticonderoga.

Beers, D. G. *Atlas of Franklin County, New York.* Philadelphia, PA., D.G. Beers & Co., 1876. 65p.; reprint, Churchville, N.Y., M. Wehle, 1977.

Reprint of 300 copies. Black and white maps. Original maps were in color. In addition to maps of townships and villages there are tables of distances, lists of post offices, population figures for 1870. Outline map of Franklin County shows many townships that have since disappeared.

Beers, D. G. *Atlas of Lewis County, New York.* Philadelphia, PA., Pomeroy, Whitman Co., 1875. 80p.; reprint, Churchville, N.Y., Martin Wehle, 1977. 79p.

Reprint of nineteenth century atlas of Lewis County, its town and villages. Map of U.S. and New York State, mileage charts for county, lists of post offices and population statistics for 1800-1870.

Beers, F. W. *Atlas of Clinton County, New York.* New York, N.Y., F. W. Beers, 1869. 38p.; reprint, Churchville, N.Y., Martin Wehle, 1977.

Reprint of nineteenth-century atlas, done in black and white inks. Format includes brief county history outline, county maps as well as maps of town and village, state map, and mileage tables for distances within Clinton County. Ink drawings and prints.

Beers, F. W. *County Atlas of Warren County, New York: from Recent and Actual Surveys and Records.* New York, N.Y., F. W. Beers Co., 1876. 86p.; reprint, Churchville, N.Y., Martin Wehle, 1977.

Reprint of county atlas first published in 1876. Maps of Warren County and its towns and villages. Three ink illus. Other miscellaneous information such as population of United States and New York State in the 1870s. Also agricultural statistics and mileage between various places within the county.

Beers, F. W. *History of Herkimer County, New York.* New York, N.Y., F. W. Beers, 1879; reprint, Ovid, N.Y., W. E. Morrison & Co., 1980. 289p.

Herkimer County is west of Hamilton County and south of St. Lawrence County. Towns of Webb, Ohio, and part of Salisbury are in the Adirondack Park. Contains extensive section on New York State with heavy emphasis on colonial and Revolutionary era history.

Beers, F. W. *History of Montgomery & Fulton Counties, N.Y.* New York, N.Y., F. W. Beers, 1878; reprint, Interlaken, N.Y., Heart of the Lakes Publishing, 1979, 1981. lxxi, 252p.

Reprint of late 19th-century county history. Such works have been valuable to genealogists and to small towns in establishing their early histories. Stratford, Caroga, Bleeker, Mayfield, Northampton, Brodalbin are Adirondack Park communities. Short essays on these communities can be found in this volume.

Beetle, David H. *Up Old Forge Way.* Utica, N.Y., Utica Observer-Dispatch, 1948; reprint, Lakemont,

N.Y., North Country Books, 1972. 183p.
Published in one volume with *West Canada Creek*. Newspaper columns. Beetle was a reporter for a Utica newspaper. *Up Old Forge Way* is about the southern Adirondacks, specifically the Fulton Chain and how it changed from wilderness to a prime resort area. Later printing in 1984.

Beetle, David H. *West Canada Creek*. Utica, N.Y., Utica Observer-Dispatch, 1946; reprint, Lakemont, N.Y., North Country Books, 1972. 158p.
Published in one volume with *Up Old Forge Way*. Beetle was a reporter for a Utica newspaper. *West Canada Creek* is about the river of the same name, which is a major tributary of the Mohawk River with its source in the Adirondacks. The book describes West Canada Creek, its communities and towns. Later printing in 1984.

Bump, Gardiner, et. al. *The Ruffed Grouse: Life History, Propagation and Management*. Albany, N.Y., New York State Conservation Department, 1947. 915p.; reprint, Harrisburg, PA., Telegraph Press, 1978. xxxvi, 915p.
Thorough and fascinating work on the ruffed grouse. Excellent photos and drawings.

Campbell, T.J. *Isaac Jogues S.J.: Discoverer of Lake George*. New York, N.Y., The American Press, 1911; reprint, s.l., Silver Buckle Press, 1992. 55p.
Biographical work of important missionary in Colonial North America. Covers activities in Eastern N.Y.

Carson, Russell M. L. *Peaks and People of the Adirondacks*. Garden City, N.Y., Doubleday, 1927. 269p.; reprint, Glens Falls, N.Y., Adirondack Mountain Club, 1973. 280p.; 1986, 279p..
Carson's description of the Adirondack High Peaks. New preface by George Marshall. Introduction by Philip Terrie Jr. A twentieth century Adirondack classic.

Chalmers, Stephen. *The Penny Piper of Saranac: An Episode in Stevenson's Life*. Boston & New York, Houghton, Mifflin, 1916. 62p.; reprint, Darby PA., Arden Library, 1979. xviii, 64p.
An essay in book format about Robert Louis Stevenson's stay in Saranac Lake, New York in the winter of 1887-88. Dr. Edward Trudeau worked with the author on this project. Stevenson wrote "A Christmas Sermon" and "The Lantern Bearers" while living in Saranac Lake. Preface by Lord Guthrie.

Chittenden, L.E. *Personal Reminiscneces, 1840-1890*. New York, N.Y., Richmond, Croscup & Co., 1893. 434p.; rcprint, Freeport, N.Y., Book For Libraries Press, 1971. ix, 434p.
Three chapters related to Adirondacks. Chapter XV: entitled "Adirondack Days-Untried Companions in the Wilderness-Their Perils and Experiences;" Chapter XVI: "The Story of Mitchell Sabattis;" and Chapter XVII on the the degradation of the Adirondack Wilderness.

Cook, Flavius J. (Joseph Cook). *Home Sketches of Essex County*. Keeseville, N.Y., W. Lansing & Son, 1858; reprint, 1989. 139p.
Early work on Ticonderoga, N.Y. Hard to find.

Coolidge, Guy O. *The French Occupation of the Champlain Valley From 1609-1759*. Montpelier, VT., Vermont Historical Proceedings, September, 1938, N.S. 6; reprint, Harrison, N.Y., Harbor Hill Books, 1979, 1989. 175p.
A classic history of Lake Champlain. Discusses French presence in northern Vermont and northern New York. Draws upon many primary sources.

Cooper, James Fenimore. *The Last of the Mohicans*. Philadelphia, PA., H.C. Carey & I. Lea, 1826. 2 v.; various ed.; reprint, Albany, N.Y., State University of New York Press, 1983. xlviii, 418p.
Historical fiction. Second volume of the *Leatherstocking Tales* about the French and Indian War. Inspired by Cooper's visit to Glens Falls and Lake George in 1824. Sympathetic treatment of Native Americans.

Covey, Frances A. *The Earl Covey Story*. New York, N.Y., Exposition Press, 1964, 1979. 164p.
Biography of versatile Lewis County native. Best known for his building skills. He designed and oversaw the building of Big Moose Community Chapel, which was completed in 1931.

Cuneo, John R. *Robert Rogers of the Rangers*. New York, N.Y., Oxford University Press, 1959; reprints, New York, N.Y., Richardson and Steinman, 1987; Ticonderoga, N.Y., Fort Ticonderoga Museum, 1988. 308p.

Biography of Robert Rogers, military leader during French and Indian War. Involved in fighting at Ticonderoga and Crown Point. Maps, illus.

Curtiss, Arthur Lester Brown. *The Life and Adventures of Nate Foster, Trapper and Hunter of the Adirondacks.* Utica, N.Y., Press of T.J. Griffiths, 1897; reprint, Harrison, N.Y., Harbor Hill, N.Y., 1976. 286p.
Biography of colorful Herkimer County personality. He was a woodsman and in later life lived in the Fulton Chain and Old Forge.

Cutting, Edith E. *Lore of an Adirondack County.* Ithaca, N.Y., Cornell University, 1944; reprint, Elizabethtown, N.Y., Denton Publications, 1972. 86p.
About Essex County. A variety of material: anecdotes, tall tales, ballads and songs.

Cutting, Edith E. *Whistling Girls and Jumping Sheep.* Cooperstown, N.Y., Farmers' Museum/N.Y. Folklore Society, 1951, 1984. 85p.
Folklore, beliefs, customs and traditions of farm life from Essex County, New York.

Davis, Brian T.C. *Bedrock Geology of the St. Regis Quadrangle.* Princeton, N.J., Princeton University, 1963. 196 lvs.; reprint, Albany, N.Y., University of the State of New York, State Education Department, 1971. 34p.
Abridged version of thesis done at Princeton in 1963. Geology of region in Franklin County, specifically the towns of Waverly, Santa Clara, Brandon, Harrietstown, and Altamont. Introduction offers brief, general physical and climatic description of the region. Bibliography.

Deming, Philander. *Adirondack Stories.* Boston, MA., Houghton, 1880; reprint, New York, N.Y., Garrett Press, 1969. 192p.
Stories about people of Adirondacks in late 1880s, written in a direct, spare style of prose.

Deming, Philander. *Tompkins and Other Folks.* Boston, MA., Houghton, 1885; reprints, New York, N.Y., Garrett Press, 1969; MSS Information Corp., 1972. 223p.
Seven short stories by Philander Deming from the late 1800s. The stories are set in the Hudson Valley or the Adirondacks.

Digby, William. *The British Invasion from the North: Digby's Journal of the Campaign of Generals Carleton and Burgoyne, from Canada, 1776-1777.* Albany, N.Y., Joel Munsell's Sons, 1887. 412p.; New York, N.Y., Da Capo Press, 1970. viii, 412p.
Introduction and Notes by James Phinney Baxter. Account of Revolutionary War action in eastern New York. Illus., index.

Dinsdale, Evelyn M. *The Lumbering Industry of Northern New York: A Geographical Examination of Its History and Technology.* Syracuse. N.Y., Syracuse University, 1963. 166 lvs.; reprint, Ann Arbor MI, UMI Reprints, 1985.
Doctoral thesis. Footnotes, maps, bibliography.

Donaldson, Alfred L. *A History of the Adirondacks, Vol. I & II.* New York, N.Y., Century Co, 1921; reprints, Harrison, N.Y., Harbor Hill Books, 1977, 1989; Fleischmanns, N.Y., Purple Mountain Press, 1992. 2 v.
Important two-volume history of Adirondacks, stressing early history and significant individuals. One of the first efforts to pull together information on the Adirondacks into one place. Lengthy bibliography in Vol . 2. "Plum" bibliography 1955-1968 built upon Donaldson's early effort. With a sketch of the author by John J. Duquette.

Dornburgh, Henry. *Why the Wilderness is Called Adirondack: The Earliest Account of the Founding of the McIntyre Mine.* Glens Falls, N.Y., Daily Times, 1885. 14p.; reprint, Harrison, N.Y., Harbor Hill Books, 1980; Fleischmanns, N.Y., Purple Mountain Press, 1992. 32p.
Early account of Adirondack Iron and Steel Company located in the High Peaks. Reprint of work first printed in 1885. Uses wood engravings from Benson Lossing's 1866 book on the Hudson River.

Dreiser, Theodore. *An American Tragedy.* New York, N.Y., Liveright, 1929. 409p.; reprint; New York, N.Y., New American Library, 1981. 828p.
Novel full of social commentary based on Gillette murder case in Adirondacks.

Drew, Hazel C. *Tales From Little Lewis.* Lyons Falls, N.Y., 1961. 48p.; rev. ed., 1969. 60p.
Accounts of Lewis County, including French presence, pioneer experience, Joshua Harris, Lyman Lyons, Welsh community in Turin, Collinsville near Lyons Falls, and logging on the Moose River. No index or table of contents. Plates, port.

Dunham, Harvey L. *Adirondack French Louie: Early Life in the North Woods.* Utica, N.Y., s.n. 1952. 200p.; rev. and enlarged ed., 1953. 212p.; reprints, Saranac Lake, N.Y., North Country Books, 1970; Sylvan Beach, N.Y., 1978; Utica, N.Y., North Country Books,1987. Var. pag.

Adirondack French Louie refers to Louis Seymour. Biography of one of the Adirondacks' more colorful characters, who lived in West Canada Creek Country. 100 plates. Map of North Woods on inside covers.

Durant, S. & H.B. Pearce. *History of St. Lawrence County, New York.* Philadelphia, L.H. Everts & Co., 1878; reprint, Interlaken, N.Y., Heart of the Lakes Publishing, 1982. 521p.

Reprint of 1878 history. Contains early history of towns of Hopkinton, Parishville, Colton, Fine, Edwards, which are wholly or partially within the Blue Line. Biographical information of interest to genealogists; early histories of towns within or near the Blue Line.

Edmonds, Walter D. *The Boyds of Black River.* New York, N.Y., Dodd & Mead, 1953; Syracuse, N.Y., Syracuse University Press, 1988. 248p.

Reprint with new preface by Edmonds. Stories first published in magazines and printed together for first time in 1953. Stories of Black River region.

Fleming, Ian. *The Spy Who Loved Me.* New York, N.Y., Viking, 1962. 211p.; reprint, London, Eng., Jonathan Cape, 1980. 180p.

James Bond novel set near Lake George.

Fox, William F. *History of the Lumber Industry in the State of New York with an Appendix; The Role of the Pioneer Lumberman.* Washington, D.C., U.S. Dept. of Agriculture, Bureau of Forestry, 1906. 59p.; reprint, Harrison, N.Y., Harbor Hill Books, 1976, 1985. 116p.

Describes the lumbering industry in New York State through the end of the nineteenth century. Topics include the primitive forest, early sawmills, the lumber market, log driving, role of the railroads. Important book for understanding the development of the Adirondacks. Appendices. Illus.

French, J. H. *Gazetteer of the State of New York.* Syracuse, N.Y., R.P. Smith, 1860. 739p.; reprint, Interlaken, N.Y., Heart of the Lakes Publishing, 1980. 751p.

County-by-county history and statistics for whole state including Adirondack counties. Assorted general information: topography, state government, canals, commerce, colleges, and businesses.

Frothingham, Octavius Brooks. *Gerritt Smith: A Biography.* New York, N.Y., Putnam, 1878; reprint, New York, N.Y., Negro University Press 1969. 381p.

Provided free land for a group of free blacks in northeastern New York.

Gilliland, William. *William Gilliland: Pioneer Settler of Willsboro on Lake Champlain.* Albany, N.Y., J. Munsell, 1863. 231p.; reprint, Elizabethtown, N.Y., Regional Museum Resources and Educational Center for Clinton, Essex Counties, 1968. iii, 48p.

Edited by Stuart D. Ludlu mtl with large large land holdings near mouth of Bouquet River on Lake Champlain. 50 copies.

Goodwin, Tony. *Guide to Adirondack Trails: High Peaks Region.* Glens Falls, N.Y., Adirondack Mountain Club, 1980, 1985, 1987, 1990. 1 v.

Covers Keene Valley, St. Huberts, Heart Lake, and peaks without trails. Appendices contain assorted information: glossary, highest 100 peaks, lean-tos, index and list of state campgrounds. Forest Preserve Series, Vol. I.

Grady, Joseph F. *The Adirondacks, Fulton Chain-Big Moose Region: The Story of the Wilderness.* Little Falls, N.Y., Press of the Journal and Courier Co, 1933; reprint, Old Forge, N.Y., North Country Books, 1966, 1972. 320p.

People, places, camps, and clubs of the southwestern Adirondacks are discussed. Information on the North Woods Club and the Adirondack League Club. Map of region on inside of front cover. Illus.

Hadden, James M. *Hadden's Journal & Orderly Books: A Journal Kept in Canada and upon Burgoyne's Campaign in 1776 and 1777.* Albany, N.Y., J. Munsell's Sons, 1884; reprint, Freeport, N.Y., Book for Library Press, 1970. 581p.

Hadden was under the command of British General Guy Carleton. Hadden's journals give the British view of events in eastern New York during the American Revolution, particularly Burgoyne's campaign. Description of battle for Valcour Bay. Maps.

Hammond, S.H. *Wild Northern Scenes, Or, Sporting Adventures with the Rifle and the Rod.* New York, N.Y., Derby & Johnson, 1857; reprint, New York, N.Y., Arno Press, 1967; reprint, Harrison, N.Y., Harbor Hill Books, 1979. 341p.

Reprint of Adirondack travel and description classic. Pre-Civil War account of Adirondack region. Hammond appreciated wilderness and foresaw the need for its protection.

Headley, Joel T. *The Adirondack, Or, Life in the Woods: A Facsimile of the 1849 Edition.* New York, N.Y., Baker and Scribner, 1849. 288p.; reprint, Harrison, N.Y., Harbor Hill Books, 1982. xi, 461p.

Early book on the Adirondacks. A facs. of the 1849 ed., with later chapters added. New introduction by Terrie places Headley in the Romantic tradition of American nature writing. Headley recounts his early visits to the Adirondacks, its people and places.

Hill, Ralph Nading. *Two Centuries of Ferryboating.* s.l., s.n., n.d.; reprint, Burlington, VT., Lake Champlain Transportation, 1972. 32p.

Two articles on Lake Champlain. One is concerned with non-military craft, and the other is a brief military history of the lake from early French explorers to the War of 1812. Hill is a well-known chronicler of Lake Champlain history. Maps, illus.

Hill, William H. *A Brief History of the Printing Press in Washington, Saratoga, and Warren Counties, State of New York.* Fort Edward, N.Y., privately printed, 1930; reprint, Harrison, N.Y., Harbor Hill Books, 1973. 117p.

Brief descriptions of newspapers printed in each county. A list of publications prior to 1825 follows each short essay. Chapter on early paper mills.

Hochschild, Harold K. *Adirondack Railroads, Real and Phantom.* Blue Mountain Lake, N.Y., Adirondack Museum, 1962. 20p.; 3rd printing, 1986.

Excerpt from *Township 34.*

Hochschild, Harold K. *An Adirondack Resort in the Nineteenth Century: Blue Mountain Lake.* Blue Mountain Lake, N.Y., Adirondack Museum, 1962. 98p.; second printing, 1976.; 3rd printing, 1988.

Excerpt from *Township 34.* Outstanding photos from an earlier time in Blue Mountain Lake, site of the Adirondack Museum.

Hochschild, Harold K. *Adirondack Steamboats on Raquette and Blue Mountain Lakes.* Blue Mountain Lake, N.Y., Adirondack Muscum, 1962. 35p.; 2nd printing, 1974.

Excerpt from *Township 34.*

Hochschild, Harold K. *Doctor Durant and His Iron Horse.* Blue Moutain Lake, N.Y., Adirondack Museum, 1962. 27p.; 2nd printing, 1976; 3rd printing, 1993.

Excert from *Township 34.*

Hochschild, Harold K. *Life and Leisure in the Adirondack Backwoods.* Blue Mountain Lake, N.Y., Adirondack Museum, 1962 122p.; 4th printing, 1990.

Rev. sections from Hochschild's book *Township 34*, which was privately printed in 1952. Much on William West Durant and the camps of the wealthy on Raquette Lake and Blue Mountain Lake in the late 1800s and early 1900s. Many excellent photos.

Hochschild, Harold K. *Lumberjacks and Rivermen: The Central Adirondacks 1850-1950.* Blue Mountain Lake, N.Y., Adirondack Museum, 1962. 88p.; 2nd printing, 1974; 3rd printing, 1993.

Excerpted from *Township 34.* People, places and methods of lumbering industry in central Adirondacks. Intriguing photos and drawings. Glossary of logging terms and Appendix on 19th century logging practices.

Hoffman, C.F. *Wild Scenes in the Forest and Prairie.* London, Eng., Richard Bentley, 1839; reprint, Upper Saddle River, N.J., Literature House, 1970. 2 v.

Very early account of travel through the Adirondacks; the Indian Pass, Mt. Marcy.

Hooker, Mildred Phelps Stokes. *Camp Chronicles.* s.l., s.n., privately printed, 1953. 83p.; reprints, Blue Mountain Lake, N.Y., Adirondack Museum, 1964, 1992. 60p.

With Intro. and Notes by Paul Jamieson. Illus. Author's account of summers on Upper St. Regis Lake.

Hough, Franklin B. *A History of Lewis County in the State of New York from the Beginning of its Settlement to the Present Time.* Albany, N.Y., Munsell and Rowland, 1860; reprint, Lyons Falls, N.Y., Lewis County Historical Society, 1993. 319p.

Hough, Franklin B. *The History of Lewis County, New York with Illustrations and Biographical Sketches.* Syracuse, N.Y., D. Mason & Co., 1883; reprint, Lyons Falls, N.Y., Lewis County Historical Society, 1993. 606p.

Hough, Franklin B. *A History of St. Lawrence & Franklin Counties, New York.* Albany, N.Y., Munsell Press, 1853; reprint, Baltimore, MD, Regional Pub. Co., 1970; Harrison, N.Y., Harbor Hill, 1970. 719p.

Facs. A combined history of Franklin and St. Lawrence County covering history, geology, local government, civic organizations, towns and early settlement.

Hurd, Duane Hamilton. *History of Clinton and Franklin Counties, New York.* Philadelphia, PA., J.W. Lewis, 1880. 508p.; reprint, Plattsburgh, N.Y., Clinton County American Revolution Bicentennial Commission, 1978. 556p.

General regional history. Ellenburg, Saranac, Black Brook, and Ausable in Clinton County and Waverly, Franklin, Bellmont, Duane, Brighton, Harrietstown, Santa Clara and Altamont in Franklin County are towns that lie within the Blue Line. Genealogists may be helped by biographical sketches of prominent, early settlers.

Hyde, Louis Fiske. *History of Glens Falls, New York and Its Settlement.* Glens Falls, N.Y., Mrs. C.F. Hyde, 1936; reprint, Glens Falls, N.Y., Hyde Collection, 1983. 347p.

Materials collected by Fiske. No table of contents, but includes index and appendices. First ed. in 1936 privately printed by author. 300 copies.

Ives, Martin V.B., *Through the Adirondacks in Eighteen Days.* New York, N.Y. & Albany, N.Y., Wynkoop, Hallenbeck, Crawford, 1899; reprint, Harrison, N.Y., Harbor Hill Books, 1985. 119p.

A turn-of-the-century work describing the north-central Adirondacks. Personal account of St. Lawrence County Assembly representative who was part of a committee which spent two and a half weeks travelling in the Adirondacks during the summer of 1898. Introduction by Neal S. Burdick provides biographical information on Ives. Illus.

Jamieson, Paul F. *The Adirondack Reader.* New York, Macmillan, 1964. 494p reprint, Glens Falls, N.Y., Adirondack Mountain Club, Inc., 1982. xvii, 525p.

Collection of some of the best writings about the region. In 1972 William Verner called it one of the four most important books published about the Adirondacks since the end of World War II.

Johnson, Crisfield. *History of Washington County, New York, with Illustrations and Biographical Sketches.* Philadelphia, PA., Everts and Ensign, 1878; reprint, Interlaken, N.Y., Heart of the Lakes Publishing, 1979. 504p.

Putnam, Fort Ann, Dresden are Washington County communities that are in the Adirondack Park. This work contains early history of the above communities, as well as the rest of Washington County.

Kalm, Peter. *Peter Kalm's Travels in North America.* var. ed. var. pag.

Classic first person accounts of parts of the region from colonial times by Swedish botanist.

Kenwell, Gerald. *French Louie: Hermit of the Adirondacks.* Amsterdam, N.Y., Ursus Press, 1983. 38p.

Tiny book. Small enough to fit in a watch pocket. Reprint of article by Alvin S. Fick that originally appeared in *The Conservationist.* Limited to 140 copies.

Koller, Lawrence R. *Shots at Whitetails.* Boston, MA., Little, Brown, & Co., 1952; reprint, New York, N.Y., Knopf, 1970. xvii, 362p.

Classic book on deer hunting. Information on guns, ammunition, and scopes outdated. However, information on deer, woodcraft, hunting techniques, safety, bow and arrow hunting, and venision still timely. Illus. by Bob Kirkus.

Lamb, Wallace E. *Historic Lake George.* Bolton Landing, N.Y., W.A. Lamb, 1946; reprint, Lake George, N.Y., Lake George Historical Association, 1984. 76p.

Father Jogues Ed. Part I covers Lake George in Colonial and Revolutionary War eras. Part II is about various islands and villages around Lake George. Illus.

Lansing, W. & Son. *The Souvenir Industrial Edition of Plattsburgh: 1897.* Plattsburgh, N.Y., W. Lansing & Son 1897; reprint, Plattsburgh, N.Y., Corner-Stone Bookshop, 1978. 124p.

Facs. rep. from 1890s about Plattsburgh with table of contents and alphabetical listing of 220 illus.

added. Describes historical, religious, economic, architectural, and social aspects of Plattsburgh near the turn of the twentieth century. Folio.

Lonergan, Carroll V. *The Northern Gateway: A History of Lake Champlain and Guide to Interesting Places in the Great Valley.* s.l., s.n., 1939. 40p., 1974. 38p.

History of the Champlain Valley from Samuel Champlain to the War of 1812. Illus, maps, tables of distances. Numerous printings.

Lonergan, Carroll V. *Ticonderoga: Historic Portage.* Ticonderoga, N.Y., Fort Mount Hope Society Press, 1959, 1975. 248p.

History of Ticonderoga. Chapter about the Battle of Ticonderoga told in the present tense. Illus.

Lossing, Benson J. *The Pictorial Field-Book of the Revolution.* New York, N.Y., Harper & Brothers, 1859; reprint, Spartenburg, S.C., Reprint Co., 1969. 2 v.

Detailed two volume history of the American Revolution. Plenty of illus.—525 in Volume I and 571 in Volume II. For those interested in Adirondack history; Lake Champlain, Saratoga and Ticonderoga discussed in Vol. I.

Lossing, Benson J. *The Pictorial Field-Book of the War of 1812.* New York, Harper and Brothers, 1868; reprint, Glendale, N.Y., Bench Mark Pub. Corp., 1970. 2 v.

Epic book about our "second war of independence with Britain." Nearly 900 illus. Chapters on events around Lake Champlain and northern New York.

Masten, Arthur H. *The Story of Adirondac.* New York, N.Y., privately printed, 1923; reprint, Syracuse, N.Y., Adirondack Museum/ Syracuse University Press, 1968. 199p.

With introduction and notes by William K. Verner. Story of iron mining town in Essex County from its founding through 1920s. Area is known for its remoteness and its wilderness.

Merriam, Clinton Hart. *The Mammals of the Adirondack Region, Northeastern New York.* New York, N.Y., Press of L.S. Foster, 1884, reprint, New York, N.Y., Arno Press, 1974. 316p.

Early book on wildlife of the Adirondack Mountain region. Chapter 1 is background information on geology, climate, physical features and botany. Chapter 2 includes brief descriptions of 51 mammals found in the Adirondacks. Information on habitat, range, prey.

Murray, Amelia M. *Letters From the United States, Cuba and Canada.* New York, N.Y., G.P. Putnam & Co., 1856; reprint, New York, N.Y., Negro University Press, 1969. 410p.

Two chapters relevant to the Adirondacks. Chapter 27 discusses Albany and Ticonderoga. Chapter 29 provides early accounts (1850s) of Saratoga, Lake George, Saranac Lake and Long Lake.

Murray, William H. H. *Adventures in the Wilderness.* Boston, MA., Fields and Osgood & Co., 1869. 236p.; reprints, Syracuse, N.Y., Adirondack Museum/Syracuse University Press, 1970, 1979, 1989. Var. pag.

Reprint of classic about the Adirondack first published in 1869. With introduction and notes by Warder H. Cadbury. Edited by William K. Verner. Murray promoted general interest in the Adirondacks with his lectures, writings and readings. Bibliographic references.

*Old Chazy: Reminiscences of Old Chazy by Descendants of the Early Settlers.* Plattsburgh, N.Y., Clinton County Farmer, 1898; reprint, Elizabethtown, N.Y., Crown Point Press, Inc., 1968. 44p.

Facsimilie of the original ed. Ten accounts of early history of Clinton County community given at a public event on August 23, 1898. Many told how various families came to settle in Chazy.

*Old Keeseville Tales.* Port Henry, N.Y., Essex Publishing Co., 1900; reprint, Elizabethtown, N.Y., Denton Publications, 1976. 99p.

Three dozen short pieces about various organizations, places and people in Keeseville, N.Y. at the turn of the twentieth century.

Palmer, Peter Sailly. *Historical Sketch of Plattsburgh, N.Y. from Its First Settlement to January 1, 1893.* Plattsburgh, N.Y., Plattsburgh Republican, 1893; reprint, Elizabethtown, N.Y., Crown Point Press, 1968. 102p.

Reprint of Palmer's article on the Village of Plattsburgh first published in the Plattsburgh Republican in 1871. Covers important events from founding to 1876. Supplement covers years 1876-1893.

Palmer, Peter S. *History of Lake Champlain: from Its First Exploration by the French in 1609 to the Close of the Year 1814.* Plattsburgh, N.Y., J.W. Tuttle, 1853. 223p.; reprint, Albany, N.Y., J. Munsell, 1866; reprint, Harrison, N.Y., Harbor Hill Books, 1983. 250p.

History of Lake Champlain by a prominent Plattsburgh resident. Book focuses on military events during three wars that shaped the future of the region and the nation: the French and Indian War, The American Revolution, and The War of 1812.

Parkman, Francis. *France and England in North America.* Boston, MA., Little, Brown & Co., 1865-1892; reprint, New York, Literary Classics of the United States, Inc., 1983. 2 v.

Parkman, Francis. *The Journals of Francis Parkman.* New York, Harper, 1947; reprint, New York, Kraus, 1969. 2 v.

Two volumes of famous historian's journals. In 1842 and 1843 Parkman visited Lake George, and Lake Champlain (Vol 1.). In 1878 Parkman visited Lake George and Ticonderoga (Chapter 2, Vol. 2). Bibliography, index.

Parkman, Francis. *Montcalm and Wolfe.* Boston, MA., Little, Brown, 1884; reprint, New York, N.Y., Viking, 1984. 2 v.

Reprint of Parkman's epic history of French and Indian War. References to various events and places in northern New York and the Adirondacks from that era. Foreword by C. Vann Woodward.

Pell, S.H.P. *Fort Ticonderoga: A Short History Compiled from Contemporary Sources.* Glens Falls, N.Y., s.n., 1935. 100p.; reprint, Fort Ticonderoga, N.Y., Fort Ticonderoga Museum, 1970. 118p.

The history of Ft. Ticonderoga from Colonial Era through American Revolution. Describes restoration of the fort and the museum. Illus. Book has been through numerous reprints.

Pinchot, Gifford. *The Adirondack Spruce: A Study of the Forest NE-HA-Sa-Ne Park.* New York, Critic Co., 1898; reprint, New York, Ayer Co.; 1907; reprint, New York, Arno Co., 1970. 157p.

Scientific study of Adirondack Red Spruce in 1898. Charts, illus.

Porter, Marjorie Lansing. *AuSable Chasm in Story and Legend.* Elizabethtown, N.Y., Denton Publications, 1954; reprint, s.l., s.n., 1967. 28p.

Lore and pictures of Ausable Chasm from 1870s. Photos of Allen Falls, the Chasm, Rainbow Falls, and Lake View House. Second edition has white and red on cover.

Reed, Frank A. *Lumberjack Sky Pilot.* Old Forge, N.Y., North Country Books, 1965. 155p.; reprint, Lakemont, N.Y., North Country Books, 1976. ix, 221p.

Story of lumber camp preachers in northern New York State. A tribute to both the preachers and the lumberjacks, depicting life in the camps in the early 20th century. Illus.

Reed, William. *Life on the Border Sixty Years Ago.* Fall River, MA., R. Adams, 1882; reissue, Saranac Lake, N.Y., Saranac Free Library, 1994. 165p.

Reprint of scarce work on pioneer life in northern Franklin County in the second quarter of the nineteenth century. Short introduction by Charles Brumley provides biographical information on author. 500 copies.

Rider, Fremont. *Melvil Dewey.* Chicago, IL., American Library Association, 1944; reprint, Boston, MA., Gregg, 1972; reprint, Ann Arbor MI., University Microfilms International, 1983. 151p.

Biography of famous librarian and educator. Contains short chapter on the Lake Placid Club.

Ritchie, William A. *The Archeology of New York State.* Garden City, N.Y., Natural History Press, 1965, 1969; rev. ed., Harrison, N.Y., Harbor Hill Books, 1980. xxxiv, 357p.

Comprehensive pre-history and history of native peoples in New York State. Maps, illus., charts. Second printing, 1980; minor corrections.

Roberts, Kenneth. *Northwest Passage.* Garden City, N.Y., Doubleday, Doran & Co., 1937. 709p.; reprint, New York, Fawcett Crest, 1981. 637p.

Historical fiction about colonial adventurer Robert Rogers during the French and Indian War. Some action set in eastern Adirondack region.

Roberts, Kenneth. *Rabble in Arms.* Garden City, N.Y., Doubleday, 1933. 870p. reprint; London, Collins, 1966. 886p.

Epic account of Burgoyne campaign during the American Revolution.

Rogers, Robert. *Reminiscences of the French War: with Robert Rogers' Journal and a Memoir of General Stark.* Concord, N.H., Father Roby, 1831. 275p.; reprint, Freedom, N.H., Freedom Historical Society, 1988. xi, 322p.

First person account of French and Indian War, recounting action from eastern New York in Lake George and Lake Champlain corridor.

Sears, George Washington. *Canoeing the Adirondacks With Nessmuk: The Adirondack Letters of George Washington Sears.* Blue Mountain Lake, N.Y., Adirondack Museum, 1962; reprint, Syracuse, N.Y., Adirondack Museum/Syracuse University Press, 1993. 177p.

Edited by Dan Brenan with revisions by Robert L. Lyon and Hallie E. Bond. Sears was a colorful figure who promoted both canoeing and the Adirondacks in the late nineteenth century.

Simms, Jeptha R. *Trappers of New York, Or, A Biography of Nicholas Stoner and Nathaniel Foster, Together with Anecdotes of Other Celebrated Hunters.* Albany, N.Y., J. Munsell's Sons, 1850. 280p.; Harrison, N.Y., Harbor Hill Books, 1980, 1987. 308p.

Stoner and Foster were well-known trappers in southern Adirondacks in early 19th century.

Smith, H.P. *History of Warren County, with Illustrations and Biographical Sketches.* Syracuse, N.Y., Mason & Co., 1885; reprint, Interlaken, N.Y., Heart of the Lakes Press, 1981. 702p.

Geography, geology and history of Warren County and its townships in southeastern Adirondacks.

Smith, William Henry (arranged and annotated by). *The St. Clair Papers: The Life and Public Services of Arthur St. Clair.* Cinncinati, OH., Robert Clarke & Co., 1881; reprint, Freeport, N.Y., Books for Library Press, 1970. 2 v.

Arthur St. Clair fought in the American Revolution, served as president of the Continental Congress and later governor of the Northwest Territory. His correspondence and papers are a valuable source of primary information on the Revolution. Chapters 1-3 deal with Lake Champlain, Ticonderoga, and the surrender of Burgoyne.

Spafford, Horatio Gates. *A Gazetteer of the State of New York.* Albany, N.Y. B. D. Packard., 1824; reprint, Interlaken, N.Y., Heart of the Lakes Publishing, 1981. 620p.

Alphabctically listed descriptions of places and geographical features of the Empire State.

Spaulding, Samuel S. *Spaulding's History of Crown Point, N.Y. from 1800-1874.* Port Henry, N.Y., Herald Print, 1874; reprint, Ann Arbor, MI., University Microfilms, 1982. 42p.

Early history of Crown Point. Information on history, mines, mills, the Champlain Canal and early settlement.

Stevenson, Robert Louis. *The Master of Ballantrae: A Winter Tale.* N.Y., G. Munro Series, 1899. 192p.; reprint, New York, Oxford University Press, 1983. xxxi, 261p.

Edited with intro. by Emma Little. Stevenson novel written while living in Saranac Lake, New York. Partially set in the Adirondacks.

Stoddard, S.R. *The Adirondacks Illustrated.* Albany, N.Y., Weeds and Parsons Co., 1874; reprint, North Adams, MA., Excelsior Print Co., 1983.

Reprint of 1874 guidebook. New preface. Numerous ink drawings by Stoddard. Various editions.

Stoddard, S.R. *Old Times in The Adirondacks.* Saranac Lake, N.Y., Adirondack Yesteryears, 1971, 1972. 152p.

A descriptive work on the Adirondacks in the late 1800s accompanied by about 40 of Stoddard's photos and numerous Stoddard drawings. Pictures of natural features such as Ausable Chasm and Saranac Lake village and Bloomingdale in 1870s are particularly evocative. DeSormo's biographical essay on Stoddard is a valuable contribution.

Street, Alfred B. *The Indian Pass.* New York, Hurd and Houghton, 1869; reprints, Harrison, N.Y., Harbor Hill Books, 1975; Fleischmanns, N.Y., Purple Mountain Press, 1993. lviii, 201p.

Nineteenth-century Adirondack classic. Travel and description in Essex County, particularly the High Peaks Region. General geographical description of northern New York as well as description of the Indian Pass, Mount Marcy and Whiteface Mt.

Street, Alfred B. *Woods and Waters; Or, the Saranac and Racket.* New York, M. Doolady, 1860; reprint, Harrison, N.Y., Harbor Hill, 1970, 1976. 345p.

Description of hunting and fishing trips to the Adirondack Region during the 1850s. Considered a classic on the region.

Sylvester, Nathaniel B. *Historical Sketches of Northern New York and the Adirondack Wilderness*. Troy, N.Y., W.H. Young, 1877; Harrison, N.Y., Harbor Hill Books, 1973, 1989. 316p.

Thirty-three short essays. Early Adirondack classic provides overview of region's history through the War of 1812. Geology, geography, and important personalities of the nineteenth century Adirondacks are discussed as well.

Sylvester, Nathaniel B. *History of Saratoga County, New York with Illustrations and Biographical Sketches*. Philadelphia, Everts and Ensign, 1878; Interlaken, N.Y., Heart of the Lakes Publishing 1979. 514p.

County history of late nineteenth century with familiar format. Much information of Colonial and Revolutionary War era in Eastern New York. Essays on the early history of Saratoga County towns including Day, Hadley, Edinburg, Corinth and Providence which are inside the Blue Line.

Thomas, Howard. *Black River in the North Country*. Prospect, N.Y., Prospect Books, 1963. 221p., 1974, 1978; reprint, Utica, N.Y., North Country Books, 1985. vi, 213p.

History of Black River which originates at North Lake in the western Adirondacks. Discusses river's role in regional history: logging, paper making, transportation, hydro-electric generation and French settlement in the Region.

Thomas, Howard. *Folklore from the Adirondack Foothills*. Prospect, N.Y., Prospect Books, 1958, 1975, 1980. 150p.

Tales, poetry and fiction intended to portray an earlier way of life to contemporary audience. Representative titles are: Streams, Sawmills, Folks, Murder, and North Woods.

Thomas, Howard. *Tales from the Adirondack Foothills*. Prospect, N.Y., Prospect Books, 1956, 1976. 150p.

Stories, biographical sketches, anecdotes and other materials from the oral tradition of the southern Adirondacks. Illus. by John Mahaffy.

Thompson, Harold W. *Body, Boots & Britches: Folk Tales, Ballads, and Speeches from Country New York*. Philadelphia, J.B. Lippincott, 1939. 530p.; reprint Syracuse, N.Y., Syracuse University Press, 1979. 538p.

Folklore from the whole of New York State divided by subject. Some Adirondack content. Author was distinguished college teacher and co-founder of New York State Folklore Society.

Todd, John. *Long Lake*. Pittsfield, MA., E.P. Little, 1845. 100p.; reprint, Harrison, N.Y., Harbor Hill Books, 1983, 1989. xxviii, 100p.

Facs. rep. Todd's early description of visits to the Long Lake area in the early 1840s. Cadbury's introduction explains why Todd came to region and book was written.

Wadsworth, Bruce. *Guide to Northville-Placid Trail*. Glens Falls, N.Y., Adirondack Mountain Club, 1980, 1986, 1988. Var. pag.

Hiking guide. Folding map in back pocket. Maps, photos accompany descriptions of various sections of the trail. Introductory chapter offers tips on hiking gear, itinerary hints, logistical considerations in planning a major hike. Forest Preserve Series, Vol. IV.

Wallace, Paul A. W. *White Roots of Peace*. Philadephia, University of Pennsylvania Press, 1946. 57p.; reprint, Saranac Lake, N.Y., Center for Adirondack Studies, North Country Community College., 1980;. Saranac Lake, N.Y., Chauncy Press, 1986. xxxvi, 66p.

Collection of Iroquois stories and legends about the founding of the Iroquois Confederacy. Illus., index. With new prologue and epilogue.

Warner, Charles Dudley. *A-Hunting of the Deer*. s.l.,s.n., 1985. 1st thus.

Reprint of 1878 essay on hunting in the Adirondacks in book form. Like Kenwell's work this is in miniature format. 300 copies.

Warner, Charles Dudley. *In the Wilderness*. Boston, Houghton, Mifflin & Co., 1878; reprint, Syracuse, N.Y., Adirondack Museum/Syracuse University, 1990. 136p.

Introduction by Alice Wolf Gilborn. Reprint of Adirondack classic. Essays with a humorous and satirical edge from the nineteenth century.

Wells, Parrish. *Dangerous Journeys 1757*. Burlington, VT., Free Press Printing Co., 1940. 95p.; reprint,

Pine Tree Press, Utica, N.Y., 1991. 99p.

Two tales. Part II takes place in 1756 during French and Indian War and chronicles escape from Montreal via Champlain Valley to Ft. Edwards.

White, William Chapman. *Adirondack Country*. New York, Knopf, 1954; reprint, Syracuse, N.Y., Syracuse University Press, 1967, 1985. 368p.

Modern classic on Adirondacks. Widely considered one of the most important books on the Adirondacks in the last 50 years. History and natural history of Adirondack Region. Last section gives month-by-month description of daily life in the Adirondacks. Heavy reliance on the use of male pronouns may date this work for contemporary readers.

White, William Chapman. *Just About Everything in the Adirondacks*. Blue Mountain Lake, N.Y., Adirondack Muscum, 1960, 1973. 101p.

Collected from White's newspaper columns. Divided into several sections titled "In the Woods," "On Farm and In Town," "On Wings, On Foot and On Wheel," and "Along Lake and Stream." Intro. by Alfred S. Dashiell.

Wikoff, Climena (comp.). *Placid Eating*. Lake Placid, N.Y., Climena M. Wikoff, 1954. 122p.; other eds., 1973, 1984. 138p.

# *Unlocated Titles*

Adirondack Economic Development Corporation. *Master Plan Final Report: Appendix E Financial Analysis: Adirondack Airport; Saranac Lake, New York.* Liverpool, N.Y., Calocerinos & Spina, 1991.

Buddington, A.F. *Guidebook For Field Trips, Petrology and Mineral Deposits, Northwestern and Northern Adirondacks.* s.l., s.n. 1977. 104p.

Conference on Low Pollution Power Systems Development. *Einhoven Technical Report.* Rockville MD., Environmental Protection Agency, 1971.

Essex County. *Essex County Directory of Social Services.* Elizabethtown, N.Y., Essex County, 1968. 52p.

Everett, A.G. *Hydro Geochemical Characteristics of Adirondack Waters Influenced by Terrestial Environments.* Rockville, MD., Everett and Associates, 1982.

Falconer, R.E. et. al. *Determination of Cloud Water Acidity at a Mountain Observatory in the Adirondack Mountains.*.Albany, N.Y., State University of New York, 1979.

Franklin County Council of Community Services. *Directory.* Malone, N.Y., The Council, 1968. 72p.

Kenney, Susan M. *Adirondack Park Private Land Use and Development Plan.* s.l., s.n., 1985.

Lake Champlain-Lake George Regional Planning Board. *Comprehensive County Plan for Washington County, 1971-1976.* Fort Edward, N.Y., Washington County Planning Board, 1971. 25 lvs.

Lake George Antique and Classic Boat Rendezvous. Lake George N.Y. *Antique and Classic Boat Rendezvous: August 27-28, 1977.* Lake George, N.Y., Lake George Antique and Classic Boat Rendezvous, 1977. 44p.

Lewis County Republican Club. *Lewis County Yearbook and Directory.* Lowville, N.Y., The Club, 1973. 73p.

Lowe, Elizabeth M. *Should There Be a Federal Role in Management of the Adirondack Park?* 1980.

New York State. Adirondack Mountain Authority. *Whiteface-Lake Placid Region, 1966-67.* Albany, N.Y., The Authority, 1966.

New York State. Department of Commerce. *Industrial Resources Survey of Lewis County.* Albany, N.Y., Department of Commerce, 1971. 172p.

Palmer, Stephen E. *Quisling and Others.* 1982. 105p.

Retired Senior Volunteer Program. *The Apple Cookbook.* Malone, N.Y., The Retired Senior Volunteer Program.

Russell D. Bailey and Associates. *Overall Economic Development Program Hamilton County, New York.* Utica, N.Y., Bailey and Associates, 1966. 54 lvs.

Warren-Hamilton Counties Action Committee for Economic Opportunity. *Report.* s.l., s.n., 1967.

Whitehead, Pamela Susan. *Ecological Linkages As a Model For Archtecture.* 28 lvs.

Wiener, R.W. *Structural Geology and Petrology of Bedrock along the Adirondack Highlands-Northwest Lowlands Boundary near Harrisville, New York.* Amherst, MA., University of Massachusetts, 1981. 163p.

# *Additional Titles*

Balmer, Randall. *Mine Eyes Have Seen the Glory: A Journey into the Evangelical Subculture in America.* New York, N.Y., Oxford Press, 1993. xii, 246p.

Betters, Francis. *A Talk with the Animals of the Adirondacks.* Wilmington, N.Y., Adirondack Sports Publications, 1994. 43p.

Bowman, Don. *Go Seek the Pow-Wow on the Mountain and Other Indian Stories of the Sacandaga Valley.* Greenfield Center, N.Y., Bowman Books, 1993. 96p.

Black River-St. Lawrence Economic Development Commission. *Second Stage Overall Economic Development Plan.* Canton, N.Y., The Commission, 1970. iv, 30 lvs.

Brumley, Charles. *Guides of the Adirondacks: A History.* Utica, N.Y., North Country Books, 1994.

Burdick, Virginia Mason. *Captain Thomas Macdonough: Delaware Born Hero of the Battle of Lake Champlain.* Wilmington, DL., Delaware Heritage Press, 1991. 100p.

Caldwell, Mark. *Saranac Lake: Pioneer Health Resort.* Saranac Lake, N.Y., Historic Saranac Lake, 1993. 45p.

Colton Historical Society. *Raquette River Recipes, Then—and Now.* Colliersville, TN., Fundright Publishing, 1987. 104p.

Douglas, Nancy A. *Sam the Adirondack Railroad Cat.* Utica, N.Y., North Country Books, 1994. 32p.

Ellenburg, N.Y. Catholic Daughters of the Americas: Court Little Rose #1300. *Ellenburg: Yesterday and Today.* Ellenburg, N.Y., 1990. 188p.

Essex County Planning Office. *Town of Jay Planning Report.* Elizabethtown, N.Y., Essex County Planning Office, 1980. 3, 113p.

Franklin, Town of. *Town of Franklin, "They Told Me So" 1987, Volume II: Founders' Day August 1, 1987.* Vermontville, N.Y., Town of Franklin. 1987. Unpaged.

Franklin, Town of. *Founders' Day Celebration: 157 Years: "They Told Me So, Volume V,"* Vermontville, N.Y., Town of Franklin, 1993. iv, 51p.

(French, J.H.) *All Name Index to the Historical and Statistical Gazeteer of New York State 1860 by J.H. French and a Listing of Geographical Names Missing in the Original Index.* Interlaken, N.Y. Heart of the Lakes Publishing, 1993. 183p.

Gerald Peters Gallery. *Keene Valley: The Landscape and its Artists: February 4 through March 11, 1994.* Sante Fe, N.M., The Gallery, 1994. Unpaged.

Goodwin, Tony. *Classic Adirondack Ski Tours.* Lake George, N.Y. Adirondack Mountain Club. 127p.

Green Albice (pseud). *Brain Bottleneck Bastion.* New York, N.Y., Vantage Press, 1969. 270p.

Healy, Trudy. *From the Black Forest to Tibet: One Woman's Mountains.* New York, N.Y., Vantage Press, 1993. 288p.

Jerome, Christine. *An Adirondack Passage: The Cruise of the Sairy Gamp.* New York, N.Y., Harper Collins, 1994. 230p.

Johannsen, Alice E. *The Legendary Jackrabbit Johannsen.* Montreal, Que., McGill-Queens University Press, 1993. 312p.

Johnsburg Historical Society. *Rivers, Rails and Ski Trails: The History of an Adirondack Town Founded in 1805.* Johnsburg, N.Y., Johnsburg Historical Society, 1994. 163p.

Lake Champlain Committee. *Planning Guide for Champlain Towns.* Burlington, VT., The Committee, 1990. 61p.

Lourie, Peter. *Hudson River: An Adventure from the Mountains to the Sea.* Honesdale, PA., Caroline House, 1992. 47p.

McGrath, Robert L. *Scenes of Placid Lake: An Exhibition in Honor of the Shore Owner's Association of Lake Placid, July 23-September 3, 1993.* Lake Placid, N.Y., Fine Arts Gallery, Lake Placid Center for the Arts, 1993. 32p.

McMartin, Barbara. *The Great Forest of the Adirondacks.* Utica, N.Y., North Country Books, 1994. 266p.

Mack, Daniel. *Making Rustic Furniture.* New York, N.Y., Sterling Publishing, 1992. 160p.

Meinke, Albert H. Jr. *Mountain Troops and Medics: Wartime Stories of a Frontline Surgeon in the U.S. Ski Troops.* Kewadin, MI., Rucksack Publishing, 1993. 372p.

Metcalfe, Anne Breen. *Leland House: An Adirondack Innovator.* Elizabethtown, N.Y., Essex County Historical Society, 1994. 68p.

New York State. Department of Environmental Conservation. *Draft Unit Management Plan for Five Ponds Wilderness Area, Buck Pond Primitive Corridor, Parker's Island Primitive Corridor, Raven Lake Primitive Corridor, Tomar Pond Primitive Corridor, Wanakena Primitive Corridor.* Albany, N.Y., Department of Environmental Conservation, 1993. 170p.

New York State. Department of Environmental Conservation. *Draft Unit Management Plan for Black River Wild Forest, Pratt-Nathan Memorial Park, J.P. Lewis Tract Easement, John Brown Tract Easement.* Albany, N.Y., Department of Environmental Conservation, 1993. 140p.

New York State. Department of Environmental Conservation. *Draft Blue Mountain Wild Forest Unit Management Plan.* Albany, N.Y., Department of Environmental Conservation, 1993. 204p.

Nimke, R.W. *The Rutland: 60 Years of Trying; Volume VII, the Addendum.* Walpole, N.H., R.W. Nimke, 1990. 1 v.

Northern Forest Land Council. *Finding Common Ground: The Draft Recommendations of the Northern Forest Lands Council.* Concord, N.H., The Council, 1994. 74p. with appendices.

Riedesel, Mrs. General. *Letters and Journals Relating to the War of the American Revolution, and the Capture of the American Troops at Saratoga.* Albany, N.Y., J. Munsell, 1867; reprint, New York, N.Y., New York Times & Arno Press, 1968. 235p.

Silver Bay Association. *Silver Bay Association: A Pictorial History, 1900-1935.* Silver Bay, N.Y., 1992. 100p.

Snyder, Patricia K. *The Underwood Club: 1908-1991.* Huntsville, ALA., 1992. 171p.

Technical Assistance Center. State University of New York at Plattsburgh. *A Guide to State, Regional, County, and Local Business Financing Programs for Northern New York.* Plattsburgh, N.Y., The Center, 1993. 153p.

Timm, Ruth. *A Collection of North Country Tales, Truths, and Trivia.* Utica, N.Y., North Country Books, 1994. 168p.

Waterman, Laura and Guy Waterman. *Backwoods Ethics.* Woodstock, VT., Countryman Press, 1993. 280p.

Waterman, Laura and Guy Waterman. *Wilderness Ethics: Preserving the Spirit of the Wilderness.* Woodstock, VT, Countryman Press, 1993, 239p.

Waterman, Laura and Guy Waterman. *Yankee Rock and Ice: A History of Climbing in the Northeastern United States.* Harrisburg, PA, Stackpole Books, 1993. 334p.

Webb, William L. *The Effects of Logging on Songbird Populations in a Northern Hardwood Forest.* Washington, D.C., The Wildlife Society, 1977. 35p.

Whitney, Philip and James F. Olmsted. *Bedrock Geology of the AuSable Forks Quadrangle, Northeastern Adirondack Mountains, New York.* Albany, N.Y., State Museum, 1993. 48p.

Wood, Bari. *Doll's Eyes.* New York, N.Y., Morrow, 1993; London, HarperCollins, 1994. 303p.

# Index

***Numbers refer to entries, not page numbers. R means the item is located in the separate section for Reprints with Plum Numbers***

-A-

## -B-

## -D-

## -E-

## -F-

## -G-

## -H-

## -I-

## -J-



## -K-

## -L-

## -N-

## -O-

## -S-

-Y-



-Z-